For Reference

Not to be taken from this room

Modern Collectible Dolls

IDENTIFICATION
&
VALUE GUIDE

VOLUME
IV

Patsy Moyer

COLLECTOR BOOKS
A Division of Schroeder Publishing Co., Inc.

The current values in this book should be used only as a guide. They are not intended to set prices, which vary from one section of the country to another. Auction prices as well as dealer prices vary greatly and are affected by condition as well as demand. Neither the author nor the publisher assumes responsibility for any losses which might be incurred as a result of consulting this guide.

On the Cover:

Clockwise from lower left: 18" composition Shirley Temple in rare tagged military style yellow and brown dress from 1935 20th Century Fox film *Little Colonel* complete with matching brown and yellow hat and pin back button, center snap shoes, $2,500.00+. Courtesy Rosemary Dent.

14" vinyl limited edition of 200 Robert Tonner Doll Company Betsy Visits Roy Rogers Ranch with brown eyes, synthetic braids, red shirt and black embroidered skirt, red leather boots, souvenir of First Betsy McCall Doll Convention, 1999, $125.00. Courtesy Marilyn Ramsey.

16½" vinyl Alexander Elise Ballerina with sleep eyes, closed mouth, synthetic hair with flowers, eyeshadow over eyes, earrings, tagged blue tutu, hard plastic body with jointed elbows, ankles, and knees, vinyl lower arms, pink ballet shoes, lovely color, circa 1957 – 1964, $400.00. Courtesy Jennifer Warren.

11½" vinyl Mattel #959 Theatre Date Barbie, green jacket and skirt with white blouse, in box, with brochure, stand, and shoes, earrings still in, turning green, circa 1964, $645.00. Courtesy Ruth Waite.

15" vinyl Ashton Drake Galleries Gene, marked on head "Gene™//© 1995 Mel Odom," created to portray a movie star, painted eyes, blond synthetic wig, jointed fashion type body, with marked Gene stand; blue suit with blue fur collar and muff, costume titled Hello Hollywood, circa 1998, $80.00 retail. Courtesy Elizabeth Surber.

Searching For A Publisher?

We are always looking for knowledgeable people considered experts within their fields. If you feel that there is a real need for a book on your collectible subject and have a large comprehensive collection, contact Collector Books.

Cover design: Beth Summers
Book design: Sherry Kraus

COLLECTOR BOOKS
P.O. Box 3009
Paducah, Kentucky 42002–3009
www.collectorbooks.com

Copyright © 2000 by Patsy Moyer

Contents

Dedication

No one person is an island — and I am no exception. I have had some very special people who have encouraged, helped, and just been my friends in the doll world. First and foremost, Pat Schoonmaker, researcher and author, has become my second mother, and who has only a positive outlook on life. Some very wonderful collectors I only see once a year are my tablemates at UFDC convention. They are the fabulous "Nifty Nine": Patty Cordon, Bernie Fricke, Angie and Angelo Gonzales, Ruth Hartwell, Judy Johnson, Lucia Kirsch, Thelma Krone, and Jean Theaker. In addition, Barbara DeFeo, Virginia Ann Heyerdahl, Robby Miller, Bev Mitchell, and Pat Schuda are just some of the collectors to whom I would like to dedicate this volume.

Credits

Introduction

As we bring to close this millennium, it is a good time to reflect on the dolls of the past 100 years. Although the exact minute, day, and time really hold no great significance for us, marking the close of an era may bring memories of our childhood, family and friends. With these, also may come forgotten memories of playtime. In this volume we will look at the some of the memorable American dolls of the last 100 years.

Looking back also may give some insight to today's collections, the dolls that are currently in favor with collectors, and give you ideas if you are contemplating becoming a collector yourself. Doll collecting ranks in the top ten of collectibles with Barbie doll finishing the millennium as the most popular doll. As with any collectible, an experienced or novice collector wants to get the most for their money. In all cases, knowledge is power.

You need that knowledge to get the best for your money. Unless you have won the lottery or made a million in software or the stock market, you probably have a limited budget. Those of us who are not independently wealthy need to know that we are spending our money wisely — so that when the time comes for us to part with our collection, it will have increased in value. Thus your next doll might be considered a portable asset.

As a novice collector you need to learn as much about doll collecting and your chosen niche as possible. This means you need to see a large number of dolls so that you can tell the good from the bad. You need to find out as much about your next doll as possible to know that you got a good buy. This book is a showcase of dolls that collectors have acquired. It will help you find an example of a certain costume and gives examples of how older dolls may look now.

Perhaps *modern* is a misnomer for dolls over 70 years old. However, some doll companies that made dolls at the turn of the century are still operating and producing today. For this book, I am grouping as modern, dolls made of composition, cloth, rubber, hard plastic, porcelain, vinyl, wood, and some other materials, as opposed to dolls of bisque, wax, wood, and china that were made before World War I. There are no easy cutoff dates and some spill over from one category to the next. This book will give you examples of dolls to compare for identification.

Collectors who want to know more about the dolls they have or want to collect, need to learn as much as possible. One way to do this is to research and arm yourself with books and magazines that deal with the subject. Another way is to seek other informed collectors. Beginning collectors should list their dolls with the prices paid, the size, marks, material, and other pertinent facts, such as originality and condition. Collectors need to be able to identify their dolls and one way to do this is by material.

Experienced doll collectors refer to a doll by whatever material is used for making the doll's head. So a composition doll has a composition head but may have a cloth, composition, or wood body. A doll with a vinyl head and a hard plastic body is a vinyl doll. The head commands the order of reference to the doll in relation to materials used to produce it. A doll made entirely of vinyl is referred to as all-vinyl.

It is nice when exact measurements are given to describe the height of the doll.

To identify a doll with no packaging or box, first examine the back of the head, then the torso, and the rest of the body, the usual places manufacturers put their marks. Some dolls will only have a mold number or no mark at all. Nursing students are often given

Introduction

the task of writing a physical description of their patient starting at the top of their head down to the bottom of their feet. This is also a good way of describing a doll and its attire.

Collectors like to meet and speak with other collectors who share their interests. For this reason we have included a Collectors' Network section in the back of this book. There are many special interest groups focusing on one area of doll collecting. These are experienced collectors who will consult with others. It is considered proper form to send a SASE when contacting others if you wish to receive a reply. If you wish to be included in this area, please send your area of expertise and references.

In addition, a national organization, the United Federation of Doll Clubs has information for doll collectors who are seeking, or wish to form, a doll club. The goals of this nonprofit organization focus on education, research, preservation, and enjoyment of dolls. They also sponsor a Junior Membership for budding doll collectors. They will put you in contact with one of 16 regional directors who will be able to assess your needs and advise you if a doll club in your area is accepting members. You may write for more information to UFDC, 10920 North Ambassador Drive, Suite 130, Kansas City, MO 64153; fax 816 891-8360 or on the 'net at www.UFDC.org.

Beginning collectors will want to learn as much as possible about dolls before spending their money. It seems prudent to investigate thoroughly all avenues regarding an addition to one's collection before actually making a purchase.

Novice collectors may wonder where to buy dolls. There are many different ways to find the doll of your dreams, including dealers or shops that will locate a particular doll for you. There are numerous focus groups that list special sales. Collector groups usually post doll shows and sales in their newsletters.

Auctions may also prove to be an aid in finding additions to your collection. Some offer absentee bidding which is most helpful if you do not live near. Some also offer phone bidding if you want to be in on the actual bidding. Auction houses usually send out catalogs and are most helpful in answering questions over the phone or fax. See Collectors' Network at the back of this book for more information.

One of the latest and greatest shopping malls is the Internet. And there is this great place called e-Bay that has thousands of dolls on auction 24 hours a day, every day, — barring electrical disturbances and Internet traffic jams. e-Bay is becoming *the* acceptable spot for collectors to shop and sell. They also feature a query that will allow you to look at prices realized in closed auctions.

Not only are books, magazines, and videos available for collectors, but simply going to museums, doll shows, and displays is a wonderful way for the collector to see dolls. To help the novice collector, simple tips on what to look for in dolls are included in this book.

Just as the most valuable quality in real estate is location, location, location; a doll collector should consider condition, condition, condition. Dolls with good color, original clothing, tags, brochures, and boxes will always be desirable. The trick is to find those dolls that also have rarity, beauty, or some other unique quality that makes them appealing to the collector. It could be that only a few were made. It could be that a collector recalls his/her childhood dolls. Or it could be that a doll's manufacture, presentation, or identity make a historical statement. Other factors can also contribute to the desirability and popularity of a doll. Cleanliness, good color, and good condition are always desirable qualities. We have included "What to look for" tips with each category.

An easy way to keep track of the money spent on doll collections is to utilize a money program on your computer, using a number and description to keep track of your doll, then entering the amount you spent. If you sell the doll or dispose of it, the doll can be checked during the reconciling procedure and will not be seen on your current inventory. This is just a very simple way to help you with your doll inventory.

This book does not mean to set prices and should only be used as one of many tools to guide the collector. It is the collector's decision alone on which doll to purchase. It is the responsibility of the collector alone to choose his or her own area of collecting and how to pursue it. This book is meant to help you enjoy and learn about dolls of our past and present and give indications of future trends. If you wish to see other categories or wish to share your collection, please write to the address in Collectors' Network in the back of the book.

Happy collecting!

Great American Dolls of the Twentieth Century

In *1900*, most dolls — china and bisque — are imported from France or Germany. A doll with sleep eyes is a big thing around the turn of the century. Mass production was limited. World War I cut back exports from Germany and France. Composition doll making begins to flourish in the United States with the war shortages of imported dolls. Effanbee, 1911+; Amberg, 1878+; Averill, 1915+; Schoenhut, 1911+; and Horsman, 1878+ were major doll makers. Just as world events speeded up the manufacture of American dolls during World War I, so new discoveries, political events and trends have influenced style, manufacturing processes, and popularity of certain dolls.

1900 – William McKinley is president. Radon is discovered, the first Browning revolvers are made, and the Zeppelin makes its trial run. The cake walk is the most popular dance.

1901 – Queen Victoria of England dies. The Boxer Rebellion ends in China. President McKinley is assassinated and Theodore Roosevelt succeeds him. The Panama Treaty is made. Walt Disney is born; Taloouse Lautrec dies, Rachmaninoff writes his Piano Concerto No 2. The century of electricity replaces the century of steam. Marconi transmits the first telegraphic radio messages. Motor-driven bicycles are invented and the first Mercedes auto is made.

1902 – The Census Bureau is created. Arthur Conan Doyle writes *The Hound of Baskerville*, Upton Sinclair writes *The Jungle*, John Steinbeck is born, and Beatrix Potter writes her *Peter Rabbit* stories. Enrico Caruso makes his first record.

1903 – A Packard car makes the first cross-country trip; Orville and Wilbur Wright make the first airplane flight. The Alaska frontier is settled; Jack London writes *The Call of the Wild*. American painter James Whistler and French painter Paul Gauguin die. *The Great Train Robbery* is the longest film made to date — it runs 12 minutes. The electrocardiograph is invented. Henry Ford starts the Ford Motor Company. Richard Steiff designs his first teddy bear.

1904 – Theodore Roosevelt is elected president. Marlene Dietrich is born. Jack London writes *The Sea Wolf*. James Barrie writes *Peter Pan*. Salvador Dali is born. *Madame Butterfly* opens in Milan. Marie Curie publishes work on radioactivity; the first ultraviolet lamp is invented. Yellow fever is eradicated and work begins on the Panama Canal. The Rolls-Royce Company is founded. Silicone is discovered. The subway is opened in New York. The 10-hour workday is established. A woman is arrested in New York for smoking a cigarette in public. Helen Keller graduates from Radcliffe.

1905 – H. G. Wells, Edith Wharton, and Oscar Wilde are writing books. The first movie theater is opened in Philadelphia. Albert Einstein formulates his Theory of Relativity. Freud publishes *Three Contributions to the Theory of Sex*. Rayon yarn is manufactured.

1906 – U.S. troops occupy Cuba. Upton Sinclair writes *The Jungle*. Paul Cezanne dies, and Swedish actress Greta Garbo is born. The term allergy is introduced. China and Britain agree to reduce the production of opium. Typhoid Mary is found and jailed. The first radio program is broadcast.

1907 – President Roosevelt bars Japanese from the U.S. Oklahoma becomes a state. The Panic of 1907 causes a run on banks. Rudyard Kipling wins the Nobel Prize for Literature. The first "Ziegfeld Follies" is staged in New York. The Boy Scouts are formed. The second Sunday in May is named "Mother's Day." *The Mutt* (later Mutt & Jeff) comic begins.

1908 – Taft is elected president; Lyndon B. Johnson and Ian Fleming are born. Lucy Montgomery writes *Anne of Green Gables*. Monet paints works of art; Matisse coins the word, "Cubism." The Zeppelin disaster occurs. General Motors Corporation is formed. Fountain pens become popular. Ford produces the first Model T of an estimated 15 million.

Dolls 1900 – 1908: Ella Gaunt Smith makes the Alabama Baby. Arnold Print Works makes cloth dolls like Palmer Cox Brownies and Art Fabric Mills makes The Life Size Doll. Babyland Rag's cloth Topsy Turvey is by E.I. Horsman and Martha Chase put sand in her cloth dolls to give a realistic feel. Emma E. Adams makes a cloth Columbian Rag distributed by Marshall Field. Illustrator Grace Drayton designs dolls for Averill and others. Ludwig Greiner of Philadelphia makes papier-mache dolls 1840 – 1900. Leo Moss of Macon, Georgia, makes ethnic black composition character dolls — some with a tear on their cheeks. Julia Jones Beecher uses silk jersey underwear to make Missionary Rag Babies. J.B. Sheppard & Co. of Philadelphia, Pennsylvania, 1860 – 1935, makes Philadelphia Babies.

27" cloth Art Fabric Mills girl with printed underwear, stitched fingers, stitch jointed, red stocking legs, black shoes, printed on bottom, "Art Fabric Mills//New York//Patented Feb. 13th, 1900," no tears, some wear, circa 1900s, $350.00.
Courtesy Debbie Crume.

1909 – Mary Pickford stars in silent films; Frederick Remington dies. Explorer Robert E. Peary reaches the North Pole. The first commercial manufacture of Bakelite marks the start of the plastic age. **Dolls:** Art competitions in Europe spark interest in character dolls and Horsman makes the character, Billiken.

1910 – The Mann Act passes, making it illegal to transport women across state lines for immoral purposes. Mark Twain, Mary Baker Eddy (founder of Christian Science) Julia Ward Howe (American suffragist) Winslow Homer, Florence Nightingale, and Leo Tolstoi die. Frank Lloyd Wright becomes well known. The opera *The Girl of the Golden West* opens in New York. The tango is a popular dance. Haley's

Great American Dolls of the Twentieth Century

Comet is seen; telephones are popular. Barney Oldfield drives a race car 133 miles per hour. The weekend becomes popular in the U.S. and Father's Day is celebrated.

Dolls: Horsman copies a German bisque to make Baby Bumps and makes Campbell Kids — used in advertising Campbell soup. Ideal makes Snookums after a *Newlyweds* comic strip character by George McManus. The manufacturer of celluloid collars and stays makes the all-celluloid Parson Jackson baby.

9½" composition Horsman Campbell Kids, molded painted features, closed smiling mouths, straw stuffed bodies and limbs, mitt hands, original clothes, circa 1910 – 1920, $500.00 for pair.
Courtesy Sue Kinkade.

1911 – There is a revolution in Central China; pigtails are abolished. Irving Berlin writes *Alexander's Ragtime Band.* The first self-starter for automobiles is developed.

Dolls: Schoenhut begins making wonderful all-wood, spring-jointed articulated dolls; the early ones have hand carved heads.

16" wooden Schoenhut model 16/301 with short blonde bob wig, painted blue eyes with large pupils, lightly feathered eyebrows, pink dots at inner eyes, nose, peach painted mouth, wooden articulated body, old dress, 1911 – 1924, $1,300.00+.
Courtesy Elizabeth Surber.

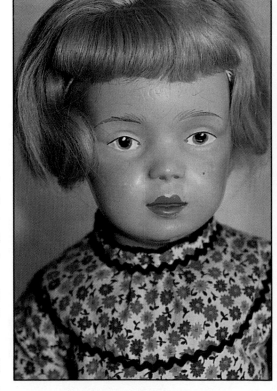

1912 – Arizona and New Mexico become states. Woodrow Wilson is elected president. Approximately 5 million people in the U.S. attend movies daily. The term "vitamin" is coined. Cellophane begins to be manufactured. The S.S. Titanic sinks on her maiden voyage — 1,513 drown. The F.W. Woolworth Company is founded. The first successful parachute jump is made.

Dolls: Effanbee makes Johnny Tu-Face with crying and laughing faces and Amberg makes Sis Hopkins, a celebrity doll based on a Rose Melville character.

1913 – Federal income tax is introduced and U.S. Federal Reserve System is established. Richard Nixon is born. Eleanor H. Porter writes *Pollyanna.* Victor Herbert presents the operetta *Sweethearts* and Jack Judge writes the song *Tipperary.* The Geiger counter is invented. Chlorophyll and jet propulsion are discovered. Albert Schweitzer opens his hospital in the French Congo. Zippers (in use since 1891) become popular. The foxtrot is the latest dance craze.

Dolls: Horsman makes Baby Butterfly with painted Oriental features. Kewpie, by Rose O'Neill, are darling characters from her writings and made in bisque, composition, and celluloid.

1914 – World War I begins when Archduke Ferdinand is assassinated. Edgar Rice Burroughs writes *Tarzan of the Apes*, Tennessee Williams is born, and Booth Tarkington writes *Penrod*. Charlie Chaplin stars in silent films. Goddard begins rocket experiments. The Panama Canal opens. Almost 10.5 million immigrants entered the U.S. since 1905.

Dolls: Louis Amberg & Sons makes John Bunny patterned after celebrity actor/comic. Skookum designed by Mary McAboy, is a composition Indian with blanket wrapped stick bodies for sale for tourists, has paper label on foot. Ideal makes Uneeda Bisquit Dolls — advertising dolls for the National Bisquit Company.

11" composition Skookums Chief, black wig, painted features, dark complexion, blanket-wrapped stick body, wooden shoes, circa 1930 – 1940, $285.00.
Courtesy Tricia Tompkins.

1915 – World War I continues. The Germans sink the *Lusitania*. Sommerset Maugham writes *Of Human Bondage*. New Orleans jazz is popular. Ford produces his millionth car and develops a farm tractor. Bell makes the first transcontinental telephone call. The U.S. Coast Guard is begun. Margaret Sanger is jailed for writing the first book on birth control. President Wilson marries Mrs. Edith Galt.

Dolls: Effanbee makes Baby Grumpy, Betty Bounce, Baby Huggums, and Pouting Bess. A composition celebrity doll Charlie Chaplin is made by Louis Amberg & Sons. Gene Carr Kids are composition comic characters taken from the Gene Carr comic. Johnny Gruelle takes a literary character from his book and designs Raggedy Ann.

16½" Volland Raggedy Ann, played with condition, circa 1920 – 1934, $1,500.00.
Courtesy Debbie Crume.

1916 – World War I continues; a German Zeppelin attacks Paris. James Joyce writes *Portrait of the Artist as a Young Man*. Jack London dies. Frank Lloyd Wright designs the Imperial Hotel in Tokyo. Charlie Chaplin and Ethel Barrymore star in films. The first Rose Bowl game is played.

Dolls: Gertrude F. Rollison makes cloth dolls. Jesse McCutcheon Raleigh, Chicago, Illinois, 1916 – 1920, makes composition dolls. Zu-Zu Kid is made by Ideal, advertising Zu-Zu Crackers for National Bisquit Company. Effanbee makes a Whistling Jim.

Great American Dolls of the Twentieth Century

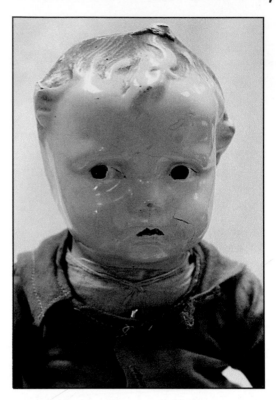

16" composition Effanbee Baby Grumpy, marked "Deco," painted blue side-glancing eyes, frowning eyebrows, pouty closed mouth, heavily molded hair, cloth body and legs, composition forearms, blue shirt, circa 1915+, $325.00.
Courtesy Janet Hill.

17" composition Raleigh Doll Co. baby, painted brown eyes, painted eyelashes, open/closed mouth with two upper painted teeth, painted brown hair, fully jointed composition body with bent legs, original white baby dress, circa 1921, $400.00.
Courtesy Nelda Shelton

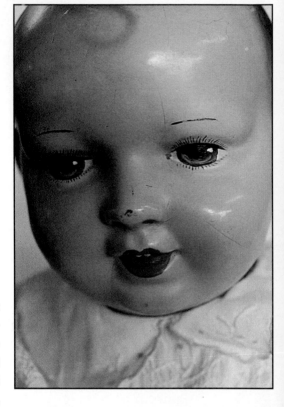

1917 – The U.S. enters World War I. John Kennedy is born. The U.S. buys the Dutch West Indies. Woodrow Wilson gets a second term. Mary Pickford stars in *The Little Princess*. Charlie Chaplin's salary reaches one million dollars. George M. Cohen writes *Over There* and the first jazz recordings are made. Bobbed hair as a fashion sweeps Britain and the U.S. Buffalo Bill Cody dies. Four women are arrested for picketing the White House for women's suffrage.
Dolls: Richard Krueger of New York makes cloth dolls with oil painted faces.

1918 – World War I finally ends leaving turmoil in Europe. The Czar and his family are executed in Russia. Dancer Vernon Castle dies. *The Four Horsemen of the Apocalypse* is a bestseller. Popular films are *Carmen* and *Shoulder Arms* (with Chaplin). Leonard Bernstein is born. Jerome Kern writes *Rock-a-bye Baby*. Airmail service is started between New York and Washington D.C. Daylight saving time is introduced. There is a worldwide flu epidemic that kills 22 million by 1920. The U.S. population is now 103.5 million.
Dolls: Effanbee copies a German bisque doll and makes a composition Baby Bud; Ideal makes a Liberty Boy.

12" composition Ideal Liberty Boy with molded painted blond hair, all-composition, spring-jointed doll with molded uniform, painted blue eyes, rosy cheeks, closed mouth, single stroke eyebrows, red accent dots at inner eye and nostrils, molded ears, jointed body with khaki painted molded U.S. World War I Army uniform, with black tie and buttons, brown molded boots, replaced felt hat, marked "Ideal" in a diamond on back, used to aid the WWI Liberty Bonds effort, circa 1918, $300.00.
Private collection.

Great American Dolls of the Twentieth Century

1919 – Theodore Roosevelt dies and prohibition passes. There are race riots in Chicago. Hugh Lofting writes the first of the *Dr. Doolittle* stories. *Madame DuBarry* is a popular film. Renoir, Andrew Carnegie, opera star Adelina Patti, and Julliard die; Julliard leaving $20 million to a school of music. Radio Corporation of America is founded. Babe Ruth is a baseball star.
Dolls: Louise Kampes Studio makes all-cloth Kamkins.

1920 – The League of Nations is formed; Warren Harding is elected president; the nineteenth Amendment gives women the right to vote, and just when you think things look right for a while, you note that Adolph Hitler is busy gaining strength in Germany. Agatha Christie, John Galsworthy, Sinclair Lewis, Carl Sandberg, Upton Sinclair, Edith Wharton, Eugene O'Neill, and F. Scott Fitzgerald all write books. The film *Polyanna* stars Mary Pickford. Jerome Kern is writing songs, and Paul Whitman and his band tour Europe. Rorschach devises the inkblot test. John Thompson invents the Tommy-gun. Robert Peary, the explorer, dies. There is a big earthquake in China killing 200,000 people. The U.S. is leading the world in industry — producing 645 million tons of coal, 443 barrels of oil, and almost 9 million automobiles. The world population is now 1.8 billion.
Dolls: Georgene Averill, who also used the name Madame Hendren, designs Wonder Mama Doll with cloth body, crier, and swing legs.

1921 – Hirohito comes into power in Japan. Aldous Huxley, D. H. Lawrence, Somerset Maugham, Eugene O' Neill, Bernard Shaw, and Virginia Woof publish books. Chaplin stars in *The Kid*. Enrico Caruso dies. A vaccine for tuberculosis is developed. Einstein gets a Nobel Prize. Ku Klux Klan activities rise in the South.
Dolls: Berwick Doll Company comes up with an amazing idea; the Famlee Doll with extra heads that could be screwed on like a light bulb. Horsman makes Jackie Coogan Kid. Hazel Drukker makes Mibs for Louis Amberg & Sons.

1922 – Mussolini marches on Rome and forms a fascist government. Willa Cather, T.S. Elliot, F. Scott Fitzgerald, John Galsworthy, James Joyce, D.H. Lawrence, and Sinclair Lewis all publish books. Booth Tarkington gets a Pulitzer Prize. The tomb of Tutankhamen is discovered, sparking Egyptian fads and interest. Some of the films are *The Loves of Pharaoh, Last of the Mohicans,* and *Nanook of the North*. Lillian Russell dies. Insulin is first used for diabetics.
Dolls: Grace Storey Putnam designed the Bye-Lo Baby made in bisque and composition and distributed by George Borgfeldt. The H.D. Lee Mercantile Company makes a composition Buddy Lee doll to display their work clothes.

1923 – Pancho Villa and President Harding die. Calvin Coolidge becomes president. Martial law in Oklahoma protects people from the Ku Klux Klan. A popular musical is *No, No, Nanette*. Films include Douglas Fairbanks in *Robin Hood*, Chaplin in *The Pilgrim*, and Colleen Moore in *Flaming Youth*. George Gershwin writes *Rhapsody in Blue* and movies add sound. Popular songs are *Yes, We Have No Bananas, Barney Google, Tea for Two,* and *I Want to Be Happy*. The first birth control clinic opens in New York. Willy Messerschmitt makes an aircraft factory in Germany. *Time* magazine begins.
Dolls: Louis Amberg makes Baby Peggy (Montgomery) based on a popular child film star.

1924 – Lenin dies; Italians favor Mussolini and fascism. The U.S. bars Japanese immigrants. Calvin Coolidge is re-elected. J. Edgar Hoover is appointed director of the FBI. Victor Herbert dies. George Gershwin writes *Lady Be Good*. Mah-Jong becomes a world craze. Will Rogers is at the height of his career. There are 2.5 million radios in use in the U.S. Ford Motor Company produces its ten millionth car.

Great American Dolls of the Twentieth Century

Dolls: Effanbee makes a composition Harmonica Joe. Ideal makes Soozie Smiles, a two-faced doll that catches the favor of the Queen of England. Louis Amberg & Son makes the Sunny Orange Maid unforgettable with a citrus orange cap molded head.

1925 – Hitler publishes *Mein Kamph*, Edna Ferber writes *So Big,* a Pulitzer Prize winning novel, and F. Scott Fitzgerald writes *The Great Gatsby*. Ernest Hemingway, Sinclair Lewis, Sommerset Maugham, and Gertrude Stein all publish works. Painter John Singer Sargent dies. Chaplin stars in *The Gold Rush*. The Charleston is a popular dance. A popular song is *Show Me the Way to Go Home*. Female fashions include shapeless dresses with skirts above the knee and cloche hats. Clarence Darrow defends John Scopes. Tennessee forbids sex education in schools. Walter P. Chrysler founds the Chrysler Corporation.
Dolls: Effanbee makes Pat-o-Pat with a mechanism to clap the hands together.

1926 – Queen Elizabeth II of Great Britain is born. A.A. Milne creates Winnie the Pooh and Ernest Hemingway writes *The Sun Also Rises*. The movie *Ben Hur* is made and Rudolph Valentino and Harry Houdini die. Popular songs are *I Found a Million-Dollar Baby in the Five-and-Ten-Cent Store, Bye, Bye, Blackbird,* and *When Day Is Done*. Kodak produces the first 16mm movie film. The permanent wave is invented.
Dolls: Georgene Averill designs Bonnie Babe made in Germany and distributed by Borgfeldt of New York. American Character makes Bottletot. Jack Collins designs Annie Rooney for the Cameo Doll Company.

1927 – Films are *The Jazz Singer* with Al Jolson, which is the first talkie, and *Flesh and the Devil* with Greta Garbo. Jerome Kern and Oscar Hammerstein II open *Show Boat* in New York. Popular songs are *Ol' Man River, My Blue Heaven, Let a Smile Be your Umbrella,* and *Blue Skies*. The iron lung is developed. Charles A. Lindbergh flies the Spirit of St. Louis nonstop to Paris. Norwegian Sonja Henie is the ice-skating champion. The fashionable dance is the slow foxtrot.
Dolls: Georgene Averill makes Snookums based on a child star of Universal-Stern Bros. movies. Horsman makes Dimples a composition doll with molded dimples.

1928 – Herbert Hoover is elected president; Chiang Kai-shek becomes president of China. *Lady Chatterley's Lover* by D. H. Lawrence causes quite a rage. Walt Disney produces the first Mickey Mouse films. Popular songs are *Bill, Am I Blue?, Makin' Whoopee, You're the Cream in My Coffee,* and *Button Up Your Overcoat*. Al Jolson's song *Sonny Boy* sells 12 million records. Penicillin is discovered. Eastman shows the first color motion pictures.
Dolls: Effanbee has Bernard Lipfert design Patsy, Lovums, and Mae Starr that has cylinder records in her torso. American Character makes Puggy with pug nose and scowling expression. Horsman makes Ella Cinders based on a cartoon character and Ideal makes Tickletoes with squeakers in each hard rubber leg.

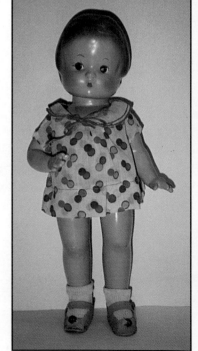

Composition Effanbee Patsy, marked "Effanbee//Patsy//Pat. Pend.//Doll" on back, painted brown side-glancing eyes, molded painted hair with molded headband, closed pouty mouth, bent right arm, jointed composition body, original balloon print dress, original shoes and socks, circa 1928, $475.00.
Courtesy Carol Elder.

Great American Dolls of the Twentieth Century

1929 – Ernest Hemingway writes *A Farewell to Arms*. Audrey Hepburn is born. *All Quiet on the Western Front* is a bestseller. Films are *Blackmail* by Alfred Hitchcock, the first musical Mickey Mouse films by Disney, and talkies kill the silent films. The musical *White Horse Inn* by Ralph Benatzky opens in Berlin. Popular songs are *Stardust, Tiptoe Through the Tulips,* and *Singin' in the Rain*. Construction begins on the Empire State Building. The New York Stock Exchange collapses causing Black Friday.
Dolls: Effanbee makes Skippy based on the comic strip character by Percy Crosby. Ideal makes Buster Brown from Richard Felton Outcault's cartoon character.

14" composition Effanbee Skippy, first advertised in 1929 as Patsy's boyfriend, painted eyes and hair, original Aviator costume with embroidered wings patch, reflecting the patriotic wartime theme, pinback button that reads "SSSS 1932 © P. L. Crosby," circa 1940s, $750.00+.
Courtesy Lilian Booth.

1930 – Films are *Blue Angel* with Marlene Dietrich, *All Quiet on the Western Front, Anna Christie* with Greta Garbo, and *The Big House* with Wallace Beery. Popular songs are *Georgia on My Mind, I Got Rhythm, Three Little Words, Time on My Hands, Walkin' My Baby Back Home,* and *Body and Soul*. The planet Pluto is discovered. Comic strips become popular.
Dolls: American Character makes Chuckles. Effanbee makes Lamkins.

1931 – Pearl S. Buck writes the bestseller, *The Good Earth*. Films are *City Lights* with Charlie Chaplin and *Frankenstein* with Boris Karloff. Clark Gable begins his Hollywood career. The Empire State Building is completed. *The Star-Spangled Banner* by Francis Scott Key becomes the national anthem. Popular songs are *Minnie the Moocher, Mood Indigo, Goodnight Sweetheart,* and *When the Moon Comes Over the Mountain*. Al (Scarface) Capone is jailed.
Dolls: Effanbee expands the Patsy line to include the composition Patsy Baby.

1932 – Franklin D. Roosevelt wins the U.S. presidential election. Caldwell writes *Tobacco Road* and Huxley writes *Brave New World*. Films are *A Farewell to Arms* with Gary Cooper, *Grand Hotel* with Greta Garbo, Johnny Weissmuller appears in his first Tarzan film, and Shirley Temple has bit parts. Popular songs are *Brother, Can You Spare a Dime?, I'm Getting Sentimental Over You, Night and Day, Let's Have Another Cup of Coffee,* and *April in Paris*. Amelia Earhart flies solo across the Atlantic. The Lindbergh baby is kidnapped.
Dolls: Cameo makes Betty Boop, a character from an animated cartoon.

12" composition Cameo Betty Boop, marked "Copyright By Fleischer Studios" on red heart label on painted dress, character head, painted eyes, molded hair, composition and wood segmented body, molded dress and high heels, circa 1932, $500.00.
Courtesy McMasters Doll Auctions.

Great American Dolls of the Twentieth Century

1933 – Adolf Hitler becomes dictator and begins building concentration camps and burns non-Nazi and Jewish books. Erskine Caldwell writes *God's Little Acre*. Films are *King Kong, Dr. Jekyll and Mr. Hyde, Little Women* starring Katherine Hepburn, and *She Done Him Wrong* starring Mae West. Popular songs are *Smoke Gets in Your Eyes, Stormy Weather, Easter Parade,* and *Who's Afraid of the Big Bad Wolf?*.
Dolls: Bernard Lipfert designs Snoozie for Ideal, with an open yawning mouth. Madame Alexander makes an all-cloth Alice in Wonderland.

1934 – Adolf Hitler promotes a blood bath in Germany. *Good-Bye Mr. Chips* is a bestseller. F. Scott Fitzgerald writes *Tender is the Night*. Films are *It Happened One Night, Of Human Bondage,* and *The Thin Man*. Shirley Temple becomes the world's little darling in *Little Miss Marker, Stand Up and Cheer, Baby, Take a Bow, Bright Eyes,* and *The Little Colonel*. Popular songs are *Blue Moon, The Continental,* and *Stars Fell on Alabama*. Marie Curie dies. Sophia Loren and the Dionne quintuplets are born. The FBI shoots Public Enemy No. 1, John Dillinger.
Dolls: Bernard Lipfert designs the composition Shirley Temple with dimples in cheeks like the popular child movie star. Effanbee comes up with a drink and wet baby that the public loves — Dy-Dee.

18" composition Ideal Shirley Temple, green sleep eyes, open mouth with teeth, dimples in cheeks, mohair wig, Stand Up and Cheer outfit of white organdy with red dots, trimmed in red, circa 1934+, $1,050.00.
Courtesy Iva Mae Jones.

1935 – President Roosevelt signs the Social Security Act. Persia changes its name to Iran. Clarence Day writes *Life with Father*. Films are *Anna Karenina* with Greta Garbo, *Mutiny on the Bounty* with Clark Gable, and *The 39 Steps* by Alfred Hitchcock. Fox Film releases Shirley Temple films *Our Little Girl, Curly Top,* and *The Littlest Rebel*. *Porgy and Bess* opens in New York. Popular songs are *Begin the Beguine, The Music Goes Round and Round, I Got Plenty o' Nuthin',* and *Just One of Those Things*. The Rumba is popular. Colleen Moore's dollhouse tours U.S.
Dolls: Madame Alexander gets the license to make the composition Dionne Quintuplets and other manufacturers promptly copy them. Effanbee costumes dolls with red braids in their line for Anne Shirley, a character from *Anne of Green Gables* movie and the *Fairy Princess* (Wee Patsy), a tie-in to Colleen Moore's dollhouse that is touring the country. Madame Alexander makes McGuffey Ana.

13" composition Madame Alexander McGuffey Ana, brown sleep eyes, open mouth with teeth, blonde human hair braided wig, in shipping box, first advertised in 1935, circa 1938, $700.00+; with four extra tagged outfits, $1,100.00.
Courtesy Rae Klenke.

Great American Dolls of the Twentieth Century

1936 – King George V of England dies. Hitler gets 99 percent vote. Margaret Mitchell's *Gone with the Wind* is a Pulitzer Prize novel. Films are *Mr. Deeds Goes to Town, San Francisco* with Clark Gable and Spencer Tracy, and *Intermezzo* with Ingrid Bergman; Shirley Temple stars in *Captain January, Poor Little Rich Girl,* and *Dimples.*
Dolls: Dewees Cochran designs the American Children.

17" composition Effanbee American Child, marked "Effanbee//American Children" on head, "Effanbee//Anne Shirley" on body, designed by Dewees Cochran, sleep eyes, closed mouth, human hair wig, separated fingers, original pink velvet dress, matching hat, a similar doll dressed in blue velvet with music box was featured in the 1939 Montgomery Ward catalog. $700.00.
Courtesy Bev Mitchell.

1937 – Recession in the U.S. Steinbeck writes *Of Mice and Men.* Walt Disney's *Snow White and the Seven Dwarfs* is released; Fox releases two Shirley Temple films *Wee Willie Winkie* and *Heidi.* Popular songs are *The Lady Is a Tramp, Whistle While You Work, A Foggy Day in London Town, The Dipsy Doodle, Harbor Lights,* and *I've Got My Love to Keep Me Warm.* Nylon is invented. Amelia Earhart is lost on her Pacific flight. The Hindenburg crashes and burns. The Duke of Windsor marries Mrs. Wallis Simpson.
Dolls: Ideal makes Betsy Wetsy and Effanbee makes Charlie McCarthy, ventriloquist dummy. Vogue makes Toddles. Rowena Haskins (Nancy Ann Abbott) makes The Nancy Ann Storybook dolls. Madame Alexander makes a celebrity doll — actress Jane Withers. Mary Hoyer starts her doll company.

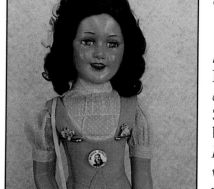

1938 – Daphne du Maurier writes *Rebecca,* Rawlings writes the *The Yearling,* and Thornton Wilder writes *Our Town.* Pearl S. Buck wins the Nobel Prize for Literature. Orson Welles's radio production of H.G. Wells's *War of the Worlds* causes panic. Films are *Rebecca of Sunnybrook Farm* with Shirley Temple and *You Can't Take It with You.* Benny Goodman's band brings new style to jazz music. Popular songs are *Flat Foot Floogie with a Floy Floy, September Song, A Tisket, A Tasket, Jeepers Creepers, Falling in Love with Love,* and *You Must Have Been a Beautiful Baby.* The 40-hour workweek is established in the U.S.
Dolls: Alexander makes the composition Flora McFlimsey. Ideal makes Disney's Snow White, celebrity dolls Deanna Durbin (a child actress) and Princess Beatrix representing Princess Beatrix of the Netherlands, Flexies that include Baby Snooks, a character by Fannie Brice, and Mortimer Snerd, Edgar Bergen's radio show dummy.

24" all-composition Ideal Deanna Durbin, marked on head "Ideal Doll//Deanna Durbin" and "Ideal Doll/25" on back, sleep eyes, open mouth with six upper teeth, felt tongue, dark brown human hair wig, in original pale blue wool jumper and purse, pink dotted Swiss blouse, pin reads "DEANNA DURBIN//A UNIVERSAL STAR," circa 1938 – 1941, $800.00+.
Courtesy Cornelia Ford.

Great American Dolls of the Twentieth Century

1939 – Germany invades Poland and starts WWII. Richard Llewellyn writes *How Green Was My Valley*; John Steinbeck writes *The Grapes of Wrath*; and Jan Struther writes *Mrs. Miniver*. Grandma Moses becomes famous in the U.S. Films are *Gone with the Wind, Good-Bye Mr. Chips, The Wizard of Oz* with Judy Garland, *The Little Princess* with Shirley Temple, and *Stagecoach*. War songs in England are *Roll Out the Barrel, Hang Out the Washing on the Siegried Line*, and *The Last Time I Saw Paris*. Popular songs are *God Bless America, Three Little Fishes, Over the Rainbow, Beer Barrel Polka*, and *I'll Never Smile Again*. Nylon stockings first appear.

Dolls: Madame Alexander makes Sonja Henie, representing the Olympic skater. Effanbee makes Historical Dolls depicting history of apparel, 1492 – 1939, Sweetie Pie, and Little Lady. Bernard Lipfert designs a celebrity doll Judy Garland as Dorothy from *The Wizard of Oz* for Ideal who also makes Disney characters Pinocchio and Jiminy Cricket.

18" composition Madame Alexander Sonja Henie, brown sleep eyes, open mouth, dimples in cheeks, blond wig, jointed composition body, satin outfit, flower ring in hair, white skates, all original, circa 1939 – 1942, $950.00.
Courtesy Flo Burnside.

1940 – Because of World War II, food is rationed in Britain; Germany invades Norway, Denmark, Holland, Belgium, and Luxembourg. Winston Churchill becomes the British Prime Minister. Franklin D. Roosevelt is re-elected president for a third term. Hemingway writes *For Whom the Bell Tolls*; O'Neill writes *Long Day's Journey into Night*. Fitzgerald dies. Films are *Grapes of Wrath, The Great Dictator, Rebecca, Gaslight, The Little Princess* with Shirley Temple, and *Fantasia* by Disney. Popular songs are *You Are My Sunshine, How High the Moon, The Last Time I Saw Paris, When You Wish Upon a Star, It's a Big Wide Wonderful World, Oh, Johnny, South of the Border, Blueberry Hill,* and *Woodpecker Song*. Penicillin is manufactured.

Dolls: Madame Alexander makes Little Shaver. Ideal uses a new material to make the Magic Skin Baby; unfortunately, this material turns black and deteriorates with age.

1941 – World War II continues as Germans invade Crete and Russia; the *Bismarck* is sunk; the Japanese bomb Pearl Harbor; the U.S. and Britain declare war on Japan; the U.S. declares war on Germany and Italy. U.S. Savings Bonds and Stamps go on sale. Films are *Citizen Kane* with Orson Welles, and *How Green Was My Valley*. Popular songs are *Bewitched, Bothered, and Bewildered, Deep in the Heart of Texas, I Don't Want to Set the World on Fire,* and *Chattanooga Choo-Choo*. Joe DiMaggio sets baseball records. Lou Gehrig dies.

Dolls: Hansi Share, in Hollywood, makes Monica dolls with human hair rooted into the composition head.

1942 – Japanese force the Bataan Death March. Millions of Jews are killed in the Nazi gas chambers; MacArthur becomes commander in chief in the Far East. Films are *Bambi* by Walt Disney and *Mrs. Miniver* with Greer Garson. Carole Lombard dies in a plane crash. Popular songs are *White Christmas, Sleepy Lagoon, Praise the Lord and Pass the Ammunition, The White Cliffs of Dover, Paper Doll,* and *That Old Black Magic*. Sugar, gasoline, and coffee rationing begin in the U.S.

Great American Dolls of the Twentieth Century

Dolls: Freundlich makes General Douglas MacArthur; Ideal makes Plassie.

18" composition Freundlich General MacArthur, painted eyes, closed mouth, molded painted hat with military insignia, jointed composition body, right arm bent to salute, original military uniform, circa 1940s, $155.00.
Courtesy McMasters Doll Auctions.

1943 – World War II continues. Betty Smith writes *A Tree Grows in Brooklyn*. Films are *Jane Eyre* with Orson Welles, *Shadow of a Doubt* by Alfred Hitchcock, and *Casablanca*. Rodgers and Hammerstein's Broadway musical *Oklahoma!* opens. Popular songs are *Mairzy Doats, Oh, What a Beautiful Mornin, People Will Say We're In Love, I'll Be Seeing You (in All the Old, Familiar Places)*, and *Comin' in on a Wing and a Prayer*. The Jitterbug becomes the hot dance in the U.S.
Dolls: Brother or Sister by Effanbee. Ideal makes Junior Miss, a large cloth soft stuffed doll, has elastic on bottom of feet so a child can dance with her.

1944 – D-Day with landings in Normandy; the Battle of the Bulge begins; Roosevelt is elected for a fourth term. Tennessee Williams writes *The Glass Menagerie*. Charles Dana Gibson, creator of the Gibson Girl, dies. Films are *Lifeboat* by Alfred Hitchcock and *Going My Way*. Popular songs are *Don't Fence Me In, Rum and Coca-Cola, Swinging on a Star, Sentimental Journey,* and *Accentuate the Positive*.
Dolls: Ideal makes all composition Bridal Party Dolls.

1945 – Okinawa is captured; Franklin D. Roosevelt dies and is succeeded by Harry S. Truman; Mussolini is killed; Hitler commits suicide; V.E. Day ends the war in Europe. The U.S. drops atomic bombs on Japan. Japan surrenders; end of World War II (war dead estimated at 35 million plus 10 million in Nazi concentration camps). General George S. Patton is killed in an automobile accident. Mary Chase writes *Harvey* and George Orwell writes *Animal Farm. The Lost Weekend* is a new film and Rodgers and Hammerstein's *Carousel* opens in New York. Be-bop comes into fashion.
Dolls: Arranbee makes composition dolls; skating costumed dolls are popular.

1946 – Robert Penn Warren writes *All the King's Men*. Films are *The Best Years of Our Lives, Gilda,* Alfred Hitchcock's *Notorious,* and *Great Expectations*. W.C. Fields dies. Irving Berlin's *Annie Get Your Gun* opens in New York. Popular songs are *How Are Things in Gloccamorra?, Tenderly, South America, Take It Away, Zip-a-dee-doo-dah, Come Rain or Shine, The Gypsy, Ole Buttermilk Sky, Shoo-Fly Pie and Apple Pan Dowdy,* and *Doin' What Comes Nacherly*.
Dolls: Alexander makes celebrity doll, Margaret O'Brien. Terri Lee is made in composition and then later in hard plastic.

1947 – Princess Elizabeth marries Philip Mountbatten, Duke of Edinburgh. Tennessee Williams's *A Streetcar Named Desire* opens. *The Diary of Anne Frank* is published. The Dead Sea Scrolls are discovered. Academy Award winning film is *Gentleman's Agreement*. Maria Callas makes her operatic debut. Popular songs are *Papa, Won't You Dance With Me?, Almost Like Being in Love,* and *I'll Dance at Your Wedding*. The

Great American Dolls of the Twentieth Century

transistor is invented. Henry Ford dies. Jackie Robinson becomes the first black in a major baseball league. Al Capone dies.

Dolls: Effanbee makes Howdy Doody and Honey. Ideal makes Sparkle Plenty, the daughter of B.O. Plenty and Gravel Gertie from the Dick Tracy comic strip.

17" composition Madame Alexander Margaret O'Brien, marked "Alexander" on head and back, blue sleep eyes, closed mouth, mohair wig in looped braids, five-piece composition body, original tagged white organdy blouse with attached slip, pink jumper, old socks, original side snap shoes, straw hat with flowers, circa 1946 – 1948, $500.00.
Courtesy McMasters Doll Auctions.

1948 – Harry S. Truman is elected president. General John J. Pershing dies. James A. Michener writes *Tales of the South Pacific*. Films are *The Naked City* and *Macbeth* with Orson Welles. Cole Porter's *Kiss Me, Kate* opens in New York. Popular songs are *Nature Boy, All I Want for Christmas Is My Two Front Teeth*, and *Buttons and Bows*. The long-playing record is invented. Orville Wright and Babe Ruth die. Prince Charles is born.

Dolls: Bernard Lipfert designs Baby Coos for Ideal with a Magic Skin body. Vogue makes Ginny.

1949 – The Berlin blockade is lifted. Nelson Algren's *The Man with the Golden Arm* and Nancy Mitford's *Love in a Cold Climate* are published. Films are *The Third Man* and *All the King's Men*. Popular songs are *Bali Ha'i, Some Enchanted Evening, I'm in Love with a Wonderful Guy, So in Love, Riders in the Sky, I Love Those Dear Hearts and Gentle People, Diamonds Are a Girl's Best Friend,* and *Rudolph, the Red-Nosed Reindeer.*

Dolls: Advance makes Wanda, the Walking Wonder with irremovable shoes and rollers and a key wind mechanism that enables her to walk. Madame Alexander makes Nina Ballerina. Bernard Lipfert designs Toni for Ideal with Toni wave set and curlers. Ideal also makes Judy Splinters, a ventriloquist doll from a TV show created by Shirley Dinsdale.

14" hard plastic Ideal Toni Walker marked "P-90//Ideal Doll" on head, "Ideal Doll//90 W" on back, designed by Bernard Lipfert, blue sleep eyes, real lashes, feathered brows, eyeshadow, painted lower lashes, closed mouth, brunette wig, five piece body, walking mechanism, blue dress, white organdy bodice, red rick-rack trim, rayon panties, Ideal marked vinyl shoes, doll is in original box, play wave set, eight curlers, partially used creme shampoo, circa 1949, $450.00.
Courtesy McMasters Doll Auctions.

1950 – President Truman gives the go-ahead to the hydrogen bomb. Ray Bradbury writes *The Martian Chronicles*. Edna St. Vincent Millay and Al Jolson die. Films are *Sunset Boulevard* and *All*

20

About Eve. Cool jazz is developed from be-bop. *Guys and Dolls* opens in New York. Popular songs are *If I Knew You Were Comin I'd 've Baked a Cake, Ragg Mopp, Sam's Story, A Bushel and a Peck, Good Night Irene, Music, Music, Music,* and *Mona Lisa*. Antihistamines become popular. 1.5 million TV sets are in the U.S. (one year later there will be approximately 15 million).
Dolls: Artisan makes Little Miss Gadabout and Raving Beauty.

1951 – J.D. Salinger writes *The Catcher in the Rye*; Herman Wouk writes *The Caine Mutiny*; and James Jones writes *From Here to Eternity*. John Erskine, Fanny Brice, and William Randoph Hearst die. Films are *An American in Paris* with Gene Kelly and *A Streetcar Named Desire* with Marlon Brando. Rodgers and Hammerstein's *The King and I* opens in New York. Popular songs are *Hello, Young Lovers, Getting to Know You, Cry, In the Cool, Cool, Cool of the Evening,* and *Kisses Sweeter than Wine*. Color T.V. is introduced in the U.S.
Dolls: Effanbee makes Tintair with white hair that could also be tinted. Ideal makes Bonnie Braids comic strip daughter of Dick Tracy and Tess Trueheart; Howdy Doody and Saucy Walker.

22" hard plastic Ideal Saucy Walker, flirty blue eyes, open mouth/two teeth, auburn saran wig, turns head from side to side, holes in body for crier, hard plastic body, original red/white print dress, circa 1951 – 1955, $175.00.
Courtesy Sally DeSmet.

1952 – King George VI of England dies. Dwight D. Eisenhower is elected president. Hemingway writes *The Old Man and the Sea*; Steinbeck writes *East of Eden*; and Edna Ferber writes *Giant*. Films are *The Greatest Show on Earth* and *High Noon* with Gary Cooper and Grace Kelly. Popular songs are *I Saw Mommy Kissing Santa Claus, Jambalaya, It Takes Two to Tango, Your Cheatin' Heart,* and *Wheel of Fortune*. The Pill for contraception is produced.
Dolls: Arthur Murray Dancing Doll comes on a wind-up platform to revolve doll to make her dance. Ideal makes Betsy McCall, designed by Bernard Lipfert, from *McCall Magazine's* paper doll and Mary Hartline from TV personality on Super Circus show.

14" vinyl Ideal Betsy McCall, marked "© McCall Corp." on head, sleep eyes, saran wig, five-piece hard plastic body, all original in box with pattern for Betsy McCall apron, unplayed with condition, circa 1952, $400.00.
Courtesy McMasters Doll Auctions.

Great American Dolls of the Twentieth Century

1953 – Queen Elizabeth II is crowned. Vietnamese rebels attack Laos. Films are *Roman Holiday* with Audrey Hepburn, *From Here to Eternity*, *The Robe* with Richard Burton, and *Julius Caesar*. Popular songs are *Doggie in the Window*, *I Believe*, *Bauble, Bangles, and Beads*, *Ebb Tide*, *Stranger in Paradise*, and *I Love Paris*. Hillary and Tenzing are the first to climb Mount Everest. Lung cancer is reported caused by smoking cigarettes. Queen Mary of England dies.

Dolls: Madame Alexander makes Winnie Walker and Margot Ballerina. American Character makes hard plastic Sweet Sue. Ideal makes Harriet Hubbard Ayers with H.H. Ayer cosmetic kit and beauty table; Joan Palooka, daughter of comic strip character, Joe Palooka; her Magic Skin body smells like baby powder. Nancy Ann Storybook makes the hard plastic Muffie.

19" hard plastic American Character Sweet Sue Bride, blue sleep eyes, closed mouth, beautiful color, red synthetic wig, flat feet, white satin dress, circa 1953, $200.00.
Private collection.

1954 – The U.S. Supreme Court rules against segregation. Tennessee Williams writes *Cat on a Hot Tin Roof*; William Golding, *Lord of the Flies*; and J.R.R. Tolkien *The Lord of Rings*. Lionel Barrymore dies. Films are *On the Waterfront*, Alfred Hitchcock's *Rear Window*, and *The Seven Samurai*. Popular songs are *Hernando's Hideaway*, *Mister Sandman*, *Young At Heart*, *Three Coins in the Fountain*, and *Hey, There*. Dr. Jonas E. Salk discovers a vaccine for polio. Twenty-nine million homes in the U.S. have TV.

Dolls: Madame Alexander makes Binnie Walker and American Character makes Ricky, Jr., son of Lucille Ball and Desi Arnez from the *I Love Lucy* television show. Effanbee makes Rootie Kazootie and Polka Dottie puppet characters from the children's television show *Rootie Kazootie*. Ideal makes Posie. American Character makes Annie Oakley, in cowgirl outfit, sells for $11.45 at Sears.

1955 – President Eisenhower has a heart attack. Blacks boycott buses in Alabama. Films are *Marty* with Ernest Borgnine, *The Rose Tattoo*, and *The Seven Year Itch*. *Damn Yankees* opens in New York. Popular songs are *The Yellow Rose of Texas*, *Davy Crockett*, *Rock Around the Clock*, *Love Is a Many-Splendored Thing*, and *Sixteen Tons*. Albert Einstein dies.

Dolls: Madame Alexander makes Cissy. Eloise is designed by Bette Gould, an interpretation of Kay Thompson's fictional character who lived at the Plaza Hotel in New York. Cosmopolitan makes Ginger. Vogue makes Ginnette.

21" cloth Eloise, a literary character from book by Kay Thompon about little girl who lived at New York Plaza Hotel, yellow yarn hair, original tagged blue skirt and white blouse, circa 1955 – 1958+, $400.00. *Courtesy Elizabeth Surber.*

1956 – Eisenhower is reelected president. Martin Luther King pushes for desegregation. Films are *War and Peace, Romeo and Juliet, Around the World in 80 Days, The King and I,* and *The Ten Commandments.* Elvis Presley becomes popular. Songs are *Blue Suede Shoes, Around the World in 80 Days, Hound Dog, I Could Have Danced All Night, Que Sera, Sera,* and *Don't Be Cruel.* The oral polio vaccine is developed. Prince Rainier of Monaco marries Grace Kelly.

Dolls: Madame Alexander makes Lissy. Arranbee makes Littlest Angel. Effanbee makes Mickey, the All American Boy. Sun Rubber makes the Bannister Baby inspired by Constance Bannister. Ideal makes Miss Revlon with high-heeled feet

18" vinyl Ideal Miss Revlon, marked "VT20//Ideal Doll," sleep eyes, lashes, pierced ears, rooted saran hair, hard plastic teenage body, original tagged pink dress, circa 1956 – 1959, $500.00.
Courtesy Cornelia Ford.

1957 – The U.S.S.R. launches Sputnik I and II. Dr. Seuss writes *The Cat in the Hat.* Films are *The Bridge on the River Kwai, The Prince and the Show-girl, Love in the Afternoon,* and *Twelve Angry Men* with Henry Fonda. Leonard Bernstein's musical *West Side Story* opens in New York. Popular songs are *Love Letters in the Sand, Young Love, Tonight, Maria,* and *Seventy-Six Trombones.* Beat and beatnik become new words to describe the Beat Generation.

Dolls: Madame Alexander makes Elise. American Character makes Betsy McCall. Shirley Temple is reissued by Ideal. Vogue makes Ginny's older sister, Jill. In Sears catalog Jerry Mahoney, 21" ventriloquist doll, sells for $13.98 and 13" Popeye sells for $3.77.

1958 – Alaska becomes a state. Tension grows over desegregation. Truman Capote writes *Breakfast at Tiffanys;* Boris Pasternak writes *Dr. Zhivago.* Films are *Cat on a Hot Tin Roof* with Elizabeth Taylor, *Marjorie*

8" hard plastic American Character Betsy McCall, marked "McCall © Corp." on back, plastic sleep eyes, closed mouth, seven-piece body with jointed knees and rigid vinyl arms, auburn rooted saran wig, original riding habit with brown pants, green vest, and red checked shirt, white scarf in hair, circa 1957, $200.00.
Courtesy Nelda Shelton.

Morningstar with Gene Kelly, and *Gigi.* The Guggenheim Museum in New York opens. The cha cha is the new dance. Popular songs are *Chipmunk Song, The Purple People Eater, Volare,* and *Catch a Falling Star.* U.S. establishes NASA.

Dolls: Madame Alexander makes Edith, the Lonely Doll. Arranbee makes Miss Coty. Deluxe Premium makes Candy Fashion and Vogue makes friends for Jill — Jan, Jeff, and Jimmy, little brother to Ginnette.

1959 – Hawaii becomes the fiftieth state. Ethel Barrymore dies. James Michener writes *Hawaii;* William

Great American Dolls of the Twentieth Century

Gibson writes *The Miracle Worker*; and Ian Fleming writes *Goldfinger*. Films are *Anatomy of a Murder, Our Man in Havana, Suddenly Last Summer,* and *Ben Hur.* Richard Rodgers composes *The Sound of Music.* Popular songs are *He's Got the Whole World in His Hands, Tom Dooley, Everything's Coming Up Roses, Mack the Knife, Personality, The Sound of Music,* and *High Hopes.* The U.S. Postmaster General bans D.H. Lawrence's *Lady Chatterley's Lover* for obscenity.

Dolls: Madame Alexander makes Marybel, The Doll That Gets Well and Walt Disney's Sleeping Beauty. Ideal makes Patti Play Pal. Mattel introduces a fashion doll, Barbie. Little do we know that this will become the bestselling doll of our time, reaching over a billion sold by the end of the century. Vogue makes a freckled face Brikette, Li'l Imp. Baby Barry Toy makes Emmett Kelly and Poor Pitiful Pearl in patched dress with a change of dress, sells for $4.97 in Sears Catalog.

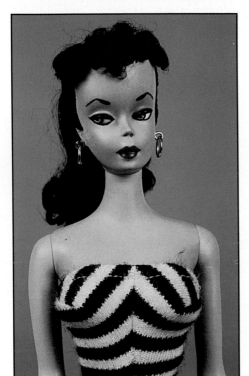

11" vinyl Mattel Number One Ponytail Barbie, #850, white irises, dark eyeliner, red lips, arched eyebrows, brunette soft hair with ringlet bangs, holes in feet, heavy solid body, circa 1959, $7,100.00+.
Courtesy McMasters Doll Auctions.

1960 – John F. Kennedy is elected president. Harper Lee writes *To Kill a Mockingbird*; William Shirer writes *The Rise and Fall of the Third Reich.* Films are *Exodus,* Alfred Hitchcock's *Psycho, The Entertainer,* and *The Apartment.* Clark Gable and Oscar Hammerstein II die. Popular songs are *Itsy Bitsy Teenie Weenie Yellow Polka Dot Bikini, The Twist, Never on Sunday,* and *Calcutta.* The first weather satellite, Tiros I, is launched by the U.S. There are 85 million TV sets in the U.S. Emily Post dies.

Dolls: Madame Alexander makes Maggie Mixup. American Character comes up with Whimsies. Mattel has a hit with a pull string talker, Chatty Cathy. Eloise Wilkins designs Baby Dear for Vogue.

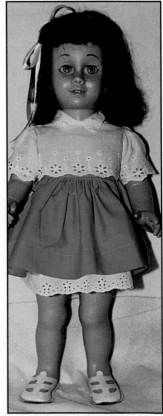

20" vinyl Mattel Chatty Cathy, hard vinyl head, blue sleep eyes, open/closed mouth with painted teeth, brunette rooted hair, hard plastic body, pull string activates voice, dressed in the Party Dress, stock #681, a blue sundress with a white eyelet bolero, petticoat, white sandal type shoes, circa 1960 – 1963, $100.00.
Courtesy Leslie Tannenbaum.

1961 – The Berlin Wall is built. Ernest Hemingway, Grandma Moses, and Gary Cooper die. Irving Stone writes *The Agony and the Ecstasy.* Films are *West Side Story, Judgment at Nuremberg,* and *The Hustler.* Popular songs are *Love Makes the World Go Round, Moon River, Where the Boys Are,* and *Exodus.*

Dolls: Madame Alexander makes Caroline, inspired by the daughter of John and Jackie Kennedy and Mimi. Ideal makes Betsy Wetsy. American Character makes Hedda Get Bedda. Ideal makes Kissy and Shirley Temple is offered in four different storybook costumes, as Little Red Riding Hood, Little Bo Peep, Cinderella, and Alice in Wonderland. Ideal makes Thumbelina and Mattel gives Barbie a boy friend named Ken.

Great American Dolls of the Twentieth Century

22" vinyl Ideal Kissy with sleep eyes, blond rooted hair, aqua check with pink trim shirt and bloomers with big Kissy label, white plastic sandals, marked on head "© Ideal Corp./K-21-L," on body marked "Ideal Toy Corp.//K22/Pat.Pend." when arms press together mouth puckers to make kiss, circa 1961 – 1964, $125.00. *Courtesy Connie Lara.*

1962 – A U.S. military council is established in South Vietnam. Katherine Anne Porter writes *Ship of Fools* and Ken Kesey writes *One Flew Over the Cuckoo's Nest.* Films are *Lawrence of Arabia, Freud, The Trial,* and *Cleopatra* with Elizabeth Taylor and Richard Burton. Marilyn Monroe dies. Popular songs are *Days of Wine and Roses, Go Away Little Girl,* and *Blowin' in the Wind.* James Meredith, a black, registers for admission to the University of Mississippi. Eleanor Roosevelt dies.
Dolls: Sears offers Angela Cartwright from the T.V. character Linda Williams on the *Danny Thomas Show,* for $3.98 and Belle Telle, that holds toy phone, battery operated, says 11 phrases, phone has record player for $12.98.

12" vinyl Ideal Tammy painted features, side-glancing eyes, rooted wig, wearing original black and white sheath dress, boxed, excellent color, circa 1963, $55.00. *Courtesy Andrea Kavanagh.*

1963 – Martin Luther King is arrested in Alabama during race riots. Lee Harvey Oswald assassinates John F. Kennedy; Lyndon B. Johnson becomes president. Jack Ruby kills Oswald as America watches on TV. American poet Robert Frost dies. Leonardo da Vinci's Mona Lisa is exhibited in New York and Washington, D.C. Films are *The Cardinal, Tom Jones, The Birds* by Alfred Hitchcock, and *Dr. Strangelove.* Joan Baez and Bob Dylan are popular singers. Popular songs are *Those Lazy, Hazy, Crazy Days of Summer, Danke Schoen, Call Me Irresponsible,* and *Eighteen Yellow Roses.* The first artificial heart is implanted.
Dolls: Madame Alexander reissues Little Shaver in vinyl and American Character makes Tressy, a grow hair doll. Deluxe Reading makes Penny Brite. Ideal makes Baby Pebbles character from the Flintstone cartoon. Ideal makes Tammy and Her Family including Mom, Dad, Tammy, Ted, and little sister Pepper. Remco makes the Littlechap Family including Dr. John, Judy, Libby, and Lisa. Sears catalog offers Fashion Queen Barbie, Ken, and Midge with tons of accessories, Betsy McCall, Ben Casey and Nurse, and Debbie Drake.

1964 – Jack Ruby sentenced to death for killing Oswald. The Warren Commission named Oswald the lone assassin. Martin Luther King wins the Nobel Peace Prize. General Douglas MacArthur, Herbert Hoover, and comedienne Gracie Allen die. Lyndon B. Johnson is elected president. Films are *Lord of the*

Great American Dolls of the Twentieth Century

Flies, A Hard Day's Night with the Beatles, *Goldfinger, Mary Poppins,* and *My Fair Lady*. The musicals *Hello Dolly!* and *Fiddler on the Roof* open in New York. Popular songs are *Hello Dolly!, I Want to Hold Your Hand, Chim Chim Cheree,* and *Fiddler on the Roof*. Elizabeth Taylor divorces Eddie Fisher and marries Richard Burton. Popular dances are the watusi, frug, monkey, funky chicken, and varieties of the twist.

Dolls: Madame Alexander makes the Fischer Quints, one boy and four girls, using Little Genius doll, in picture box with pink blanket/bottles, and Brenda Starr the red-headed reporter from the comics. Hasbro makes G.I. Joe action figures. Ideal makes a vinyl Bamm-Bamm, a character from the Flintstone cartoon. Mattel makes Baby Pattaburp who drinks from magic bottle and burps when patted and Shrinkin' Violette, a cloth pull-string talker. Remco makes the Beatles: Paul McCartney, Ringo Starr, George Harrison, and John Lennon, with guitars bearing their names. Sears catalog offers Bonomi Fashion dolls, several versions of Thumbelina, bendable leg Barbie, and accessories for her and Ken.

16" cloth Mattel Shrinkin' Violette, felt features, long thick yellow yarn hair, pull-string-talker mouth moves, eyelids flutter, says 11 phrases, marked "Copyright 1963 by The Funny Company," circa 1964, $45.00.
Courtesy Sue Amidon.

1965 – Jack Ruby, Winston Churchill, Malcolm X, and Nat King Cole die. President Johnson signs the Medicare bill. Norman Mailer writes *An American Dream*. Films are *Help!* with the Beatles, *Othello, Dr. Zhivago,* and *The Sound of Music*. Popular songs are *King of the Road, It Was A Very Good Year, Downtown,* and *A Hard Day's Night*. A relay switch malfunctions in Ontario and the northeastern United States and parts of Canada lose electrical power affecting 30 million people, causing a noticeable increase in birth rate nine months later.

Dolls: Hasbro makes sad Little Miss No Name with a tear on cheek. Little Miss Echo, battery operated recorder in torso, sells in Sears catalog for $14.99. Horsman makes Mary Poppins, a character played by Julie Andrews in the movie. Patty Duke a television celebrity comes with her own phone, $2.97 in Sears catalog. Ideal makes Samantha from the TV show *Bewitched*. Marx makes Johnny West Family of Action Figures. Mattel makes a pull string talker Drowsy in sleepers and Baby First Step, battery operated, who walks by herself.

1966 – A 48-hour Christmas truce is observed in Vietnam. Truman Capote writes *In Cold Blood* and Jacqueline Susann writes *Valley of the Dolls*. Films are *A Man for All Seasons* and *Who's Afraid of Virginia Woolf?*. Walt Disney dies. Popular songs are *Born Free, Eleanor Rigby, Strangers in the Night,* and *Ballad of the Green Berets*. *Anthony and Cleopatra* opera and the musical play *On a Clear Day You Can See Forever* opens in New York. Miniskirts come into fashion. Color TV becomes popular. The U.S. population totals 196 million.

Dolls: Mattel makes Liddle Kiddles. Sears catalogs offer mod dolls: Color Magic Barbie, Francie, Tiny Kissy, and Ideal's Glamour Misty.

1967 – Martin Luther King leads civil rights marches. Ira Levin writes *Rosemary's Baby*; Thornton Wilder *The Eighth Day*; and Harold Pinter *The Homecoming*. Bert Lahr, Vivien Leigh, Jayne Mansfield, and

Spencer Tracy die. Films are *Bonnie and Clyde, In the Heat of the Night, Guess Who's Coming to Dinner* with Katherine Hepburn and Spencer Tracy, and *The Taming of the Shrew*. Singers Nelson Eddy and Woody Guthrie die. Musical *Cabaret* opens in New York. Mickey Mantle hits his 500th career home run. Twiggy takes U.S. fashion by storm.

Dolls: Ideal has comic strip heroines Wonder Woman, Mera — Queen of Atlantis, Bat Girl, and Super Girl. Mattel makes a hit with Buffy and Mrs. Beasley characters from TV sitcom *Family Affair*. Mattel also makes Baby's Hungry, battery operated, eyes move and lips chew when magic bottle or spoon is put to mouth, and Cheerful Tearful. Remco makes Heidi and Friends, press button and dolls wave.

1968 – Martin Luther King is assassinated; James Earl Ray is arrested. Senator Robert F. Kennedy is assassinated in Los Angles; Sirhan Sirhan is arrested. Charles Portis writes *True Grit* and Arthur Hailey *Airport*. Tallulah Bankhead and Helen Keller die. Films are *Funny Girl, The Odd Couple, In Cold Blood, 2001: A Space Odyssey,* and *Oliver!*. Popular songs are *Cinderella Rockefella, Hey Jude,* and *Mrs. Robinson*. Aretha Franklin and Jimi Hendrix are popular. Jacqueline Kennedy marries Aristotle Onassis.

Dolls: Shindana, a division of Operation Bootstrap, Inc. founded after Watts's riots, is the first manufacturer of black ethnically correct black dolls like Baby Nancy. Ideal makes Little Lost Baby. Mattel makes Baby Small Talk which says eight phrases and Tippee-Toes which is battery operated and rides accessory tricycle and horse. Remco makes Baby Grows a Tooth who grows her own tooth, battery operated. Randy Reader, battery operated, recites 15 rhymes as she reads from book. Tippy Tumbles by Remco does somersaults, has batteries in pocketbook.

1969 – Dwight D. Eisenhower dies. Edward Kennedy drives a car off a bridge at Chappaquiddick Island killing Mary Jo Kopechne. Mario Puzo writes *The Godfather*. Judy Garland and Boris Karloff die. Films are *Midnight Cowboy, MacKenna's Gold, Easy Rider, Butch Cassidy and the Sundance Kid, They Shoot Horses, Don't They?* and *M.A.S.H.* Woodstock attracts more than 300,000. Popular songs are *A Boy Named Sue, Hair, Aquarius,* and *In the Year 2525.* Neil Armstrong walks on the moon. Joseph Patrick Kennedy dies. Charles Manson is arrested for the killing of actress Sharon Tate and others.

Dolls: Deluxe Reading makes the Dawn series. Ideal makes Crissy, Beautiful Crissy. Mattel makes Baby Sing-a-long, Bozo the Clown, 23 Skiddoo, and Teachy Keen, all pull string talkers. Dancerina by Mattel, is battery-operated and dances with control knob on head, and Julia a nurse, from T.V. sitcom, *Julia*.

1970 – The National Guard kills four students at Kent State. Earle Stanley Gardner, Francis Parkinson Keyes, and Gypsy Rose Lee die. Burt Bacharach wins two Academy Awards in popular music with *Butch Cassidy and the Sundance Kid* and *Raindrops Keep Falling on my Head*. Movies are *Paint Your Wagon, True Grit,* and *Woodstock*. TV sets in use throughout the world estimated at 231 million.

Dolls: Eegee makes Baby Carrie with plastic carriage or carry seat. Remco makes Baby Tender Love, and Jumpsy.

1971 – The 26th Amendment gives 18-year-olds the vote. The Pentagon Papers appear in *The New York Times*. Erich Segal writes *Love Story*; Herman Wouk *The Winds of War*; and Bernard Malamud *The Tenants*. Films are *A Clockwork Orange, The French Connection,* and *The Conformist*. Louis Armstrong and World War II hero Audie Murphy die. Cigarette ads are banned from U.S. television.

Dolls: Ideal makes Belly Button Babies; Bizzie Lizzie who when plugged into power pack, irons, vacuums, uses feather duster; and Velvet, Crissy's cousin, a pull string talker. Mattel makes Baby Beans.

Great American Dolls of the Twentieth Century

1972 – Watergate scandal begins. It will bring down President Nixon. Governor George C. Wallace is shot. J. Edgar Hoover, Harry S. Truman, the Duke of Windsor, Jackie Robinson, and Charles Atlas die. Tom O'Horgan directs *Jesus Christ Superstar*; and Tom Moore directs *Grease* in New York. The Supreme Court rules against capital punishment. Films are *Cabaret* with Liza Minnelli and *The Godfather* with Marlon Brando. *All in the Family* is the leading TV show in the U.S.
Dolls: Cinnamon by Ideal, Velvet's little sister, has growing hair.

1973 – Agnew resigns as vice president; Gerald Ford is named to replace him. Edward G. Robinson, Chic Young (creator of the *Blondie* comic strip), Pablo Picasso, Betty Grable, popular songwriter Walter E. Rollins (*Frosty the Snowman*), and Walt Kelly (creator of *Pogo* cartoon strip) die. You can go to the movies and see *The Sting, A Touch of Class,* and *Last Tango in Paris* with Marlon Brando. Lyndon B. Johnson, Pearl Buck, J.R.R. Tolkien, and Irene Ryan, Granny on the TV show *Beverly Hillbillies*, die.
Dolls: Ideal makes Harmony (arm strums guitar, head moves, battery operated with changeable record in her amplifier) and Tiffany Taylor (top of head turns to change color of hair). Mego makes Star Trek TV Series Captain Kirk, Dr. McCoy, Klingon, Lt. Uhura, Mr. Scott, and Mr. Spock action figures.

1974 – President Nixon resigns and Gerald R. Ford becomes president. Peter Benchley writes *Jaws* and Carl Bernstein and Bob Woodward *All the President's Men.* Samuel Goldwyn, Agnes Moorehead, Tex Ritter, Cass Elliot, Jack Benny, Dizzy Dean, and Charles A. Lindbergh die. This year's movies are *Harry and Tonto, Alice Doesn't Live Here Anymore, Chinatown, Clarence Darrow,* and *The Godfather, Part II* with Al Pacino. Streaking becomes a fad in the U.S.
Dolls: Blythe, by Kenner, has a pull string that changes color of eyes, and oversized head on smaller body. Mattel makes The Sunshine Family including father, Steve; mother, Stephie; and Baby Sweets, who reflect the 1970s era of oil crisis, thrift, bicycles, sewing clothes, or selling crafts from their van.

11½" hard plastic Kenner Blythe, pull string opens and closes eyes and changes color from blue to yellow to green to pink, closed mouth, lack synthetic wig, large head, small body, vinyl arms, mint-in-box, circa 1972, $100.00.
Courtesy Cathie Clark.

1975 – The U.S. ends two decades of military involvement in the Vietnam War. Egypt reopens the Suez Canal. Two assassination attempts are made on President Ford. Thornton Wilder, Rod Sterling, Susan Hayward, and Aristotle Onassis die. James R. Hoffa disappears. Moviegoers can see *Jaws, Nashville* with Lily Tomlin, *Hearts of the West,* and *The Sunshine Boys* with George Burns. Queen Elizabeth II knights Charlie Chaplin. The cost of a first class stamp increases from 10 cents to 13 cents.
Dolls: Dyn-O-Mite, J.J. Talking Doll, a pull string talker of celebrity Jimmy Walker of T.V. sitcom, *Good Times,* is made by Shindana. Six Million Dollar Man figures by Kenner, from TV show starring Lee Majors, include Bionic Man, Jaime Sommers the Bionic Woman, and Oscar Goldman with exploding briefcase.

1976 – The U.S. and Russia sign a nuclear treaty. The U.S. celebrates the Bicentennial. North and South Vietnam are reunited with Hanoi the capital. *A Chorus Line* wins a Pulitzer and a Tony award. Rev. Moon ends U.S. ministry. The Academy Award goes to *One Flew Over the Cuckoo's Nest*. Films this year are *All the President's Men* and Sylvester Stallone in *Rocky*. Mystery writer Agatha Christie, Lily Pons, Guy Lombardo, Howard Hughs, J. Paul Getty, Mao Tse-tung, Richard Daley, and Rosalind Russell die. Concorde schedules supersonic service to Washington, D.C. Israel rescues 103 hostages at Entebbe in Uganda. The Air Force Academy admits 155 women. Jimmy Carter is elected president. Leon Uris writes *Trinity* and Alex Haley writes *Roots*. Legionnaires disease kills 29 at a Philadelphia convention. The Orient Express has its last run.
Dolls: Sonny and Cher by Mego represent husband and wife TV personalities Sonny and Cher Bono. O. J. Simpson by Shindana is packed with football athletic gear.

1977 – The Energy Department is established. G. Gordon Liddy is released from prison. *Roots* is shown on T.V. Warner von Braun, Joan Crawford, Elvis Presley, Toots Shor, Anthony Eden, Bing Crosby, Maria Callas, Charlie Chaplin, Groucho Marx, and Ethel Waters die. The U.S. space shuttle, *Enterprise,* makes its first manned flight. Two planes collide in Tenerife, 570 people die. Colleen McCullough writes *The Thorn Birds*. New movies are *Star Wars, Saturday Night Fever,* and *Oh God* with George Burns. The U.S. launches space probe and tests a neutron bomb. Seattle Slew wins the Triple Crown. The U.S. population reaches 216 million.
Dolls: Mattel makes dolls of TV celebrities Donny & Marie Osmond; *Welcome Back Kotter's* Barbarino played by John Travolta, Mr. Kotter portrayed by Gabe Kaplan, Eptein & Horshack played by Robert Heges and Ron Palillo. Shindana makes Marla Gibbs who portrays Florence on T.V. sitcom, *The Jeffersons*. Mego makes Lenny & Squiggy characters from the *Laverne & Shirley* sitcom played by Michael McKean and David L. Lander.

1978 – The U.S. and China establish full diplomatic relations. Herman Wouk writes *War and Remembrance*. A Gutenberg Bible sells for $2 million. Faith Baldwin, Charles Boyer, Hubert Humphry, Golda Meir, Dan Dailey, Edgar Bergen, Norman Rockwell, Willy Messerschmitt, Gene Tunney, and Margaret Meade die. Thor Heyerdahl sails the ocean in a reed boat. The first test tube baby is born in England. The tanker *Cadiz* spills oil. The first female general is named — Margret Brewer, a Marine. Liza Minnelli wins an award for her performance in *The Act*. You can see movies with John Travolta in *Grease, National Lampoon's Animal House,* and *Coming Home*. California passes Proposition 13. There is a rash of rich and famous weddings — King Hussein, Princess Caroline, and Christina Onassis. Princess Margaret gets a divorce. Jim Jones has his People's Temple followers commit suicide after shooting Rep. Leo Ryan in Guyana. Love Canal is named a disaster era. The world's population is now 4.4 billion with 200,000 added daily.
Dolls: Mattel makes Cheryl Ladd and Kate Jackson dolls from the popular TV show, *Charlie's Angels,* Grizzly Adams portrayed by Dan Haggerty, and Jimmy Osmond, the youngest brother of Donny & Marie. Mego makes dolls of Gene Simmons, Ace Frehley, Peter Cris, and Paul Stanley from the band Kiss.

12½" vinyl Mego Ace Frehley, Paul Stanley, Peter Cris, and Gene Simmons from the band Kiss, and all-vinyl, fully jointed, rooted hair, painted features and makeup, circa 1978, $150.00 each.
Courtesy McMasters Doll Auctions.

Great American Dolls of the Twentieth Century

1979 – The Three Mile Island nuclear accident happens. The government severs military ties with Nicaragua. Egypt and Israel sign a peace treaty. Inflation heats up. The Department of Education is formed. Arthur Fedler and John Wayne die. Iran takes American hostages. The government bails out Chrysler.

Dolls: Mattel makes more personality dolls: Debby Boone, singing star whose record *You Light Up My Life* sold millions, Kristy McNichol who plays on *Family* from 1976 – 1979, and Mork & Mindy, from 1978 – 1982 T.V. sitcom starring Robin Williams and Pam Dawber.

1980 – The Soviets invade Afghanistan. Mt. St. Helens erupts in Washington state. Ronald Reagan is elected president. Mae West dies. A mentally disturbed youth shoots John Lennon. The U.S. boycotts the Moscow Summer Olympics. Jesse Owens dies.

Dolls: Mattel makes Guardian Goddesses, take-offs of the *Wonder Woman* T.V. series. Fisher Price makes Mickie and Becky.

1981 – Iranian hostage crisis ends as Reagan assumes office. Reagan is shot outside the Washington Hilton in D.C. The first woman, Sandra Day O'Connor, is appointed to the Supreme Court. Two Libyan jets are shot down. IBM introduces the personal computer. Reagan fires the striking air traffic controllers. Cholesterol is linked to heart disease. Boxer, Joe Louis dies.

Dolls: Tomy makes Kimberly with long blond rooted hair. Effanbee makes John Wayne for the Legend Series, with Stetson and rifle.

17" vinyl Effanbee John Wayne Commemorative Doll, marked "WAYNE//3N5.//19©81" on back and head, painted blue eyes, molded painted hair, fully jointed, felt cowboy hat, plastic rifle, hangtag, mint in box, circa 1981, $95.00.
Courtesy Millie Carol.

1982 – Secretary of State Alexander Haig resigns. The U.S. Marines land in Beirut. An Air Florida jet crashes into a bridge in Washington, D.C. Someone puts cyanide in Tylenol capsules and seven die. Braniff airlines files bankruptcy. Some banks fail. Reagan proposes an MX missile deployment scheme. We have the first space shuttle flight and the first artificial heart. Ayn Rand and Satchel Paige die.

Dolls: Effanbee makes celebrity dolls John Wayne in calvary uniform and Mae West.

1983 – A car bomb destroys the U.S. embassy in Beirut. The USSR shoots down a South Korean airliner. The U.S. invades Grenada. The U.S. withdraws from UNESCO. Cable TV and video are popular. Ira Gershwin and Harry James die. The final episode of M.A.S.H. is shown. Sally Ride is the first American woman in space. A holiday is named for Martin Luther King Jr.

Dolls: Cabbage Patch dolls Babyland General Hospital, Cleveland, GA., Xavier Roberts Little People, are cloth, needle sculptures. #99 The Great Gretzky by Mattel portrays Canadian hockey player Wayne Gretzky with skates and stick.

Great American Dolls of the Twentieth Century

23" cloth Xaiver Roberts Cabbage Patch Little People, with red yarn pigtails, red dotted dress, excellent condition, circa 1983, $125.00.
Courtesy Joanne Morgan.

1984 – Ronald Reagan is re-elected. U.S. Marines withdraw from Lebanon. Donald Duck turns 50. Ansel Adams and Count Basie die. The AIDS virus is identified. A vaccine for chicken pox is developed. Los Angeles holds the Olympics.
Dolls: Effanbee makes Louis Armstrong for the Great Moments in Music Series and Winston Churchill from the Great Moments in History.

1985 – Reagan imposes sanctions on South Africa for apartheid. The Titanic is located on the ocean bottom. Henry Cabot Lodge, Roger Maris, Orson Welles, and Rock Hudson die. Videocassette recorders are popular. The U.S. dollar is devalued. Leaded gasoline is banned. Christa McAuliffe is chosen to be the first civilian on a space shuttle mission.
Dolls: Mattel makes The Heart Family, vinyl, Mom, Dad, and baby, with the slogan, "Fun is being part of the family that's all Heart," through 1990. Mattel makes Princess of Power fantasy creature Etheria, Angella, Bow, Castapella, Catra, Double Trouble, Glimmer, and Frosta and many accessories. Playmates makes Cricket, a talker with recorder and World of Wonder makes Pamela a battery operated talking doll. Hasbro makes Jem with truly outrageous costumes and makeup.

1986 – Sanctions are imposed and the U.S. makes air strikes against Libya. Averill Harriman, Benny Goodman, Cary Grant, and Rudy Vallee die. Rehnquist is named Chief Justice of the Supreme Court. The Iran Contra affair is exposed. Christa McAuliffe and others die in the Challenger accident. The U.S. Congress names the rose as the official flower. Scientists make genetic engineered organism. Ivan Boesky is brought down in a Wall Street scandal.
Dolls: Kirsten, Samantha, and Molly from the American Girl Collection are made by Pleasant Company, all representing girls set in a historical period, with books and accessories available.

1987 – America celebrates the 200th anniversary of the Constitution. Congress overrides President Reagan's veto of the Clean Air Act. The Senate blocks nomination of Robert Bork to the Supreme Court. The English musical *Les Miserables* comes to the U.S. Fred Astair and Andy Warhol die. Alan Greenspan is appointed to head the Federal Reserve. Reverend Jimmy Baker is forced to resign his television ministry due to sex and money scandals.
Dolls: Worlds of Wonder makes Julie, a battery operated talking doll. Mattel makes Hot Looks, vinyl models with cloth bodies who work for the Hot Looks Modeling Agency: Chelsea, Elkie, Mimi, Stacey, and Zizi.

1988 – George Bush is elected president. A terrorist bomb brings down a Pan Am 747 over Lockerbie, Scotland. Oliver North is indicted in the Iran-Contra Affair. Ronald Reagan, George Bush, and Mikhail Gorbachev have a summit in New York. On Broadway you can see *Phantom of the Opera*. Aspirin is touted to reduce heart attacks. There are droughts in the Midwest. Jimmy Swaggart is the next television minister brought down by a sex scandal. Super Wal-Marts and Super K-Marts become the rage.
Dolls: Happy Holiday Barbie in red long gown is issued by Mattel.

Great American Dolls of the Twentieth Century

1989 – U.S. forces enter Panama and capture Manuel Noriega for drug trafficking. The Cold War ends. The Supreme Court says flag burning is not a crime. The Exxon Valdez oil spill occurs. *Batman* and *Superman* are popular movies. There is a major earthquake in Northern California. Alar is thought to be a carcinogen and banned for use on apples. Hurricane Hugo wrecks havoc. Pete Rose is banned from baseball.
Dolls: The Little Mermaid Disney character by Mattel.

1990 – Iraq invades Kuwait and Bush sends troops to the Persian Gulf. Oliver North's conviction is overturned. U.S. sends aid to Russia. NASA launches the Hubble space telescope satellite. GM starts building the Saturn automobile.
Dolls: Meritus makes Michelle, star of TV sitcom *Full House*, as portrayed by the Olson twins. Galoob makes Baby Face with different expressive character faces.

1991 – Operation Desert Storm is used by the U.S. to defeat Iraq in the Persian Gulf War; General Norman Schwarzkopf leads troops. Clarence Thomas wins confirmation to the Supreme Court. Four L.A. policemen beat black motorist Rodney King. Biosphere II, Pan Am, and Eastern Airlines fold. Jeffrey Dahmer, a serial killer, confesses. Magic Johnson, basketball star, announces he is HIV positive. The Navy is accused of sexual harassment in the Tailhook scandal.
Dolls: The Pleasant Company introduces Felicity of 1774 in the American Girl Collection. Mattel makes Disney characters Cinderella & Prince Charming and Beauty & the Beast .

1992 – Bill Clinton is elected president. U.S. troops are sent to Somalia to keep order. In Oregon, republican Bob Packwood comes under fire for sexual harassment. Star of the Tonight show, Johnny Carson, retires. Hurricane Andrew causes a lot of damage. Boxer Mike Tyson is convicted of rape.
Dolls: Mattel makes Neptune Fantasy Barbie designed by Bob Mackie, Aladdin & Jasmine from the animated *Aladdin* film, and *Beverly Hills, 90210* characters from the T.V. series which include Brandon Walsh, Brenda Walsh, Donna Martin, Dylan McKay, and Kelly Taylor. Wendy Lawton makes a porcelain Pascha named after the Russian word for Easter.

1993 – Terrorists bomb the New York World Trade Center. Attorney General Janet Reno is sworn in. The Motor voter law passes. A "don't ask; don't tell" policy is adopted in the military regarding homosexuality. The NAFTA bill passes. This is the year that the Internet and home computers become popular. Federal officers fire on David Koresh and his Branch Davidian followers resulting in the massacre of 88 men, women, and children.
Dolls: The Pleasant Company's American Collection makes Addy, a black girl from 1864. Lawton Doll Company makes Flora McFlimsey and Snow White. Mattel makes Disney characters Snow White and the Seven Dwarfs.

1994 – Cohorts of Tonya Harding attack Nancy Kerrigan during ice-skating practice. The California Northridge earthquake occurs. On T.V. O.J. Simpson is seen eluding police after being accused of killing his ex-wife Nicole and a friend. Susan Smith drowns her children in Florida and blames a carjacker. An unruly American teenager who drew graffiti on cars in Singapore is caned for punishment. Michael Jackson marries Lisa Marie Presley. Cubans and Haitians flee to America. Serial killer John Wayne Gacy is executed; Jeffrey Dahmer is murdered in prison. Richard Nixon and Jacqueline Kennedy Onassis die.
Dolls: The Lawton Doll Company makes Emily and her Diary and Katie and her Kewpie. Mattel makes Queen of Hearts Barbie.

Great American Dolls of the Twentieth Century

1995 – The U.S. sends peace-keeping forces to Bosnia. The O.J. Simpson trial begins on television (he is acquitted). There is a heat wave in the Midwest. Newt Gingrich named speaker of the house. Jonas Salk and Mickey Mantle die. The Internet is popular — seen as the information highway.

Dolls: Ashton Drake makes Gene, designed by Mel Odom, who portrays a woman of the 1940s – 1950s era that goes to Hollywood to become a film star. Bitty Baby is added to the American Girl Collection by the Pleasant Company. Georgetown makes Alison, Megan, Heather, and Keisha the Magic Attic Club designed by Robert Tonner, children who discover a trunk of costumes in the attic. Wendy Lawton of the Lawton Doll Company makes Patricia and her Patsy. Mattel makes Pocahontas, John Smith, Nakoma, and Kocoum from the animated film. Playmate makes Baby So Beautiful with many combinations of hair and eye color.

1996 – Commerce Secretary Ron Brown killed in Bosnia in a plane crash. The Unabomber, Ted Kaczynski, is arrested. A seven-year old girl, Jessica Dubroff dies in an attempt to set an age record for flying cross-country. Value-Jet 592 crashes in the Everglades. TWA flight 800 explodes and crashes off Long Island. Clinton has legal troubles with the Whitewater Scandal. Spiro Agnew, Alger Hiss, Gene Kelly, and George Burns die. A terrorist explodes a pipe bomb at a park during the Summer Olympics in Atlanta.

14" vinyl Robert Tonner Betsy McCall, auburn rooted hair, brown glass eyes, closed smiling mouth, rigid vinyl body, dressed in raspberry velveteen dress with matching shoes and headband, 1996 Modern Doll Convention in Las Vegas, NV, $100.00.
Private collection.

Dolls: Mattel makes Disney characters Cruella De Vil, portrayed by Glenn Close in the film *101 Dalmations*, and *Hunchback of Notre Dame* from the animated film. Ashton Drake makes Sparkling Seduction Gene in glittering long gown, winner of the 1996 Young Designers of America Award. The Robert Tonner Doll Company makes a vinyl 14" Betsy McCall in red and white scissor dress.

1997 – Princess Diana is killed in a auto accident in Paris. The world mourns the loss of Mother Theresa. Global warming and El Nino are blamed for weather extremes. Hong Kong is returned to China. A cloned sheep, Dolly, is born. Timothy McVeigh is convicted of the Oklahoma City bombing. Space probe Pathfinder takes pictures of Mars and sends them home. Septuplets are born in Iowa to the McCaugheys. Tiger Woods wins the Masters tournament. Jimmy Stewart and Robert Mitchum die. As the Hale Bopp comet passes, 39 members of the Heaven's Gate cult commit suicide to catch a heavenly ride to the next millennium.

Dolls: Josefina is added to the Pleasant Company's American Girls Collection, she depicts a girl growing up in 1824 Mexico. Mattel makes Harley Davidson Barbie and Barbie Loves Elvis. The Alexander Doll Company makes the Coca Cola Carhop. Vogue Doll Company makes Ginny Barbecues. Wendy Lawton makes The Lawton Travel Doll.

1998 – Clinton receives an Impeachment vote in the House. A drug to prevent impotency, Viagra, is announced. El Nino continues to make severe weather changes. John Glenn returns to space in a much-publicized *Discovery* shuttle mission. Mark McGuire and Sammy Sosa set new baseball records. Asian economies falter, the tobacco industry has lawsuits. The Y2K crisis looms.

Great American Dolls of the Twentieth Century

Dolls: Vogue makes a Bobby Soxer Ginny. Ashton Drakes makes Hello Hollywood and Incognito Gene. Wendy Lawton makes Petra & Pinocchio.

15½" vinyl Ashton Drake Galleries Gene marked "Gene ™//© 1995 Mel Odom" on head, created to portray a movie star, painted eyes, blond synthetic wig, jointed fashion type body, with marked Gene stand, wearing Incognito, red and white print cotton frock, red buttons, petticoat, purse/gold chain, red polka-dot scarf, sunglasses, nylons, earrings, shoes, from the 1955 era designed by Timothy Alberts, 1998 doll and costume issue price $79.95.
Courtesy Elizabeth Surber.

1999 – John Kennedy, Jr., his wife, and sister-in-law are killed in a plane crash off Martha's Vineyard. Wilt Chamberlain dies. e-Bay is recognized as the leader in online auctions.
Dolls: Robert Tonner Doll Company introduces Ann Estelle adapted from a Mary Englebrite character and a new fashion doll, Tyler Wentworth.

2000 - And what will the new millennium hold? Looking back, Raggedy Ann remains a favorite, Kewpies still have their charm, but the most popular doll in sales volume, with a reported over one billion dolls sold, has to be Barbie. Starting the new century, a big revival of interest is noted for fashion dolls such as Gene, Tyler Wentworth, Brenda Starr, and Cissy. Ashton Drake's Gene may well be the doll to put a dent in Barbie doll's crown as the most popular doll of the new century.

Advertising Dolls

Companies often use dolls as a means of advertising their products, either as a premium or in the form of a trademark of their company. This entrepreneurial spirit has given us some delightful examples. Not meant primarily as a collectible, but as a means to promote products or services, the advertising doll has been around since the late 1800s, and continues to be a viable form of advertising. Advertising dolls now can be made just for the collector — look at the Christmas ornaments that advertise Barbie, space adventurers, and the McDonald's restaurant premiums in their Happy Meal boxes. All of these dolls or figurines that promote a product or service are called advertising dolls. Early companies that used dolls to promote their products were Amberg with Vanta Baby, American Cereal Co. with Cereta, American Character with the Campbell Kids, Buster Brown Shoes with Buster Brown, Ideal with Cracker Jack Boy and ZuZu Kid, Kellogg's with a variety of characters, and many others.

What to look for:

This is a wonderful field for collectors as you may find dolls others overlook. Dolls can be of any material, but those mint-in-box or with original advertising will remain the most desirable. Cloth should have bright colors, no tears, little soil, and retain printed identifying marks. On dolls of other materials, look for rosy cheeks, little wear, cleanliness, and originality, original tags, labels, boxes, or brochures. Keep dates and purchasing information when you obtain current products. This information will add to the value of your collectibles.

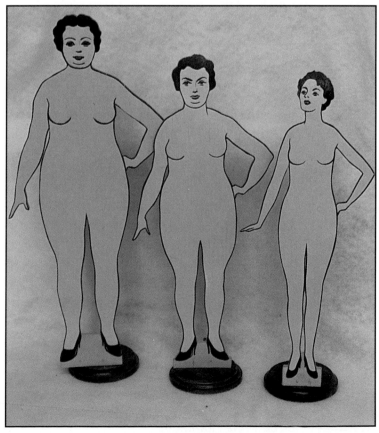

14" – 12½" girdle mannequins, painted wooden ladies in black high heels and black hair, 1940s, largest to smallest: $30.00, $25.00, $20.00.
Private collection.

23" composition Miss Curity (possibly R & B), blue sleep eyes, blond mohair wig, rosy cheeks, all original with original stand, mint in box, circa 1940s to 1951, $875.00.
Courtesy Peggy Millhouse.

14" vinyl black premium doll, black wig, closed mouth, red accent dots at nostrils, gold hoop earrings, dressed as Egyptian prince with red and navy turban, red costume with navy jacket, gold slippers, has gold label on hat marked "S," this was given as a premium in Germany from the Sarrotti Chocolate factory, circa 1965, $75.00.
Courtesy Rita Donohue.

Buddy Lee

Buddy Lee is a display doll made for the H. L. Lee Company to promote Lee uniforms and was first offered to dealers in 1922. The Lee Company's most popular dolls were the Cowboy and Engineer reflecting their production of denim jeans and overalls. The early 12½" dolls were made in composition and the later 13" in hard plastic about 1949. This is one doll that really appeals to men — especially men who wore uniforms in their work on the railroad, at gas stations, and Coca-Cola plants. It was discontinued in 1962. Collectors can look for outfits including Coca-Cola, Phillips 66, Sinclair, MM, Standard, John Deere, TWA, Cowboy, Engineer in striped and plain denim, and also two versions (farmers) dressed in plaid shirt and jeans.

Left: 16" hard plastic Cowboy, painted side-glancing eyes, molded painted hair, dressed in red and black plaid shirt, jeans, black cowboy hat, all original, circa 1950s, $400.00.
Right: 16" composition Engineer, painted side-glancing eyes, molded painted hair, dressed in bib overalls, cap, all original, circa 1940s, $400.00.
Courtesy Martha Sweeney.

12" composition Engineer, painted side-glancing eyes, all original in tagged cap and overalls, circa 1922, $325.00.
Courtesy Mary Evelyn Graf.

13" hard plastic Gas Station Attendant, with Phillips 66 labeled shirt and hat, painted side-glancing eyes, all original, circa 1950s, $1,200.00.
Courtesy Marie Swedeen.

12" hard plastic, marked "Buddy Lee" on back, "Union Made//Lee//Sanforized" on tag on pants, stiff neck, brown painted side-glancing eyes, closed smiling mouth, molded painted hair, hard plastic body jointed at shoulders only, dressed in the original scarce Coca-Cola outfit with cap, circa 1948+, $650.00.
Courtesy McMasters Doll Auctions.

Alexander Doll Co.

The Alexander Doll Company made news on the financial pages as reorganization from their 1995 chapter 11 bankruptcy led new management to use the Japanese "kaizen" flow-type manufacturing. The company is owned by TBM Consulting Group and is located in the Harlem section of New York City. The new management has redesigned the production flow in the turn-of-the-century Studebaker plant to allow groups of workers to oversee the manufacturing process from start to finish on selected items. Instead of one person doing one job all day, the group works together to finish dolls within their group, thus increasing productivity and cutting costs.

The financial and production changes seem not to have slowed the interest in Alexander dolls which have increased in popularity under the guidance of the Alexander Doll collector's club, a company-sponsored marketing tool that also has been used successfully by both Effanbee during the 1930s and more recently by Vogue with their Ginny club.

Beatrice and Rose Alexander began the Alexander Doll Co. in about 1912. They were known for doll costumes, and began using the "Madame Alexander" trademark in 1928. Beatrice A. Behrman became a legend in the doll world with her long reign as the head of the Alexander Doll Company. Alexander made cloth, composition, and wooden dolls, and after World War II they made the transition to hard plastic and then into vinyl.

The doll world was shocked these past few years with skyrocketing prices paid for some wonderful collectible Alexander dolls at auction including $56,000.00 for an 8" hard plastic doll re-dressed as the Infante of Prague. Alexander's rare and beautiful dolls continue to attract young collectors. Alexander dolls continue to increase in value as shown by one-of-a-kind fully documented special dolls as they appear on the market. These should continue to gain in value with the support of the avid Alexander fans. And there seems to be no lack of them as premier events by the growing Madame Alexander Doll Club are held around the country. For information, write: Madame Alexander Doll Club, P.O. Box 330, Mundelein, IL 60060. Telephone: 847-949-9200; fax 847-949-9201.

One of the Alexander company's luckiest breaks came when they obtained the exclusive license to produce the Dionne Quintuplets dolls in 1934. The Alexander Dionne Quintuples were introduced in 1935, and were made in both cloth and composition, as babies and as toddlers. Some of the rarer sets are those in the bathtub or with the wooden playground accessories like the carousel or Ferris wheel. Other companies tried to fill out their lines with matching sets of five identical dolls even though this brought copyright suits from Madame Alexander. Quintuplet collectors collect not only dolls, but clothing, photographs, and a large assortment of other related memorabilia.

Quint News is published quarterly at $10.00 per year by Jimmy and Fay Rodolfos, founders of a nonprofit group, Dionne Quint Collectors, PO Box 2527, Woburn MA 01888.

For photos of Alexander and other quintuplets see the Quintuplet section.

What to look for:
Alexander cloth dolls should be clean, all original, with bright colors. In newer Alexander dolls only mint, all original dolls with brochures, tags, boxes, and accessories bring top prices.

Composition Alexander dolls may have minute crazing, but must have good color, original clothes, labels, tags, and brochures to bring the highest prices. Buy dolls with severe cracking, peeling, or other damage *only* if they are all original or tagged.

Dolls made of painted hard plastic are transitional and may be mistaken for composition. Hard plastic dolls should have good color, tagged outfits, and be all original. The newer the doll, the closer to mint it should be. Alexander dolls were produced in the 1970s and 1980s with few changes — and collectors can find many of these dolls. The dolls from the 1950s and early 1960s are eagerly sought after as well as the limited edition special event dolls.

Composition

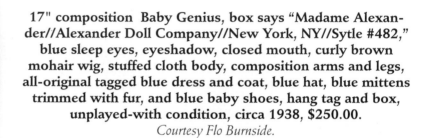

17" composition Baby Genius, box says "Madame Alexander//Alexander Doll Company//New York, NY//Sytle #482," blue sleep eyes, eyeshadow, closed mouth, curly brown mohair wig, stuffed cloth body, composition arms and legs, all-original tagged blue dress and coat, blue hat, blue mittens trimmed with fur, and blue baby shoes, hang tag and box, unplayed-with condition, circa 1938, $250.00.
Courtesy Flo Burnside.

Left: 17" composition Bridesmaid, marked "Mme. Alexander" on head, brown sleep eyes, eyeshadow, closed mouth, mohair wig, tagged pink taffeta dress, all original, circa 1939 – 1944, $675.00.
Right: 20" composition Bride, blue sleep eyes, eyeshadow, closed mouth, mohair wig, tagged bride dress, nylon overlay, veil, flowers in hand, all original, circa 1942 – 1943, $525.00; both Wendy Ann faces, both five-piece composition bodies.
Courtesy McMasters Doll Auctions.

13" composition Kate Greenaway (Princess Elizabeth), marked "13" on back, sleep eyes, open mouth with teeth, feather on bonnet tagged "Madame Alexander//New York//All Rights Reserved," rose colored dress, all original, circa 1938 – 1943, $700.00.
Courtesy Iva Mae Jones.

15½" composition Flora McFlimsey, marked "Madame Alexander//Flora McFlimsey," sleep eyes, open mouth with four teeth, freckles, composition body, original clothes and straw hat, leather shoes, heavy crazing, circa 1938, $350.00.
Courtesy Nelda Shelton.

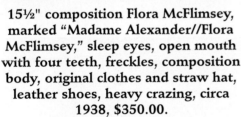

19" composition McGuffey Ana marked "Princess Elizabeth //Alexander Doll Co." on head, sleep eyes, open mouth with teeth, blond human hair wig in braid with curls around forehead, tagged blue dress with yellow pinafore, original except for replaced socks, circa 1937 – 1943, $750.00.
Courtesy Donna Nance.

24" composition Little Colonel, brown sleep eyes, open mouth with teeth, human hair wig, all original organdy dress and bonnet, Alexander oval hang tag reads "Madame Alexander Presents//Trade Mark//Little Colonel//Alexander Doll Co. N.Y.," all original, circa 1935+, $950.00.
Courtesy Oleta Woodside.

19" composition Princess Elizabeth, blue sleep eyes, open mouth with teeth, tagged Madame Alexander yellow dress and matching bonnet, excellent condition, circa 1937 – 1941, $750.00.
Courtesy Margaret Johnson.

19" composition Scarlett O'Hara, blue sleep eyes, closed mouth, auburn wig, composition body, red dress, circa 1939 – 1946, $400.00.
Courtesy Martha Sweeney.

13½" composition Princess in tagged pink moire taffeta costume, circa 1940 – 1942, human hair wig, brown sleep eyes, real lashes above, painted lashes below, closed mouth, circa 1940 – 1942, $535.00.
Courtesy Debbie Crume.

14" composition Sonja Henie, marked "Madame Alexander//Sonja Henie" on back of head, brown sleep eyes, eyeshadow, open mouth with four upper teeth, blond mohair wig in original set, five-piece composition body, tagged blue flowered taffeta skating dress, gold skates, blue ribbon in hair, original trousseau case with red ski jacket, blue pants, striped shirt, knit cap, wooden skis, ski poles, pink nightgown, bra, girdle, circa 1939 – 1942, $3,100.00.
Courtesy McMasters Doll Auctions.

14" composition Scarlett, marked "Madame Alexander" on head (Wendy Ann), blue sleep eyes, eyeshadow, closed mouth, black wig, tagged original green dress and hat, shoes, circa 1941 – 1943, $650.00.
Courtesy Kate Treber.

14" composition Wendy Ann, blue sleep eyes, closed mouth, blond human hair wig, hair in net, tagged organdy clothes, mint in box, circa 1935 – 1948, $600.00+. *Courtesy Rae Klenke.*

Hard Plastic

18" painted hard plastic Binnie Walker, sleep eyes, wig, with tagged red coat, leopard muff and hat, circa 1954 – 1955, $275.00.
Courtesy Cornelia Ford.

20" hard plastic Cissy, blue sleep eyes, closed mouth, pierced ears, dark blond synthetic wig, jointed vinyl arms, yellow dress and overcoat, black shawl, diamond ring, circa 1956, $325.00.
Courtesy Mary Sakraida.

14" hard plastic Cinderella (Margaret face) with blond wig, blue sleep eyes, blue star trimmed ball gown, braid tiara on head, circa 1950 – 1951, $800.00.
Courtesy Debbie Crume.

20" hard plastic Cissy, eyeshadow over blue sleep eyes, closed mouth, dark blond synthetic wig, yellow formal, rhinestone necklace and headband, vinyl arms, hard plastic body, circa 1955 – 1959, $295.00.
Courtesy Mary Sakraida.

Alexander Doll Co.

20" hard plastic Cissy Bride from Fashion Parade Series, eyeshadow over blue sleep eyes, closed mouth, dark brown synthetic wig, vinyl arms jointed at elbows, hard plastic body, circa 1956, $500.00.
Courtesy Sally DeSmet.

20" hard plastic Cissy #2095, wearing long summer gown of sheer white organdy, trimmed with rows of lace and rosebuds, red satin sash and purse, white straw hat, tagged "Cissy," circa 1955, $1,000.00.
Courtesy Karrin Schaulin.

16" hard plastic Elise Bride with short dark curly hair, blue sleep eyes, tulle bodice, puff sleeves, marked "Alexander" on head, "Madame Alexander" on back, circa 1960s, $345.00.
Courtesy Debbie Crume.

15" hard plastic black Cynthia, brown sleep eyes, black wig, has tagged original pink dotted Swiss organdy dress, circa 1952, $850.00.
Courtesy Cornelia Ford.

12" hard plastic Lissy in pink #1250 Afternoon Party Dress, sleep eyes, closed mouth, auburn wig, circa 1956, $300.00.
Courtesy Debbie Crume.

15" hard plastic Elise Bridesmaid, blue sleep eyes, closed mouth, blond synthetic wig, pierced ears, soft vinyl arms jointed above elbows, pink dress with lace/flowers, circa early 1950s, $325.00.
Courtesy Mary Sakraida.

15" hard plastic Margot Ballerina, head marked "Alexander," blue sleep eyes, closed mouth, blond wig, pink tutu, flowers in hair, cloverleaf hang tag, hard to find, circa 1953 – 1955, $950.00
Peggy Millhouse photo.
Courtesy Sidney Jeffrey Collection.

21" hard plastic Margaret, green sleep eyes, closed mouth, auburn mohair wig, net on hair, original long white tagged Alexander dress, pink hat with flowers, circa 1950s, $350.00.
Courtesy Mary Sakraida.

Alexander Doll Co.

30" hard plastic MiMi, wearing tagged MiMi dress, marked "Alexander 19©61," sleep eyes, closed mouth, earrings, brown rooted hair, jointed wrists, multi-jointed body, white dress with red rick-rack, circa 1961, $500.00.
Courtesy Cornelia Ford.

18" hard plastic McGuffey Ana (Margaret face), head marked "ALEX," blue sleep eyes, red braided wig, original clothing, straw hat with flowers, cloverleaf hang tag, circa 1955 – 56, $750.00.
Peggy Millhouse photo.
Courtesy Sidney Jeffrey Collection.

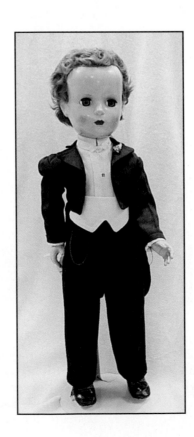

17½" hard plastic Prince Philip, Beaux Arts Creations, brown sleep eyes, closed mouth, reddish blond wig, Alexander tagged tuxedo, circa 1953, $575.00.
Courtesy Mary Sakraida.

24" hard plastic Winnie Walker in tagged blue costume with matching hat and shoes, synthetic wig, blue glassine eyes, painted lashes below, real lashes above, closed mouth, circa 1953 – 1954, $500.00.
Courtesy Cornelia Ford.

Vinyl

21" vinyl Coco Renoir, marked "Alexander// 19©66" on head, amber sleep eyes, real lashes, closed smiling mouth, original hair in original set, vinyl fashion-type body jointed at shoulders and waist, bent right leg, tagged aqua taffeta dress and matching bonnet, original underclothing, nylon stockings and black velvet shoes, diamond ring on left hand, circa 1966, $700.00.
Courtesy McMasters Doll Auctions.

16½" vinyl Elise Ballerina with sleep eyes, closed mouth, synthetic hair with flowers, eyeshadow over eyes, earrings, tagged blue tutu, hard plastic body with jointed elbows, ankles, and knees, vinyl lower arms, pink ballet shoes, lovely color, circa 1957 – 1964, $400.00.
Courtesy Jennifer Warren.

15" vinyl Elise Bride (with Mary-bel face), blue sleep eyes, pierced ears, closed mouth, blond synthetic wig, jointed at elbows/knees/ankles, white bridal gown/veil, pearl necklace, circa 1962 only, $350.00.
Courtesy Mary Sakraida.

21" vinyl Godey Portrait (Coco), marked "Alexander//19©66" on back of head, blue sleep eyes, closed smiling mouth, blond hair in original set, vinyl body jointed at shoulders and waist, bent right leg, dressed in tagged red taffeta dress with black velvet jacket, black velvet bonnet with net trim and red roses, stockings, red velvet shoes, made only in 1966, $950.00.
Courtesy McMasters Doll Auctions.

21" all vinyl Portrait Goya (Jacqueline face), blue sleep eyes, eyeshadow, closed mouth, blond synthetic wig, ring on right hand, multi-tiered pink formal, pink hat, Alexander hang tag, circa 1969, $450.00.
Courtesy Mary Sakraida.

Amberg, Louis & Sons

Louis Amberg and Sons were in business from about 1878 until 1930. They were located in Cincinnati, Ohio, prior to 1898, and in New York City after that. They used other names before 1907. Amberg imported dolls made by other firms. They were one of the first manufacturers to produce all American-made dolls in quantities. As early as 1911, they made cold press composition dolls with straw-stuffed bodies and composition lower arms. In 1915 they introduced a character doll, Charlie Chaplin, which was a big hit for them. In 1918 Otto Denivelle joined the firm and introduced a hot press baking process for making composition dolls. Mibs, a soulful composition child with molded hair and painted eyes, was introduced in 1921. The company was soon making mama and Baby Peggy dolls. In 1927, they introduced the Vanta baby, which promoted Vanta baby clothing. In 1928 Amberg patented a waist joint and used several different heads on this torso, one of which was called the It doll. In 1930, Amberg was sold to Horsman who continued to make some of the more popular lines.

What to look for:

Amberg produced some very interesting composition characters, and being able to recognize these early dolls will be a plus for you. Labeled clothing, good color, and minimal crazing are points to keep in mind when searching flea markets, estate sales, or garage sales for these dolls.

13" composition Charlie Chaplin, portrait head, painted side-glancing eyes, molded painted hair, composition hands, cloth body and legs, tagged, all original, circa 1915, $625.00.
Courtesy Martha Sweeney.

22" composition Vanta Baby, marked "Vanta Baby//Amberg," sleep eyes, molded painted hair, open/closed mouth with two teeth, cloth body with bent limb composition baby legs, original pink baby dress and bonnet, advertised in Sears catalog, circa 1927 – 1930, $350.00.
Courtesy Sharon Harrington.

American Character

American Character Doll Co. (1919+, New York City) first made composition dolls. In 1923 they began using Petite as a tradename for mama and character dolls. They later made cloth, hard plastic, and vinyl dolls. Sweet Sue, Tressy, Mary Makeup, and other dolls with high heels and fashion-type figures all reflect the focus on women as objects of beauty that remains an ongoing theme in dolls.

What to look for:

Composition American Character dolls should have good color, little crazing, and tagged original outfits or appropriate copies of original costumes using natural or period fabrics.

Hard plastic and vinyl dolls should have great color, be clean, and should be dressed in original costumes with tags, labels, and brochures. The newer the doll, the more complete and closer to mint it must be to command higher prices. Reject soiled or nude dolls unless they have wonderful color and you have original clothes you can use to re-dress them.

Cloth

21" cloth Eloise tagged "Eloise//1st Edition//American Character," mask face, painted black eyes, crooked painted smile, yellow yarn hair, cloth body, white shirt, black felt skirt, circa 1950s, $175.00.
Courtesy Nelda Shelton.

Composition

16" composition Carol Ann Beery, marked "Petite// Sally" on head, "Petite" on back, green sleep eyes, real lashes, closed mouth, red mohair wig with braid across top, five-piece composition body, celebrity doll, named for daughter of Hollywood actor, Wallace Beery, white pique dress trimmed in blue, matching sunsuit and bonnet, socks, snap shoes, all original, circa 1935, $440.00.
Courtesy McMasters Doll Auctions.

American Character

15" Puggy, marked "A//Petite Doll" on back of head, original cowboy costume, painted eyes, closed mouth, molded painted blond hair, circa 1929+, $650.00+. *Courtesy Elizabeth Surber.*

12½" Sally, marked "Sally//A Petite Doll," brown painted side-glancing eyes, closed rosebud mouth, painted brown hair, original tagged green dress, matching shoes, circa 1930+, $200.00. *Courtesy Janet Hill.*

Hard Plastic and Vinyl

17" hard plastic baby, marked "AMER.CHAR," blue sleep eyes, closed rosebud mouth, blond mohair wig over molded hair, hard plastic head, arms, and legs, cloth body with ma-ma crier voice, re-dressed in vintage doll clothes with matching bonnet, childhood doll of Sheryl Schmidt, circa 1948 – 1950, $100.00. *Courtesy Sheryl Schmidt.*

12" hard plastic Tiny Tears, marked "Amer. Char. Doll//Pat. No. 2,675,644" on back of head, blue sleep eyes, holes for tears, open mouth for bottle, rosy cheeks, rooted hair, five-piece rubber body, original pink/white dress, booties, bonnet, pacifier, flannel diaper, romper, terry washcloth, clothes pins, bubble pipe, Ivory soap, sponge, rattle, plastic bottle, mint with case, circa 1950 – 1962, $505.00. *Courtesy McMasters Doll Auctions.*

24" vinyl Toodles toddler with follow-me sleep eyes, heavy eye-lashes, multi-stroke eyebrows, rosy cheeks, curly synthetic hair with pigtails, re-dressed in sun-suit, circa 1960s, $125.00.
Courtesy Dolores Ortega.

21" hard plastic Sweet Sue walker, unmarked, synthetic rooted saran skull-cap wig, sleep eyes, eyeshadow, all original, circa 1954 – 1956, $400.00.
Courtesy Cornelia Ford.

22" hard plastic Sweet Sue walker, marked "Amer. Char. Doll" with vinyl arms, jointed elbows, molded breasts, jointed knees, synthetic rooted skull-cap, saran wig, sleep eyes, eye-shadow, all original, hang tag, circa 1954 – 1956, $400.00.
Courtesy Cornelia Ford.

21" hard plastic Sweet Sue, blue sleep eyes,
light brown synthetic hair, unmarked, has
extra plastic model case with shoes, peach
long outfit, circa 1957, $350.00.
Courtesy Cornelia Ford.

19" hard plastic Sweet Sue Bride, blue
sleep eyes, closed mouth, beautiful color,
red synthetic wig, flat feet, white satin
dress, circa 1953, $200.00.
Private collection.

10½" vinyl unmarked Toni, sleep eyes, rosy
cheeks, dark blond synthetic wig, in original
strapless undergarment, circa 1958+, $110.00.
Courtesy Lee Ann Beaumont.

19" vinyl multi-face American Doll & Toy Corp. Whimsie Hedda Get Bedda with three faces, revealed by turning knob on top of vinyl capped head, sleeping face, sick, and smiling faces, marked on stuffed head "Whimsey//American Doll & Toy Corp//19©60," no joints at arms, stitch-jointed legs, circa 1960s, $105.00.
Courtesy Debbie Crume.

21" vinyl Whimsie Bessie the Bashful Bride, marked "WHIMSIE//AMER. DOLL & TOY CO." on head, molded painted closed eyes, closed smiling mouth, rosy cheeks, synthetic wig, one-piece stuffed vinyl body with molded head, short white dress with net overlay, veil, white sandals, hang tag, the box says "whimsies//little people full of fun," all-original in box, circa 1960 – 1961, $250.00.
Courtesy Amanda Hash.

Rubber

16" hard rubber Toodles with oilcloth type body, molded and painted dark brown hair, sleep brown eyes with eyeshadow above, open mouth, composition limbs, has original booklet and original dress (not shown), note hole in foot for possible disposal of water on this drink and wet doll, circa 1938, $75.00. *Courtesy Matea O. Todd.*

Arranbee

Arranbee Doll Co. was located in New York from 1922 until 1958. It was sold to Vogue Doll Co. who used the molds until 1961. Some of their bisque dolls were made by Armand Marseille and Simon & Halbig. They made composition baby, child, and mama dolls. Early dolls have an eight-sided tag. They went on to make hard plastic and vinyl dolls, many using the R & B trademark. Some hard plastic and vinyl dolls (Littlest Angel and Li'l Imp) were made for Vogue by the Arranbee division and may be marked by either.

Composition

What to look for:

Composition dolls should have good color, only very fine crazing if any, and original clothes or appropriate copies. Always look for mint-in-box and tagged dolls in excellent to mint condition. Hard plastic and vinyl dolls should be clean with bright rosy cheek color, tagged or labeled clothes, preferably with brochures and/or boxes to command higher prices in the future.

22" composition Dream Baby, tin sleep eyes, open mouth, composition head, arms, and legs, cloth body, all-original tagged pink dress with matching bonnet, white baby shoes, circa 1927+, $575.00.
Courtesy Martha Sweeney.

11" all-composition Debu' Teen, unmarked, sleep eyes, closed mouth, red mohair wig, in red skating outfit, circa 1940, $275.00.
Courtesy Peggy Millhouse.

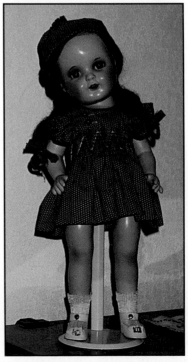

18" composition Nancy, marked on head "Nancy," brown sleep eyes, open mouth with teeth, auburn human hair braided wig, all original in red dress and hat, mint in box, box marked "Nancy by Arranbee," circa 1938 – 1941, $350.00.
Courtesy Sally DeSmet.

18" composition Nancy, sleep eyes, open mouth, dark brown wig, blue velvet coat and hat, silk dress, all original, circa 1930, $450.00.
Courtesy Martha Sweeney.

17" composition Skater, marked "R&B," blue sleep eyes, eyeshadow, closed mouth, red human hair wig, knitted sweater and hat, white skirt, ice skates, circa 1939 – 1940, $250.00.
Courtesy Sheryl Nudelman.

14" composition skater, mohair wig, sleep eyes, eyeshadow over eyes, real lashes over eyes, painted lashes under eye, closed mouth, original costume, circa 1945, $275.00.
Courtesy Yvonne Burgess.

14" composition Nancy Lee, marked "R & B" very faint on back of head, brown sleep eyes with real lashes, painted lower lashes, closed mouth, auburn mohair wig in original set, five-piece composition body, original long yellow dress with gold polka dots, matching bonnet, yellow taffeta underclothing, ribbons on wrists, socks, and shoes, circa 1939+, $250.00.
Courtesy McMasters Doll Auctions.

Hard Plastic and Vinyl

11" hard plastic Littlest Angel Cross Country Skier, in royal blue gabardine ski outfit with red trim, cap with pompon, wooden skis and poles, marked "R & B" on torso, circa 1950s, $125.00.
Courtesy Sally DeSmet.

14" hard plastic Nancy Jane bride, blue sleep eyes, rosy cheeks, closed mouth, red wig, mint in box, marked "Made in USA" on back torso in a circle, impossible to identity without marked box, circa 1950s, $500.00.
Courtesy Sally DeSmet.

14" vinyl Nancy Lee with sleep eyes, synthetic wig, closed mouth, distinctive eyebrows, real lashes above and painted lashes below, red accent dots at nose, toddler body, pretty cheek color, unmarked, circa 1950s, $75.00.
Courtesy Lenora Sweet.

17" hard plastic Nancy Lee Skater, blue sleep eyes, closed mouth, auburn mohair wig, red outfit with white felt trim with blue and red yarn trim, matching gloves, white skates, all original in box, circa 1949, $500.00.
Courtesy Flo Burnside.

18" hard plastic Nanette, sleep eyes, closed mouth, blond synthetic wig, black lace evening costume, circa 1949 – 1959, $275.00.
Courtesy Peggy Millhouse.

Artist Dolls

These are original, one of a kind, limited edition, or limited production dolls of any medium (cloth, porcelain, wax, wood, vinyl, or other material) made for sale to the public. While a hot debate goes on in some doll-making and collecting circles as to the exact definition of an artist doll, we will use the above definition in this category. Some dolls appear to be works of art and some collectors may wish to have just that in their collection. Others define a doll as a play object and like to collect them for such. You, as a collector, are free to make your own decision to suit yourself. Still we can all appreciate the creativity which these talented artists exhibit.

What to look for:

One should remember that as with all collectibles, a well-made object of beauty will always be appealing. Some, not all, will increase in value. Study the dolls to find what you like. Some may only be popular fads.

A doll that is artistically done, in proper proportion stands a greater chance of increasing in value over time. You can enjoy it as part of your collection, rather than acquiring it entirely as an investment.

With artist dolls, one needs six examples or more of the artist's work to show the range of their talent. The artist doll category, however, does offer something for everyone.

Alphabetically by Maker

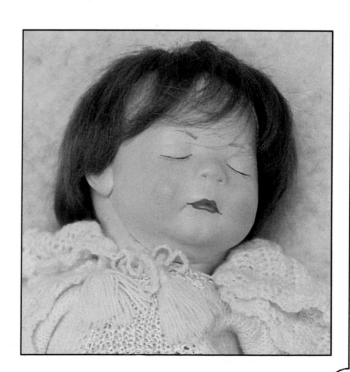

16" cloth Sleeping Baby by Christine Adams, tagged "Christine Adams//Tiny Tots//Hand Made Dolls," mask face, features are hand painted in oils, red human hair wig, stitched fingers, all hand-knitted clothes, circa 1980, $1,000.00.
Private collection.

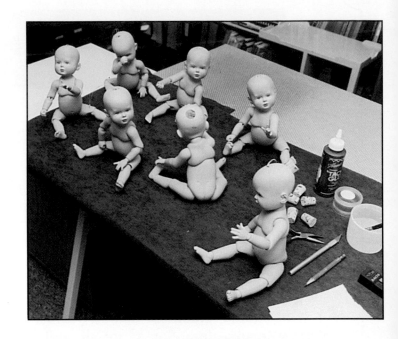

**11" porcelain Hannah by Martha Arm-
strong-Hand, inspired by her youngest
granddaughter, blue eyes, brown hair, all
jointed (15 joints), circa 1999, $2,500.00.**
Courtesy Martha Armstrong-Hand.

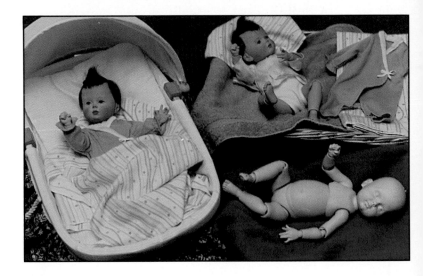

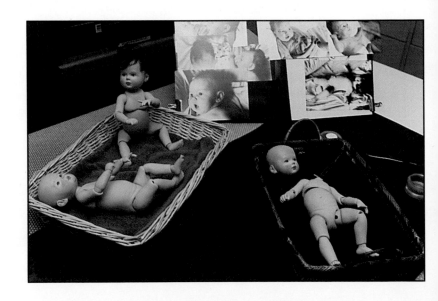

Elizaveta, 28" cloth doll by Alexandra of Moscow, represents a bride from northern Russian in period costume, circa 1989+, $275.00.
Courtesy Tonny Blair.

28" cloth Alexandra of Moscow, Darya, a copy of newly-wed woman from the Vononezh Province during the second half of the ninteenth century, circa 1989+, $275.00.
Courtesy Judy Korynasz.

Artist Dolls

12" super sculpy Mary's Lamb by Betsey Baker, doll is hand sculpted with painted blue eyes, rosy cheeks, open mouth with teeth, red braided wig, blue dress and cap, holding an apple, books, and a purse, the lamb is super sculpy on wire armature, one of a kind, circa 1998, $250.00.
Courtesy Betsey Baker.

17" paper clay Puss in Boots by Betsey Baker, sculpted/painted features, wire armature body, sculpy paws, boots, tail, black cape, purple shirt with lace cuffs and collar, gold and purple pants, black molded boots, one of a kind, circa 1997, $350.00.
Courtesy Betsey Baker.

3 – 4" resin and polymer clay Cynthia Baron Designs Alice in Wonderland chess set, an amazing example of creativity with 32 pieces, pawns of resin, all other pieces individually sculpted, circa 1998, $6,000.00.
Courtesy Cynthia Baron.

14" polymer clay Cynthia Baron Designs Gathering Humpties & Golden Egg, painted eyes, wigged, closed smiling mouth, black peaked hat with white feather, rose striped long dress, white apron, hold Humpty egg in one hand, basket with more in another, $1,600.00.
Courtesy Cynthia Baron.

6" resin Cynthia Baron Designs original Comedienne, limited edition of 100, fully articulated on wired body, jointed neck and waist, painted features, $195.00, circa 1999.
Courtesy Cynthia Baron.

16" polymer clay Cynthia Baron Designs Jolly Old Elf with painted features, white beard, dark red gold trimmed robe, holds marionette in one hand, doll in another, surrounded by toys, circa 1999, $2,400.00.
Courtesy Cynthia Baron.

6" resin Cynthia Baron Designs original Mother Goose, limited edition of 100, fully articulated on wired body, jointed neck and waist, painted features, $195.00, circa 1999.
Courtesy Cynthia Baron.

Artist Dolls

14" wood Harriet Tubman, a black leader in the underground railroad led 300 slaves to freedom. Hand carved by Los Angeles teacher, Floyd Bell, cloth body with wire armature, wooden hands and feet, signed on shoulder plate, "1994, Floyd Bell," $1,000.00.
Courtesy Cornelia Ford.

24" polymer clay Cynthia Baron Designs intricately designed Punchinelli, standing nineteenth century masked figure with painted features, holds clown in one hand a stack of toys in the other, circa 1999, $2,400.00.
Courtesy Cynthia Baron.

16" cernit Cheryl D. Bollenbach Baby Sitter, finely sculpted features, wire armature throughout bodies, gray wig in long braids, colorful leather costume, holds papoose in cradleboard on back, 1999, $600.00.
Courtesy Cheryl Bollenbach.

21" cernit Cheryl D. Bollenbach Man-Dan Warrior, finely sculpted features, black wig, feather headdress, colorful bead, feathers, fur, and leather costume, 1999, $1,000.00.
Courtesy Cheryl Bollenbach.

20" brown cloth pillow-type Prizy child, hand crafted by Laura Clark, with embroidered features, black floss curls with ribbons, floral print body, elongated legs and arms, circa 1999, $28.00.

24" latex/composition Portrait Doll by Dewees Cochran, painted blue eyes, closed mouth, auburn wig, white dress with red stitched trim, bottom of stand reads "Honeysuckle//Natl. Molded Products Co.//N.Y., N.Y.," circa 1950s, $2,500.00.
Courtesy Jane Horst.

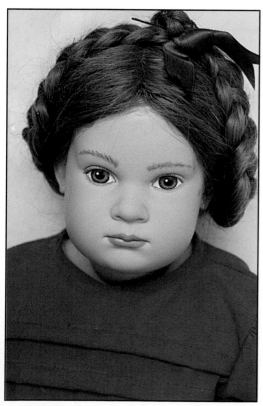

28" hard vinyl Annette Himstedt Barefoot Children Madina, glass eyes, closed mouth, marked "Madina// AnnetteHimstedt/©" on neck, red wig, vinyl shoulder plate, cloth body, vinyl arms and legs, original black dress with green apron, bead earrings, circa 1995, Tenth Anniversary Collection, $600.00.
Courtesy Elizabeth Surber.

22" hard vinyl Lotta II by Sabine Esche of Sigikid Co., limited edition of 500, painted eyes, closed mouth, auburn human hair braided wig, nicely made dress, cloth body, circa 1980s, $1,500.00.
Private collection.

26" black vinyl Fatou by Annette Himstedt, marked on head, glass eyes, vinyl and cloth body with vinyl limbs, dark wig, original rose dress with white pinafore, oval peach tag reads, "Puppenkinder//Annette Himstedt//Fatou," circa 1986, bare feet, $1,100.00.
Courtesy Cornelia Ford.

26" black vinyl Ayoka by Annette Himstedt, marked on head, glass eyes, vinyl and cloth body with vinyl limbs, dark wig with individual braids and colorful beads, original yellow and turquoise costume, bare feet, circa 1990, $1,100.00.
Courtesy Cornelia Ford.

24" paper clay over gourd Dreaming Grandmother by Lillian Hopkins, one-of-a-kind, circa 1998, $1,500.00.
Courtesy Lillian Hopkins.

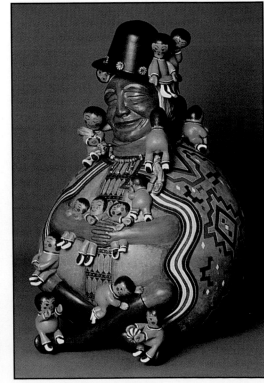

7½" paper clay over gourd Son of Raven by Lillian Hopkins, one-of-a-kind, circa 1998, $800.00. *Courtesy Lillian Hopkins.*

15" painted snake gourd Singing Geisha by Lillian Hopkins, one-of-a-kind, circa 1999, $500.00. *Courtesy Lillian Hopkins.*

8" super sculpy Frolicking Frogman by Marilynn Huston, sea sponge yellow hair, black goggles, circa 1998, $325.00. *Courtesy Marilynn Huston.*

16" super sculpy The Bay Lady by Marilynn Huston, brown eyes, gray karakul sheep hair wig, closed mouth, gray sweater, plaid scarf, red and blue dress, black knit hat, carrying a sewing basket, circa 1998, $595.00. *Courtesy Marilynn Huston.*

Artist Dolls

19" black wooden, Lisa Christina by Janci with painted side-glancing brown eyes, human hair wig with colorful beads on numerous braids, bangs, colorful costume of fruits on dark background, cross-stitched apron, red shoes, circa 1994, $350.00.
Courtesy Cornelia Ford.

8" super sculpy The Turtle Jockey by Marilynn Huston, jester riding a turtle, wool hair, open/closed mouth, circa 1998, $395.00.
Courtesy Marilynn Huston.

17" – 18" cloth Five Clowns and a Model T by Joyce Patterson, signed "Joyce Patterson//1999," hand-painted features, cloth bodies, circa 1999, $1,095.00.
Courtesy Joyce Patterson.

15" cloth Lovers' Quarrel by Joyce Patterson, signed "Joyce Patterson//1998," hand-painted features, cloth bodies, included with the dolls is a handmade round wooden bistro table with a bottle of champagne, two glasses, and a metal ashtray, one-of-a-kind, circa 1998, $350.00.
Courtesy Joyce Patterson.

18" cloth A Taste of Texas Barbecue by Joyce Patterson, signed "Joyce Patterson//1996," hand-painted features, cloth bodies, barbecue pit is a handmade birdhouse purchased and painted black, small accessories to represent cooking utensils, small props to represent serving of the barbecue, potato salad, bread, beans, eating utensils and condiments, iced down beer, circa 1996, $600.00.
Courtesy Joyce Patterson.

18" solid wood carved Cave Man by W. Harry Perzyk, anatomically correct, handmade glass eyes, silk hair fastened to the head by individual hairs, handmade clothes, one-of-a-kind, circa 1999, $2,500.00.
Courtesy W. Harry Perzyk.

24" porcelain King Ethiopia by W. Harry Perzyk, fully sculpted, anatomically correct, handmade glass eyes, silk hair fastened to the head by individual hairs, handmade clothes, one-of-a-kind, circa 1999, $1,500.00.
Courtesy W. Harry Perzyk.

20" wood carved Date Masumune, the One-Eyed Dragon, by W. Harry Perzyk, sixteenth century Japanese warrior sitting, handmade glass eyes, silk hair fastened to the head by individual hairs, handmade costume, one-of-a-kind, $6,950.00.
Courtesy W. Harry Perzyk.

20" carved porcelain Masasige by W. Harry Perzyk, a Japanese warrior of the eleventh century, handmade glass eyes, silk hair fastened to the head by individual hairs, handmade clothes, one-of-a-kind, circa 1999, $950.00.
Courtesy W. Harry Perzyk.

24" porcelain Wolf Man by W. Harry Perzyk, anatomically correct, handmade glass eyes, silk hair fastened to the head by individual hairs, handmade clothes, one-of-a-kind, circa 1999, $1,500.00.
Courtesy W. Harry Perzyk.

24" wood carved The Last Emperor of China — Puyi, by W. Harry Perzyk, solid carved wood, anatomically correct, handmade glass eyes, silk hair fastened to the head by individual hairs, handmade clothes, one-of-a-kind, circa 1999, $10,000.00.
Courtesy W. Harry Perzyk.

14½" Auntie Maim by Daryl Poole, one-of-a-kind signed original, head, hands, and feet are of premo sculpy, soft sculpted body over wire armature, staff is premo sculpy, bullwhip is leather, circa 1998, $895.00.
Courtesy Daryl Poole.

15" Eggs by Daryl Poole, one-of-a-kind signed original, head, hands, and feet are of premo sculpey, he has a soft-sculpted body over wire armature, chefs' hat, gray apron, white shirt and pants, circa 1998, $695.00.
Courtesy Daryl Poole.

16" Maestro's Day Off by Daryl Poole, one-of-a-kind signed original, head, hands, and feet are of premo sculpey, he has a soft-sculpted body over wire armature, birdhouse and pole are 17½" tall, circa 1997, $795.00.
Courtesy Daryl Poole.

14" Makin' a List, Checkin' It Twice by Daryl Poole, one-of-a-kind signed original, head, hands, and feet are of premo sculpey, he has a soft-sculpted body over wire armature, chair is premo sculpey, circa 1998, $795.00.
Courtesy Daryl Poole.

17" in Fimo by Sarah Russell, finished in washes of acrylics, pastels, and wax, circa 1997, $1,800.00.
Courtesy Sarah Russell.

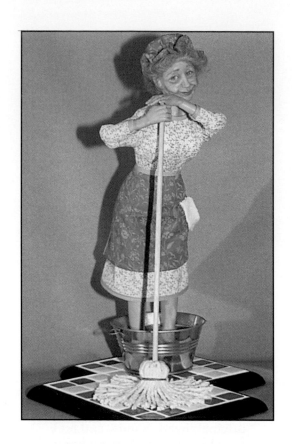

16" Creall-therm N.A. Hurry, by Sandy Simonds, one-of-a-kind, molded painted features, red synthetic wig, canvas body stuffed with polyfill, wire armature, red polka dot outfit, fingernail polish, red purse and high-heels, pearl necklace, circa 1999, $1,050.00.
Courtesy Sandy Simonds.

17" Creall-therm Wanda's Aching Feet by Sandy Simonds, one-of-a-kind, molded painted features, gray wig, canvas body with polyfill, wire armature, white cloth print dress with green apron and cap, standing in metal pail, leaning on wooden mop, circa 1998, $1,100.00.
Courtesy Sandy Simonds.

16" stone clay Willie and the Spring Collection by Sandy Simonds, one-of-a-kind, molded painted features, brown hair, canvas body stuffed with polyfill, wire armature, green suit, black felt hat, suede belt and shoes, holding cardboard boxes with fabric shoes and tissue, circa 1998, $1,200.00.
Courtesy Sandy Simonds.

6" all wood Angelita by Sherman Smith, with painted features, comb on head, dressed in white dotted print, the official 1963 U.F.D.C. Region 2 souvenir doll, a copy of the 1820 – 1830 wooden doll, circa 1963, $125.00.
Courtesy Elizabeth Surber.

15" vinyl Dorothy & Toto by Marjory Spangler, created exclusively for The Enchanted Doll House, limited edition production, sleep eyes, long lashes, auburn braided synthetic wig, blue and white poly-cotton jumper, bright red shoes that sparkle, with shaggy plush brown dog as Toto, the certificate of authenticity and registration says this is doll #8 created on March 15, 1982, $70.00.
Courtesy Dickee Burror.

7" all-wood Sherman Smith Mary Poppins dressed by Mrs. Smith, circa 1960s, $150.00.
Courtesy Elizabeth Surber.

15" porcelain Linda Lee Sutton Dianna Rose, marked "Linda Lee Sutton//©1999" on back of head, blue paperweight eyes, blond wig, cloth body with porcelain arms and legs, stands in the shadow of her very own topiary rose, inspired from Jackson's & Perkins's own limited edition (Coral and Pink) rose bush sold in the summer of 1998 to admirers of Princess Diana, limited edition of 10, circa 1999, $650.00.
Courtesy Linda Lee Sutton.

15" all-composition Pinocchio by Marjory Spangler, prototype 7 of 8, painted side-glancing eyes, closed mouth, black synthetic wig, black painted boots, jointed at elbows/knees, red and blue velvet outfit and cap, circa 1985, $165.00.
Courtesy Dickee Burror.

15" porcelain Linda Lee Sutton Emily on the Oregon Trail, marked "Linda Lee Sutton Originals//©1999" on back of head, paperweight eyes, curly blond wig, porcelain shoulder plate, arms and legs on an armature cloth body, prairie dress and sun bonnet of coral, pastel teal, and white, comes with blanket and wagon, artists' interpretation of the Legend of the Blue Bucket Lost Gold Mine on the Oregon Trail, limited edition of 20, circa 1999, $650.00.
Courtesy Linda Lee Sutton.

28½" porcelain Linda Lee Sutton Jolly Jingles Santa, marked "Linda Lee Sutton Originals//© 1999" on back of head, winking, beard and wig made of angora mohair, cream wool slacks, synthetic lamb coat trimmed in real furs, porcelain arms, sculpted shoes, long handle underwear and his buttons help him to keep track of time, limited edition of 15, circa 1999, $885.00.
Courtesy Linda Lee Sutton.

18" porcelain Linda Lee Sutton Little Cattail, marked "Linda Lee Sutton Originals//© 1999" on back of head, dark brown paperweight eyes, black flowing braids, dressed in soft leathers, sitting on a lava foam rock, called pumas, from Crater Lake in Oregon, one of the Seven Wonders of the World, cloth body, seated in a synthetic cattail arrangement, limited edition of 20, circa 1999, $675.00.
Courtesy Linda Lee Sutton.

21" porcelain Linda Lee Sutton Sara Jill, marked "Linda Lee Sutton Originals//©1999" on back of head, big brown paperweight eyes, closed mouth, blond human hair French braided wig, posable cloth body with porcelain arms and legs, coral silk dress with embroidered cream silk with three porcelain roses attached framing her face, limited edition of 10, circa 1999, $750.00.
Courtesy Linda Lee Sutton.

14" porcelain Clo — Cloth Seller by Goldie Wilson of Original Dolls by Goldie, limited edition of 5, detailed and hand painted, head, shoulder plate, arms, and legs are porcelain, cloth body with wire armature, one-of-a-kind costume, sitting on trunk holding wicker basket, circa 1999, $995.00.
Courtesy Goldie Wilson.

30" porcelain Linda Lee Sutton See Santa of the Sea, marked "Linda Lee Sutton Originals//© 1999" on back of head, is a sculpture of close family friend, Ron Converse, who himself loves the oceans and lakes, porcelain on an armatured body, tie-dyed angora mohair wig, brown paperweight eyes, carrying a sack full of ocean memories, limited edition of 10, circa 1999, $895.00.
Courtesy Linda Lee Sutton.

10" King Henry VIII by Frances Popenoe Wood, elaborately dressed, circa 1970s, $200.00.
Courtesy Elizabeth Surber.

9½" terra cotta and kaolin doll by Frances Popenoe Wood, old lady in night gown and cap, carries cat and candlestick, gray mohair wig in long pigtails, circa 1974, her dolls sell for $175.00 to $300.00.
Courtesy Jean Rice Thompson.

Georgene Averill

Georgene Averill (ca 1915+, New York City) made composition and cloth dolls operating as Madame Georgene Dolls, Averill Mfg. Co., Georgene Novelties, and Madame Hendren. Her first line included dressed felt dolls. She also made Lyf-Lyk and the Wonder line, and patented the Mama doll in 1918. She designed dolls for Borgfeldt, including Bonnie Babe. Her Peaches was a Patsy-type doll. A very talented designer and maker, she made wonderful cloth and composition dolls. The family had ties to Arranbee, as some in-laws worked in production at that firm. Averill's line of whistling dolls with bellows in the cloth body was clever and made to portray different occupations or ethnic backgrounds.

What to look for:
Georgene made dolls of cloth, composition, or early plastic type materials. Georgene Averill was known for her felt costumes and composition mama dolls with swing legs and criers. Search for bright and clean cloth dolls and labeled or tagged costumes on composition dolls with rosy cheeks and little crazing.

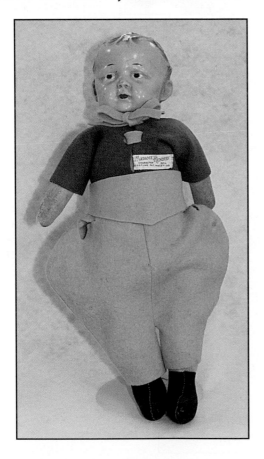

15" composition Baby Huggums with flange head, molded painted hair, intaglio eyes, closed mouth, cloth excelsior stuffed body, felt costume tagged "Madame Hendren// Character Doll//Costume Pat. May 9th 1916," $275.00.
Courtesy Janet Hill.

4½" all-bisque Bonnie Babe with sleep eyes, molded hair, open/closed mouth, in pink molded painted one strap shoes and white socks, appropriately dressed in pink silk and old lace, circa 1926+, $1,200.00.
Courtesy Connie Lee Martin.

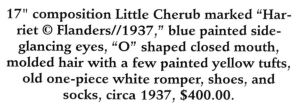

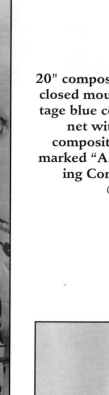

20" composition mama doll with sleep eyes, closed mouth, mohair wig, cloth body, vintage blue cotton floral print dress and bonnet with felt and embroidery trim, composition lower limbs, a family doll, marked "A.M. Co." for Averill Manufacturing Company, circa 1920s, $325.00.
Courtesy Evelyn Broderick.

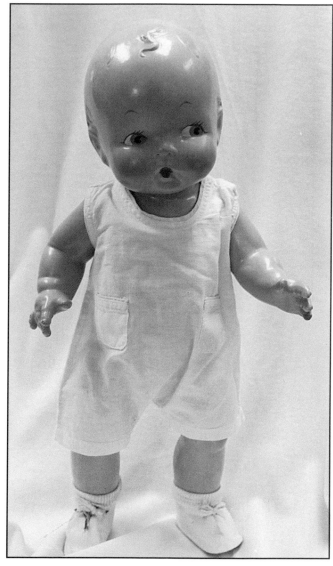

17" composition Little Cherub marked "Harriet © Flanders//1937," blue painted sideglancing eyes, "O" shaped closed mouth, molded hair with a few painted yellow tufts, old one-piece white romper, shoes, and socks, circa 1937, $400.00.
Courtesy Janet Hill.

Barbie

Mattel began making Barbie doll in 1959 in Hawthorne, California. As we near the end of the century she remains a top collectible as children have grown up and become avid collectors of their childhood dolls. Of interest to collectors, also, are the fashion trends reflected by Barbie doll's seemingly endless wardrobe.

Marks:
1959 – 62: *BARBIE TM/PATS. PEND.// © MCMLVIII//by//Mattel, Inc.*
1963 – 68: *Midge TM © 1962//BARBIE ® / © 1958//BY//Mattel, Inc.*
1964 – 66: *© 1958//Mattel, Inc. //U.S. Patented//U.S. Pat. Pend.*
1966 – 69: *© 1966//Mattel, Inc.//U.S. Patented//U.S. Pat. Pend//Made in Japan*

Description of the first five Barbie dolls:
Number One Barbie, 1959
11½" solid heavy vinyl body, faded white skin color, white irises, pointed eyebrows, soft ponytail, brunette or blond only, black and white striped bathing suit, holes with metal cylinders in balls of feet to fit round-pronged stand, gold hoop earrings.

Number Two Barbie doll, 1959 – 1960
11½" solid heavy vinyl body, faded white skin color, white irises, pointed eyebrows, no holes in feet, some with pearl earrings, soft ponytail, brunette or blond only.

Number Three Barbie doll, 1960
11½" solid heavy vinyl body, some fading in skin color, blue irises, curved eyebrows, no holes in feet, soft ponytail, brunette or blond only.

Number Four Barbie doll, 1960
11½", same as #3, but solid body of skin-toned vinyl, soft ponytail, brunette or blond only.

Number Five Barbie doll, 1961
11½", vinyl head, now less heavy, hard plastic hollow body, firmer texture saran ponytail, and now also redhead, has arm tag.

What to look for:
It is still possible to assemble outfits from loose pieces and sell or trade your extras. The limited edition dolls with runs of under 2,000 or the fad that hits the collector's fancy, such as the Harley Davidson Barbie, are the dolls that will increase in price. This is one category that is so broad you are sure to find a niche that will keep you happy.

11½" vinyl number two Barbie, #850, brunette, soft hair, ringlet bangs, white irises, dark eyeliner, red lips, arched eyebrows, same as number one but no holes in feet, marked "Barbie™/Pats.Pnd./©MCMLVIII/by Mattel/Inc.," mint in box, circa 1959, $6,350.00.
Photo courtesy McMasters Doll Auctions.

11½" vinyl number one Ponytail Barbie with blond soft hair, white irises with dark blue eyeliner, red lips, high arched eyebrows, holes in bottom of feet and copper tubing in legs, heavy whitish solid body, dressed in black and white striped swimsuit, stock No. 850, boxed, marked, "Barbie™//Pats. Pend//© MCMLVIII//by Mattel//Inc.," circa 1959, $4,800.00.
Courtesy McMasters Doll Auctions.

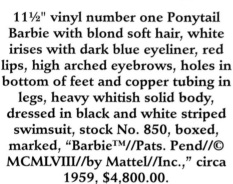

11½" vinyl number four Ponytail Barbie, brunette, blue irises, red lips, gentle curve eyebrows, blue eyeliner only, black and white swimsuit, vinyl retains tan tone, marked: "Barbie™//Pats. Pend.//© MCMLVIII//by Mattel//Inc.," circa 1960, $800.00.
Courtesy McMasters Doll Auctions.

11½" vinyl number three Ponytail Barbie with blue irises, red lips, gentle curve eyebrows, brown eyeliner, heavy solid body may turn white, dressed in black and white swim suit, marked "Barbie™//Pats. Pend.//© MCMLVIII//by Mattel//Inc.," boxed, stock No. 850, circa 1960, $1,025.00.
Courtesy McMasters Doll Auctions.

11½" vinyl Bubble Cut Barbie, boxed, blond, blue irises, red lips, gentle curve eyebrows, black and white swimsuit 1961 only, marked, "Barbie™//Pats. Pend.//© MCMLVIII//by Mattel Inc.," stock No. 850, $375.00.
Courtesy McMasters Doll Auctions.

11½" vinyl number five Ponytail Barbie, blue irises, blue eyeliner, gentle curve eyebrows, bangs have larger curls, red lips, hollow lightweight body keeps pink color, marked "Barbie™//Pats. Pend.//© MCMLVIII//by Mattel Inc.," circa 1961, $775.00.
Courtesy McMasters Doll Auctions.

11½" vinyl Bride's Dream Barbie, marked "©1964//Barbie™//© 1958//by//Mattel, Inc.," stock #947, box marked "Imported from Japan," boxed, circa 1964, $900.00.
Courtesy Delores Kelly.

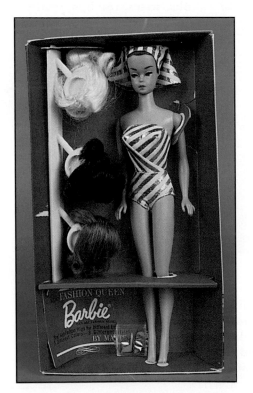

11½" vinyl Fashion Queen Barbie, straight leg, painted side-glancing blue eyes, blue eyeshadow, painted brunette hair with removable blue band, pearl earrings, fingernail and toenail paint, original gold and white striped one-piece strapless swimsuit with matching turban, wedgies with gold uppers, white wig stand with titian wig, brunette wig, white wig, near mint condition in box, circa 1963 – 1964, $215.00.
Courtesy McMasters Doll Auctions.

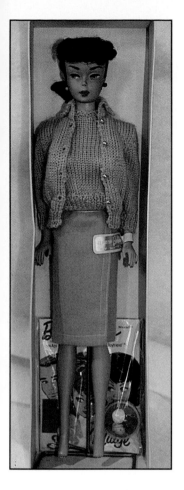

11½" vinyl #957 Knitting Pretty Barbie, the pink version, in box, with wrist band, bowl of yarn, brochure and stand, corrosion of green from earrings has migrated to eye, circa 1964, $675.00.
Courtesy Ruth Waite.

11½" vinyl #959 Theatre Date Barbie, green jacket and skirt with white blouse, in box, with brochure, stand, and shoes, earrings still in, turning green, circa 1964, $645.00.
Courtesy Ruth Waite.

11½" vinyl Swirl Ponytail Barbie, straight leg, painted side-glancing blue eyes, blue eyeshadow, coral lips, brunette hair in original set in ponytail with ribbon and swirl of hair across forehead, hairpin, cellophane head bag, fingernail and toenail paint, red nylon swimsuit, wrist tag, red open toe shoes in cellophane bag, gold metal stand, Exclusive Fashion booklet, near mint in box, circa 1964 – 1965, $725.00.
Courtesy McMasters Doll Auctions.

11½" vinyl American Girl Barbie, blond, beige lips, wearing #933 Movie Date dress with blue and white stripes and bow accents, ends of eyebrows slightly faded, toe rub, left leg does not bend, sticky spot on hair, circa 1965, $325.00.
Courtesy McMasters Doll Auctions.

11½" vinyl Twist 'n Turn Barbie, bendable legs, blue painted side-glancing eyes, rooted eyelashes, light brown brows, deep pink lips, blush, ash blond hair, finger and toe paint, wearing original orange two-piece swimsuit with net cover-up, circa 1967, $285.00.
Courtesy McMasters Doll Auctions.

11½" vinyl Hair Fair Barbie on bendable leg body, marked "© 1966//Mattel, Inc.," blue painted side-glancing eyes, rooted lashes, light brown brows, pink lips and blush, one dangle earring in left ear, blond hair pieces, brunette wig, wearing Smasheroo dress and fur coat, near mint condition, circa 1967, $185.00.
Courtesy McMasters Doll Auctions.

11½" vinyl Walk Lively Barbie, #1182, bendable legs, blue painted eyes, rooted eyelashes, brown brows, pink lips and blush, blond shoulder length hair with side part and ends curled under, two-piece sleeveless red pantsuit with two thin brown gold buckle belts, yellow vinyl shoulder bag, red pilgrims, circa 1972, $105.00.
Courtesy McMasters Doll Auctions.

11½" vinyl Live Action Barbie on Stage, #1152, painted blue eyes, rooted eyelashes, pink lips and blush, bendable arms and legs, blond hair with brown suede headband across forehead, original multicolor long sleeve top of pink, fuchsia, and orange, brown suede waistband with long fringe, brown plastic bracelets with fringe, matching multicolor pants, brown high top shoes, gray plastic microphone on stand, NRFB, circa 1971, $275.00.
Courtesy McMasters Doll Auctions.

11½" vinyl Francie, bendable legs, blond hair with clear plastic band, brown eyes, rooted eyelashes, pink lips and blush, hair in loose flip to shoulders with bangs, one-piece aqua stretch Helanca swimsuit with green and fuchsia blocks and floral print, wrist tag, wire stand, booklet, gold paper label, NRFB, circa 1966, $425.00.
Courtesy McMasters Doll Auctions.

11½" vinyl Walking Jamie, bendable legs, brown painted eyes, rooted lashes, brown brows, pink lips, brunette hair with side part, shoulder-length flip tied with pink scarf, original yellow and orange knit dress, orange elastic belt, orange mid-calf boots in plastic bag, clear plastic stand, instruction booklet, wrist tag, near mint in box, circa 1970, $265.00.
Courtesy McMasters Doll Auctions.

11½" vinyl Live Action Christie, bendable arms and legs, painted brown-orange eyes, rooted eyelashes, black brows, orange lips and blush, long black hair with sheer orange scarf, original multicolor purple, lilac, orange, gold pattern crop top with long extended sleeve fringe, matching pants, wrist tag, near mint, circa 1971, $175.00.
Courtesy McMasters Doll Auctions.

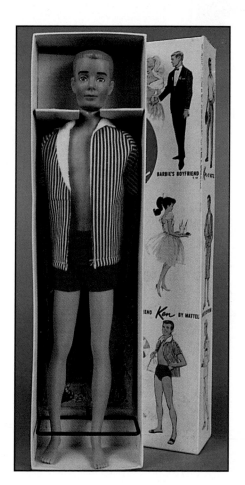

12" vinyl Ken with blond painted hair, painted eyes, red and white beach jacket and red cotton trunks, marked "Ken T.M.//Pats. Pend//© MCMLX//by//Mattel//Inc.," stock no. 750, boxed, circa 1962, $75.00.
Courtesy McMasters Doll Auctions.

12" vinyl Busy Ken with painted brown hair, blue eyes, wearing orange stretch tank top with brown vinyl belt, blue jeans, tennis shoes, marked on head "© 1968 Mattel Inc.," body marked "© 1968//Mattel, Inc.//U.S. & For.Patd/Other pats//Pending//Hong Kong," has wrist tag, circa 1971, $50.00.
Courtesy McMasters Doll Auctions.

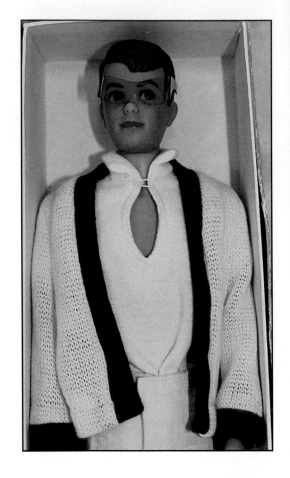

11½" vinyl Allan, boxed with tennis racket and balls, brown molded painted hair, painted eyes, closed mouth, wears tennis outfit, green sunshade, circa 1964, $75.00.
Courtesy Sarah Munsey.

11½" vinyl Mod Hair Ken, #4234, Montgomery Ward's issue, bendable legs, painted blue eyes, brown brows, pink lips, smiling mouth with painted teeth, brunette hair with side part, plastic band around hair, wearing red nylon swim trunks, also included is blue/black tuxedo jacket, black pants, nylon shirt, black bowtie, black shoes and socks in plastic bag, doll wrapped in white tissue with "Made in Hong Kong" yellow sticker, brown shipping box, circa 1974, $145.00.
Courtesy McMasters Doll Auctions.

11½" vinyl Live Action Ken on Stage, #1172, blue painted eyes, brown brows, peach lips, molded/painted brown hair, multicolor turquoise, purple, blue, green and gold long sleeve shirt, open in front with a hook-and-eye closure, yellow gold satin pants, brown fringe vest, brown loafers, wrist tag, gray plastic microphone on stand, NRFB, circa 1971, $175.00.
Courtesy McMasters Doll Auctions.

11½" vinyl Allan, straight legs, #1000, brown painted eyes, reddish brows, peach lips, molded painted reddish-brown hair, multicolor horizontal stripe beach jacket with white terry cloth facing bonded to collar, blue swim trunks, blue cork sandals in cellophane bag, wrist tag, white cover booklet, black wire stand, cardboard inserts, near mint in box, circa 1964, $95.00.
Courtesy McMasters Doll Auctions.

12" black vinyl Talking Brad with painted and molded black hair, brown eyes, black brows, closed mouth, multicolor v-neck short sleeve top, orange trunks, marked on head, "© 1968 Mattel," on body "© 1968//Mattel, Inc.//U.S. & For Patd//Other Pats//Pending//Hong Kong," non talking, circa 1969, $70.00.
Courtesy McMasters Doll Auctions.

9" vinyl Skipper, bendable leg, #1030, painted turquoise side-glancing eyes, light brown brows, peach lips, titian hair with middle part and bangs, brass headband, cellophane on head, one-piece navy stretch swimsuit with white and red striped bib shaped insert with anchor design, circa 1965, $80.00.
Courtesy McMasters Doll Auctions.

9" vinyl Skooter in box, with wrist tag, brochure, extra outfit, brown painted eyes, freckles, closed smiling mouth, black rooted hair in ponytails, original red two-piece short set, straight legs, circa 1965, $125.00.
Courtesy Sarah Munsey.

9" vinyl Living Fluff with blond hair in original set, ribbon, pink lips, bendable arms and legs, wears one-piece outfit, circa 1971, $75.00.
Courtesy McMasters Doll Auctions.

6" vinyl Tutti, #3550, painted blue eyes, pink lips, cheek blush, brunette hair with side part and bangs, pink hair ribbon, bendable posable body, pink and white checked sleeveless sundress with white ruffled hem, matching hat, white shoes, pink plastic brush and comb in plastic bag, wrist tag, NRFB, circa 1967, $100.00.
Courtesy McMasters Doll Auctions.

6" vinyl Todd, painted eyes, pink lips, titian hair, bendable posable body, wearing striped jacket, white shirt, blue shorts and socks, white tennis shoes, wrist tag, NRFB, circa 1967, $100.00.
Courtesy McMasters Doll Auctions.

9" vinyl Pose 'N Play Skipper and her Swing-A-Rounder Gym, #1179, blue eyes, brown brows, pale pink lips, short pigtails tied with blue ribbons, pin curls at ears, bangs, cellophane on head, blue and white sleeveless playsuit/swimsuit with blue buttons, bendable arms and legs, wrist tag, accessories, NRFB, circa 1972, $95.00.
Courtesy McMasters Doll Auctions.

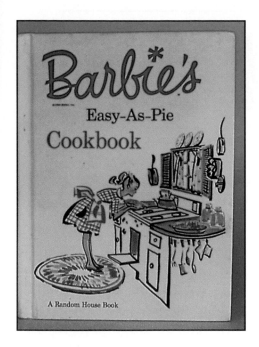

Barbie shower mitt with fine powdered soap, includes pink/white terrycloth mitt in clear plastic bag (unopened), six waxed pouches of powdered soap, paper advertisement for toiletries, in cardboard box with sleeve, boxed date 1961, $65.00.
Courtesy McMasters Doll Auctions.

Barbie's Easy-As-Pie Cookbook by Cynthia Lawrence, Random House, copyright 1964, $135.00.
Courtesy McMasters Doll Auctions.

Vinyl Barbie record tote, black vinyl, black plastic handles and ten paper record holders, paper record index attached to front binding, dated 1961, $65.00.
Courtesy McMasters Doll Auctions.

#4041 Barbie & Francie Color Magic Fashion Fun, includes Color Magic A & B Changer, metal spoon, two brushes with sponge ends, yellow plastic bowl, booklet, straw hat with attached yellow scarf, print shirt and skirt, pink pants with print trim, pink flat shoes, NRFP, package date 1965, $350.00.
Courtesy McMasters Doll Auctions.

Betsy McCall

1952 – 1953: Betsy McCall was based on the May 1951 *McCall* magazine paper doll. The doll was designed by Bernard Lipfert for Ideal with a vinyl head, strung hard plastic Toni body, and rooted saran wig. Marked: *McCall Corp* ® on head and *Ideal Doll//P-90* on back. **1957 – 1963**: American Character made an 8" hard plastic doll with a seven piece body. Some had rooted skull caps. American Character also made 14", 20," and 36" vinyl dolls in 1959. All were marked *McCall Corp*. In 1961 they made 22" and 29" Betsy, as well as, 36" Linda and 39" Sandy McCall. **1964**: Uneeda made an 11½" unmarked all vinyl Betsy with a teenage body. **1974**: Horsman made 12½" vinyl Betsy dolls marked *Horsman Doll Inc//19 ©67* on head, *Horsman Dolls Inc.* on torso. Horsman also made a 29" walking doll marked © *Horsman Dolls 1974*. **1986**: Rothschild made an 8" and 12" hard plastic 35th Anniversary Betsy. **1996**: Robert Tonner made a 14" vinyl Betsy, as well as, some porcelain special editions. Tonner introduced an 8" hard plastic Betsy in 2000.

What to look for:

Vinyl Betsy McCall dolls should be clean, retain color in the cheeks, and have original clothes. The large size can still be found in good condition. If you can't find an old one, try the new ones from Robert Tonner.

Ideal

American Character

8" hard plastic American Character Betsy McCall, blue sleep eyes, synthetic wig, seven-piece body with jointed knees, white dress, blue felt coat, pink felt hat, black stockings and shoes, circa 1957+, $200.00. *Courtesy Mary Sakraida.*

14" vinyl Ideal Betsy McCall with dark wig, closed mouth, brown sleep eyes, real lashes above, painted eyelashes at outer eye, original dress, with trunk and extra wardrobe, circa 1952, $325.00.
Courtesy Sally DeSmet.

8" hard plastic American Character Betsy McCall, marked "McCall © Corp." on mid back, plastic sleep eyes, closed mouth, seven-piece body with jointed knees and rigid vinyl arms, auburn rooted saran wig, long white dress with black bodice and lace over skirt, circa 1957, $200.00.
Courtesy Nelda Shelton.

8" hard plastic American Character Betsy McCall, marked "McCall © Corp." on mid back, plastic sleep eyes, closed mouth, seven-piece body with jointed knees and rigid vinyl arms, blond saran wig, original red sunsuit with white polka dots and towel, circa 1957, $175.00.
Courtesy Nelda Shelton.

19" vinyl American Character Betsy McCall marked "McCall 19©58 Corp." in a circle, with closed mouth, green sleep flirty eyes, reddish rooted hair, wears original red and green dotted Swiss street dress, circa 1958 – 1962, $325.00.
Courtesy Cornelia Ford.

14" vinyl American Character Betsy McCall, marked "McCall//19©58//Corp." on head, blue sleep eyes, auburn rooted saran hair, rigid vinyl walker, slim body, flat feet, re-dressed in green dress with lace, circa 1958, $250.00.
Courtesy Nelda Shelton.

Betsy McCall

22" vinyl American Character Betsy McCall, sleep eyes, rooted hair, in blue cotton dress with nylon apron, no marks, circa 1962, $250.00.
Courtesy Sally DeSmet.

22" vinyl American Character Betsy McCall, brown sleep eyes, closed mouth, rooted wig, jointed at wrists, waist, knees, and ankles, all-original red dress with black rickrack, white shirt underneath, black shoes, circa 1962, $325.00.
Courtesy June Allgeier.

22" vinyl American Character Betsy McCall, brown sleep eyes, rooted brown saran hair, swivel waist, wrists, and ankles, original plaid dress, circa 1962, $325.00.
Courtesy Sue Robertson.

FEATURED MONTHLY IN THE PAGES OF McCALL'S MAGAZINE

BETSY McCALL

A WELL-KNOWN QUALITY DOLL AT A NEW, LOW PRICE!

- Fantastically flexible...has jointed waist, hips, upper thighs, ankles, shoulders and wrists
- Poses in scores of positions...bends, balances—even on one leg
- Durable plastic, extremely lightweight, with glamorous rooted hair
- Practical 20" size, "See-thru?" gift packaged for point-of-sale display and self-service

#120 *Plaid flannel dress, white linen button-trimmed yoke and matching white cuffs. With black leotards, shoes and hair bow.*
Min. Pk. ....1 doz.
Approx. Wgt...............39 lbs.
Suggested
retail price $10.98

#320 *Tassel-trimmed red corduroy dress, white cotton collar and sleeves. With panties, shoes and socks.*
Min. Pk. ....1 doz.
Approx. Wgt...............39 lbs.
Suggested
retail price $10.98

#420 *Pink ballerina costume with satin bodice, bouffant tulle tutu. With startling pink leotards and satin slippers.*
Min. Pk. ....1 doz.
Approx. Wgt...............39 lbs.
Suggested
retail price $10.98

#220 *Vibrant-color cotton dress and collar, fringe-edged white nylon pinafore. With panties, shoes and socks.*
Min. Pk. ....1 doz.
Approx. Wgt...............39 lbs.
Suggested
retail price $10.98

American Doll and Toy catalog page featuring Betsy McCall from 1962.
Courtesy Margaret Stewart.

Betsy McCall

Horsman

29" vinyl Horsman Betsy McCall, marked "Horsman Dolls//1974," painted eyes, applied lashes, open/closed mouth, painted teeth, blond rooted hair with two ponytails, side part, white eyelet blouse, black shirt with "BMc" in red on front belt, red slip-on shoes, in marked blue two-tone box, box says "Betsy McCall — She WALKS with you," circa 1974, $275.00.
Private collection.

Robert Tonner

Left: 14" vinyl Robert Tonner Scissor Betsy, marked "Betsy McCall// by//Robert Tonner// ©Gruner & Jahr USA PUB.," rooted auburn hair, plastic eyes, closed smiling mouth, rigid vinyl body, red and white scissor dress with matching shoes and headband, circa 1996, $75.00.

Right: 14" porcelain Betsy McCall in pink party dress with matching hair bows, black shoes and white socks, limited edition of 250, circa 1996, $600.00.
Courtesy Margaret Stewart.

14" vinyl Robert Tonner Betsy McCall, left, and Betsy's cousin Barbara McCall, right, marked "Betsy McCall//by//Robert Tonner//©Gruner & Jahr USA PUB.," rigid vinyl bodies, Betsy McCall has brown rooted hair, brown plastic eyes, blue and white seersucker with matching hat, Barbara McCall has blond rooted hair, blue plastic eyes, and pink and white seersucker with matching hat, circa 1997, $75.00 each.
Courtesy Margaret Stewart.

Left: 14" vinyl Robert Tonner Betsy McCall, limited edition of 300, navy coat with white collar, matching hat, $95.00.

Right: 10" vinyl Robert Tonner Linda McCall, limited edition of 325 (first introduction of Linda), $140.00.

Plush stuffed dachshund dog Nosey with white matching collar, limited edition of 50, $18.00. All three from the 1998 UFDC Convention in New Orleans.
Courtesy Margaret Stewart.

Left: 14" vinyl Robert Tonner Barbara McCall, center: Betsy McCall, and right: 10" Linda McCall, rooted hair, plastic eyes, closed smiling mouth, rigid vinyl bodies, Barbara in turquoise gingham, Betsy in hot pink gingham, long hair, and Linda in lavender gingham with Betsy's plush stuffed dachshund dog, Nosey, circa 1998, Barbara – $70.00, Betsy – $70.00, Linda – $77.50, Nosey – $18.00.
Courtesy Margaret Stewart.

Left: 14" vinyl Robert Tonner Betsy McCall, limited edition of 50, rooted hair, plastic eyes, closed smiling mouth, rigid vinyl body, in lavender print dress at Robert Tonner's Club High SocieTea function at Expo East, circa 1998, $75.00.

Right: 10" vinyl Robert Tonner Linda McCall, limited edition of 10, blond rooted hair, closed smiling mouth, lavender print dress, centerpiece for Tonner Club High SocieTea function at Expo East, circa 1998, $55.00.
Courtesy Margaret Stewart.

Two 14" porcelain Robert Tonner Betsy McCall dolls, brown rooted hair, brown plastic eyes, closed smiling mouths.
Left: Betsy in pink party dress, limited edition of 250, circa 1996, $600.00.

Right: Betsy in Town & Country, limited edition of 250, circa 1997, $595.00 retail.
Courtesy Margaret Stewart.

Betsy McCall

14" vinyl Robert Tonner Betsy McCall dolls, rooted hair, plastic eyes, closed smiling mouths.

Left: Tennessee Waltz, white dotted Swiss formal for 1997 Collectors' United Winter Wonderland, limited edition of 200, $75.00.

Right: Betsy at Summer Camp, denim shorts, white sweatshirt, whistle around neck, 1998 Collectors' United Winter Wonderland, limited edition of 150, $75.00.
Courtesy Margaret Stewart.

14" vinyl Robert Tonner Betsy McCall dolls, rooted hair, plastic eyes, closed smiling mouths. Left to right: Limited edition of 200, raspberry velveteen dress, matching shoes and headband, for 1996 Modern Doll Convention in Las Vegas, $100.00. Sailor Betsy, limited edition of 100, white sailor suit and hat, 1997 Modern Doll Convention in San Diego, $100.00. Kimono Betsy, limited edition of 125, red kimono for 1998 Modern Doll Convention in Orlando, $125.00.
Courtesy Margaret Stewart.

14" vinyl Robert Tonner, Betsy Goes to Branson in pink and white striped dress and white pinafore, Dolly Dears show in Branson, MO, limited edition of 100, rooted hair, brown plastic eyes, closed smiling mouth, rigid vinyl body, circa 1997, $85.00.
Courtesy Margaret Stewart.

14" vinyl Robert Tonner Betsy McCall, Santa Fe Betsy in blue top, red flowered skirt, Santa Fe style belt with conchos, beaded necklace, sandals, limited edition of 100, for the third Santa Fe Doll Art Convention, rooted red hair, brown plastic eyes, closed smiling mouth, rigid vinyl body, circa 1997, $150.00.
Courtesy Margaret Stewart.

14" vinyl Robert Tonner Betsy McCall dolls, rooted hair, plastic eyes, closed smiling mouths, rigid vinyl bodies.

Left: Betsy Poodle Skirt, limited edition of 100, 1998 Expo West sale doll, $100.00.

Right: Betsy Goes to the Tea Party, limited edition of 100, 1998 Expo West sale doll, pink organza embroidered dress, $100.00.
Courtesy Margaret Stewart.

14" vinyl Robert Tonner Betsy Goes to Broadway, navy velveteen dress with matching shoes, limited edition of 50 at Collectors' United Kaffee Klatch with Robert Tonner, red rooted hair, brown plastic eyes, closed smiling mouth, rigid vinyl body, circa 1997, costume price $40.00.
Courtesy Margaret Stewart.

14" vinyl Robert Tonner Betsy McCall dolls, rooted hair, plastic eyes, closed smiling mouths, rigid vinyl bodies.

Left: Betsy Goes to Her Favorite Theme Park, limited edition of 200 for Walt Disney World Doll & Teddy Bear Convention, 1996.

Center: Betsy Mousketeer, original mousketeer outfit, limited edition of 200 for Walt Disney World, 1997.

Right: Betsy Loves Minnie, limited edition of 300 for Walt Disney World, 1998.
$200.00 each.
Courtesy Margaret Stewart.

14" vinyl Robert Tonner Betsy McCall dolls, rooted hair, plastic eyes, closed smiling mouths, rigid vinyl bodies.

Left: Robert Tonner's Club Sundaes on Saturday function at 1998 Expo West, limited edition of 75, pink and white pinstripe carhop uniform with apron, costume price $55.00.

Right: Centerpiece Betsy at the Hop for Tonner Club Sundaes on Saturday function at Expo West, limited edition of 15, felt jumper with music notes and rickrack, 1998, $125.00.
Courtesy Margaret Stewart.

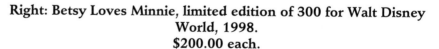

Betsy McCall

14" vinyl Robert Tonner Betsy McCall dolls, rooted hair, plastic eyes, closed smiling mouths, rigid vinyl bodies.

Left: Pink checked dress with pink flower print pinafore, matching checked pockets and shoes, for 1998 Portland Doll Luncheon, limited edition of 225, $125.00.

Right: Blue checked dress with blue flower print pinafore, matching checked pockets and shoes, centerpiece at 1998 Portland Doll Luncheon, limited edition of 25, $250.00. *Courtesy Margaret Stewart.*

14" vinyl Robert Tonner Sailor Betsy, black rooted hair, brown plastic eyes, closed smiling mouth, rigid vinyl body, in white sailor suit and hat, 1997 Modern Doll Convention in San Diego, $100.00. *Private collection.*

14" vinyl Robert Tonner Betsy McCall, plastic eyes, closed smiling mouth, rooted hair, rigid vinyl body, wearing style No. 99557, Going to Linda's Party, pink floral brushed cotton party dress, pearl accents and white shoes with pink bows, white stockings, pink bow in hair. Costume circa 1999, $34.99. *Photo courtesy Robert Tonner Doll Company.*

14" vinyl Robert Tonner Betsy McCall in Perfectly Suited, style No. 99502, plastic eyes, closed smiling mouth, rigid vinyl body, French suit of pink cotton pique and jet black crepe with gold buttons, white tights, smart black flats, black patent leather bag, circa 1999, doll and costume $90.00.
Photo courtesy Robert Tonner Doll Company.

14" vinyl Robert Tonner Betsy McCall, plastic eyes, closed smiling mouth, rooted hair, rigid vinyl body, wearing style No. 99550, Making Gingerbread, long sleeve print dress with a print pinafore, ribbon in hair, tights, brown shoes. Costume circa 1999, $34.99.
Photo courtesy Robert Tonner Doll Company.

14" vinyl Robert Tonner Betsy McCall, plastic eyes, closed smiling mouth, rooted hair, rigid vinyl body, wearing style No. 99551 Going Sailing, blue and white pinstripe dress with a big sailor collar, trimmed in red with white polka dots around the hem and collar and a big bow on front, red shoes, white tights, red bow in hair. Costume circa 1999, $34.99.
Photo courtesy Robert Tonner Doll Company.

14" vinyl Robert Tonner Betsy McCall, plastic eyes, closed smiling mouth, rooted hair, rigid vinyl body, wearing style No. 99549, Pretty in Pink, pink tulle and velvet gown with matching hair ribbon. Costume circa 1999, $34.99.
Photo courtesy Robert Tonner Doll Company.

Betsy McCall

14" vinyl Robert Tonner Betsy McCall, plastic eyes, closed smiling mouth, rooted hair, rigid vinyl body, wearing style No. 99558, Big City Shopping, crimson red dress coat, black trim on collar and cuffs, buttons, black hat, black shoes, white stockings.
Costume circa 1999, $34.99.
Photo courtesy Robert Tonner Doll Company.

14" vinyl Robert Tonner Betsy McCall, plastic eyes, closed smiling mouth, rooted hair, rigid vinyl body, wearing style No. 99555, Betsy's Halloween Party, pumpkin colored dress and jack-o-lantern apron, black eye mask, pumpkin.
Costume circa 1999, $34.99.
Photo courtesy Robert Tonner Doll Company.

14" vinyl Robert Tonner Betsy McCall, plastic eyes, closed smiling mouth, rooted hair, rigid vinyl body, wearing style No. 99553, It's Cold Outside, green knit sweater and matching cap, purple tights, socks, boots.
Costume circa 1999, $34.99.
Photo courtesy Robert Tonner Doll Company.

14" vinyl Robert Tonner Betsy McCall in Betsy Goes Hiking, style No. 99503, plastic eyes, closed smiling mouth, rigid vinyl body, printed flannel jacket, corduroy overalls, peach turtleneck, hiking boots, circa 1999, doll and costume $79.99.
Photo courtesy Robert Tonner Doll Company.

14" vinyl Robert Tonner Betsy McCall, plastic eyes, closed smiling mouth, rooted hair, rigid vinyl body, wearing style No. 99556, Summertime Separates, mix-and-match daisy print separates, yellow twin set with pants and jumper, yellow vinyl bag with daisy buttons. Costume circa 1999, $34.99.

Photo courtesy Robert Tonner Doll Company.

14" vinyl Robert Tonner Betsy McCall, plastic eyes, closed smiling mouth, rooted hair, rigid vinyl body, wearing style No. 99552, Rainy Days, lilac raincoat with floral print, matching hat and umbrella, red boots. Costume circa 1999, $35.99.

Photo courtesy Robert Tonner Doll Company.

14" vinyl Robert Tonner Betsy McCall in Betsy Goes to Scotland, style No. 99504, plastic eyes, closed smiling mouth, curly rooted hair, rigid vinyl body, black velvet jacket trimmed in gold with a classic tartan kilt, white lace blouse, knee socks, matching hat, black shoes, circa 1999, doll and costume $90.00.

Photo courtesy Robert Tonner Doll Company.

14" vinyl Robert Tonner Betsy McCall, plastic eyes, closed smiling mouth, rooted hair, rigid vinyl body, wearing style No. 99554, Walking Nosey, corduroy parka with black tights and snow boots, Nosey has matching outfit with red leash. Nosey, $18.00. Outfit circa 1999, $35.99.

Photo courtesy Robert Tonner Doll Company.

Betsy McCall

14" vinyl Robert Tonner Betsy McCall in Christmas Cotillion, style No. 99505, plastic eyes, closed smiling mouth, rooted hair, rigid vinyl body, plaid taffeta gown with velvet bodice and gold trim, gold petticoats, red velvet slippers with gold trim, carries her handkerchief in a plaid taffeta purse, circa 1999, doll and costume $79.99.
Photo courtesy Robert Tonner Doll Company.

Left: 14" vinyl Robert Tonner Cabana Barbara, long rooted blond hair, center 10" Cabana Linda, short rooted blond hair, and right, 14" Cabana Betsy, short brown rooted hair, all with plastic eyes, closed smiling mouths, rigid vinyl bodies, jersey swimsuits, white terry cloth cover-ups with matching trim, matching sandals, circa 1999, $69.99. Cabana Barbara No. 99506, $69.99, Cabana Linda No. 99508, $64.99, Cabana Betsy No. 99501, $69.99.
Photo courtesy Robert Tonner Doll Company.

10" vinyl Robert Tonner Linda McCall in Linda's Birthday Party, style No. 99510, blue plastic eyes, closed smiling mouth, rooted hair, rigid vinyl body, soft pink print party dress, pearl smocked yoke, lacy white petticoat, lace patterned tights, white velvet shoes decorated with satin rosettes and a tiny pearl, doll and costume, circa 1999, $74.99.
Photo courtesy Robert Tonner Doll Company.

14" vinyl Robert Tonner Barbara McCall in Barbara Goes to Holland, style No. 99507, plastic eyes, closed smiling mouth, rooted hair, rigid vinyl body, blue and white print dress with eyelet apron and matching hat, wooden shoes, doll and costume, circa 1999, $89.99.
Photo courtesy Robert Tonner Doll Company.

10" vinyl Robert Tonner Linda McCall, blue plastic eyes, closed smiling mouth, rooted hair, rigid vinyl body, dressed in style No. 99559, Bundle Up, pink fleece swing coat, hood and cuffs are trimmed in fluffy white fur, pink bow tied under her chin, white tights, pink patent Mary Janes. Costume circa 1999, $34.99.
Photo courtesy Robert Tonner Doll Company.

10" vinyl Robert Tonner Linda McCall, blue plastic eyes, closed smiling mouth, rooted hair, rigid vinyl body, dressed in style No. 99561, Day at the Shore, bright cotton print sunsuit with a ruffle and striped bow, matching hat, white canvas slip-ons, matching white canvas tote. Costume circa 1999, $34.99.
Photo courtesy Robert Tonner Doll Company.

10" vinyl Robert Tonner Linda McCall, blue plastic eyes, closed smiling mouth, rooted hair, rigid vinyl body, dressed in style No. 99560, Linda Picks a Posy, navy cotton floral print dress with buttons down front, trimmed in lace, floral petticoat, bloomers, navy velvet shoes with purple flowers, white stockings. Costume circa 1999, $34.99.
Photo courtesy Robert Tonner Doll Company.

8" vinyl Robert Tonner Merry and Kerry McCall, Betsy's twin baby brother and sister, inset acrylic eyes, soft vinyl bodies, blond hair, dressed in gingham seer-sucker outfits, Merry in a pink dress and Kerry in blue bibbed overalls, both with white shoes, circa 1999, $39.99 ea.
Photo courtesy Robert Tonner Doll Company.

10" vinyl Robert Tonner Linda McCall in Send in the Clown, style No. 99509, blue plastic eyes, closed smiling mouth, rooted hair, rigid vinyl body, cotton clown suit, starched pink taffeta collar trimmed in gold rickrack, sparkled purple pompons, tall matching clown hat, gold clown shoes with pompons, gold eye mask, doll and costume, circa 1999, $74.99. *Photo courtesy Robert Tonner Doll Company.*

Black Dolls

A great collectible category is black dolls. Black dolls almost always place over white dolls in competition. Fewer of these survived and finding one in mint condition is harder to do. These come in many different mediums and offer a wide range of collecting possibilities in cloth, composition, hard plastic, porcelain, rubber, and vinyl.

Shindana, 1968 – 1983, Los Angeles, California

After the Watts riots in Los Angeles, Shindana Toys was formed in 1968, the first major manufacturer of black dolls with ethnically correct features, high quality, covering a wide selection of babies, children, and adults. Shindana was a division of Bootstrap Inc., a non-profit black community organization founded by Lou Smith and Robert Hall. Its motto was "Learn Baby, Learn!" and they presented positive images of black children. It ceased production in 1983 and with a short 15-year span of operation, only a few of these dolls are still available. Dolls may be marked *Div. Of//Operation Bootstrap, Inc, USA//©1968 Shindana* or other Shindana marks.

What to look for:

Condition is still the number one factor in great collectible dolls. From finding a Leo Moss papier mache/composition to a modern vinyl, black dolls can be an intriguing part of your collection. Almost any out of production black doll mint in the box will remain a good collectible and may increase in value. Check for marks to find those Shindana dolls — they included the infamous O.J. Simpson as well as other celebrities. Do not overlook black dolls at garage sales and flea markets and other sales.

Shindana

15" vinyl Kim Jeans 'n Things, marked "17//©1969//Shindana Toys//Div. Of Operation// Bootstrap Inc. U.S.A.//K" on head, painted brown eyes, closed mouth, long black rooted hair, tie-dye jacket and skirt, white top with pink flower print, circa 1976, $45.00.
Courtesy Susan Dubow.

15" vinyl Malaika (means Angel in Swahili), rooted black hair, jointed vinyl body, wears fashion design by Aajib, marked "© 1969//Shindana Toys//Division of Operation Bootstrap USA," circa 1969, $75.00.
Courtesy Cornelia Ford.

Celluloid

2½" tall crawling celluloid baby, 3½" long, painted side-glancing eyes, molded black curly hair with painted bows, red and white original dress, windup mechanism allows baby to crawl, circa 1930s, $50.00.
Courtesy Elizabeth Surber

Composition

9½" composition Effanbee Mammy, has one-piece torso and head, wire spring upper arms, oversize molded boots attached to side of torso, hands fit metal carriage with rubber wheels (also comes with composition carriage), circa 1947+, $600.00.
Courtesy Cornelia Ford.

13½ composition Horsman Peterkins, marked "EIH Co. Horsman," painted brown side-glancing eyes, closed smiling mouth, molded painted hair, cloth torso, jointed composition arms/legs, red and white outfit and hat, circa 1929, $225.00.
Courtesy Dorothy Bohlin.

Black Dolls

Hard Plastic

Rubber

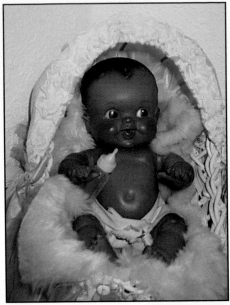

10" rubber Sun Rubber Co. Amosandra from *Amos & Andy* radio/TV series, eyes painted to left, molded painted curly hair, nursing mouth, jointed rubber baby body, circa 1949, $45.00.
Courtesy Kate Treber.

Vinyl

6" hard plastic Knickerbocker Hawaiian Girl, marked "Knickerbocker" on back, painted side-glancing eyes, black mohair wig, green grass skirt, circa 1950s, $35.00.
Private collection.

35" vinyl Ideal Patti Play Pal marked "Ideal Toy Corp. © G-35," rotational molded vinyl head, blow-molded vinyl body, jointed wrists, vinyl hands, brown sleep eyes, straight saran rooted black hair with bangs, individual fingers, original red checked dress and white pinafore, circa 1981 (reissued from 1959 mold), $175.00.
Courtesy Cornelia Ford.

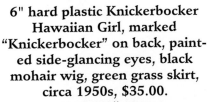

19" vinyl Beatrice Wright child, with black curly wig, brown sleep eyes, rigid vinyl body, marked on head, "Beatrice Wright//© 1967," circa 1967, $75.00.
Courtesy Cornelia Ford.

Cameo

Joseph L. Kallus's company operated from 1922 to 1930 in New York City and Port Allegheny, Pennsylvania. They made composition dolls with segmented wooden or cloth bodies as well as all-composition dolls.

What to look for:

Look for composition dolls with little crazing, no cracks, no pealing paint, good cheek color, original tagged costumes that are not faded or soiled. When looking at vinyl, look for clean dolls with good color, and costumes that are clean and bright. Wooden segmented dolls are a great collectible and sometimes overlooked by collectors focusing on better-known dolls.

12" composition Giggles, painted blue side-glancing eyes, closed smiling mouth, molded/painted hair with hole for bow in back, five-piece composition body, yellow organdy dress with lace trim, white lace-trimmed taffeta underclothing, original socks and shoes, yellow ribbon in hair, box marked "Kewpie Doll//design and copyright by Rose O'Neill//9613//"Giggles"//Des.," cardboard tag reads "Designed and Copyright by Rose O'Neill, a Cameo doll," circa 1946, $425.00.
Courtesy McMasters Doll Auctions.

15" vinyl Scootles pair, with side-glancing painted eyes, molded hair, closed smiling mouth, marked "JLK A 64//© Cameo" in blue and white striped costumes, with red trim, circa 1964, $200.00.
Courtesy Mary Curik.

Celebrity Dolls

Celebrity dolls must represent real people — they cannot be a literary, comic, or cartoon character. They must represent someone who lived. To still be considered a celebrity doll, the doll may represent the person who plays the character on television, in the movies, or in a play. Abraham Lincoln was a real person so the Lincoln doll can be entered in the celebrity doll category. Princess Diana was a real person, so again, the doll that represents her can be considered a celebrity doll.

Charlie McCarthy was never alive — he represents an object and although he is famous as a ventriloquist's dummy from the movies, he is not a celebrity doll and would be disqualified in competition if placed in that category. Dorothy of Oz fame is not a celebrity doll — but Judy Garland, who portrayed the Dorothy character in the Wizard of Oz film, is regarded as a celebrity doll. Mickey Mouse is not a live person, he is a Disney cartoon or comic character and is not considered a celebrity doll.

This is an exciting, fun, very interesting category of collecting. While Shirley Temple is a celebrity, she is so collectible and so famous, the doll usually has its own category. The same is true for the Dionne Quints. Avid Quint and Shirley fans usually collect all sorts of accessories, ephemera, and related memorabilia as well as the dolls. You can collect just television or movie celebrities, athletes, black dolls, or whoever catches your fancy.

What to look for:

Condition and originality highly influence the collecting status of these dolls as well as associated boxes, labels, brochures, and other paper products. Look for clean dolls with original tagged or labeled costumes, good color and related items that enhance the collector's knowledge of the doll.

Alphabetically by Celebrity

11" vinyl Horsman Mary Poppins from character portrayed by Julie Andrews in the Walt Disney movie, dark rooted hair, side-glancing painted blue eyes, marked "H" on head, vinyl arms, rigid vinyl body and legs, blue felt coat, hat, tapestry bag, umbrella, pictured in Sears 1965 catalog, $35.00.
Courtesy Elizabeth Surber.

12" composition Ideal Fanny Brice as Baby Snooks, marked "Ideal Doll" on back of head, designed by Joseph Kallus, painted blue eyes, open/closed laughing mouth, molded/painted hair with loop for bow, wooden torso, flexy wire arms and legs, composition hands, wooden feet, original blue print clothing with organdy collar and tie, circa 1939, $285.00.
Courtesy McMasters Doll Auctions.

7½" hard plastic Daniel Boone tagged "Carlson Dolls," blue sleep eyes, closed mouth, all original with rabbit fur hat, simulated leather costume, gun, Carlson made these type dolls 1950s – 1970s, $15.00.
Courtesy Peggy Millhouse.

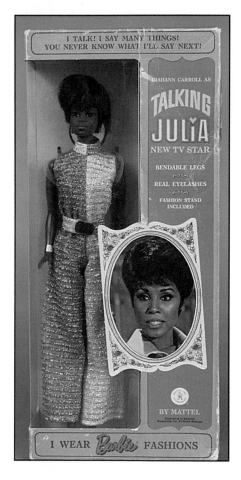

11½" vinyl Mattel Talking Julia, as portrayed by Diahann Carroll, the first black performer who was the star of a regular TV series, bendable legs, brown eyes, rooted eyelashes, pink lips, cheek blush, oxidized red hair, wearing silver and gold pantsuit with belt, wrist tag, clear plastic stand, mint in box, circa 1969, $220.00.
Courtesy McMasters Doll Auctions.

11½" vinyl Galoob Rose DeWitt Bukater *Titanic* Motion Picture Collector Doll, painted blue eyes, closed mouth, long curly red rooted hair, jointed, wearing a maroon gown with black lace and trim, holding a sheer black shawl, box says "James Cameron Film//TITANIC//14 Academy Award Nominations in 1997//(star)//Winner of 11," mint in box, circa 1998, $80.00.
Courtesy Leslie Tannenbaum.

14" composition Horsman Jackie Coogan, painted side-glancing eyes, closed mouth, molded painted hair, original pants tagged "Jackie Coogan Kid," turtleneck sweater, all original, circa 1921 – 1922, $450.00. *Courtesy Martha Sweeney.*

14" vinyl Danbury Mint Princess Diana, shown with some of her wardrobe, painted blue eyes, 21 sets of clothing and complete accessories, red trunk marked "Princess Diana," circa 1988, $750.00. *Courtesy Sue Robertson.*

12½" vinyl Sharpgrade Ltd. LJN Toys Boy George, English rock star, with painted features, rooted hair, purple eyeshadow, original Colors by Number costume with red boots, unmarked but comes with yellow stand marked "Boy George; ©1984 Sharpgrade Ltd. LJN Toys," $125.00. *Courtesy Cornelia Ford.*

15" all-composition Ideal Deanna Durbin, marked "DEANNA DURBIN//IDEAL DOLL" on head and "15//IDEAL DOLL" on back, sleep eyes, dark eyeshadow, open mouth with six teeth and felt tongue, dark brown human hair wig, fully jointed, all original, circa 1938 – 1941, $425.00. *Courtesy Flo Burnside.*

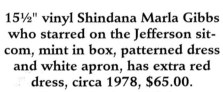

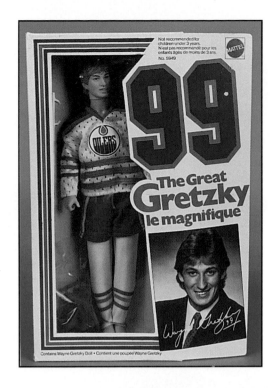

12" vinyl Mattel Wayne Gretzky with the Edmonton Oilers, painted blue eyes, pink lips, painted teeth, painted blond hair, original hockey outfit, NRFB, circa early 1980s, $75.00.
Courtesy McMasters Doll Auctions.

15½" vinyl Shindana Marla Gibbs who starred on the Jefferson sitcom, mint in box, patterned dress and white apron, has extra red dress, circa 1978, $65.00.
Courtesy Antoinette Whelan.

17" porcelain Mary Kay doll made to represent founder of the Mary Kay Cosmetics Company, blond wig, blue glass eyes, dressed in long trademark pink gown with feather boa, unmarked, circa 1990s, $175.00.
Courtesy Cornelia Ford.

11½" vinyl LJN Toys Inc. FloJo representing athlete Florence Griffith Joyner, with black rooted hair, painted brown eyes, open/closed mouth in smile with teeth, dressed in one-leg tights, missing shoe, circa 1989, $8.00.
Courtesy Michelle Lyons.

20" vinyl Emmett Kelly's Willie the Clown, by Baby Barry, all original in box marked "# 715 //Emmett Kelly's//Willie the Clown// Baby Barry Toy// NYC," complete with clothespin tie clasp, black derby hat, green shirt, gold check vest, brown jacket with cloth label, blue patched pants, sewn on black felt shoes, circa late 1950s, $325.00.
Courtesy Elizabeth Surber.

11" vinyl Mattel Twiggy, painted blue eyes, heavily painted rooted lashes below, pink lips, open/closed smiling mouth with painted teeth, rooted light blond hair, vinyl head, arms, and legs, plastic torso, fully jointed with a twist waist, original yellow, blue, and green knit dress with yellow plastic boots, circa 1967, $115.00. *Courtesy McMasters Doll Auctions.*

5" hard plastic Hollywood Doll Co. Roy Rogers and Dale Evans, marked "star//Hollywood Doll Co.," sleep eyes, molded painted hair on Roy Rogers, red mohair wig on Dale Evans, fingers molded together, original western clothes, circa 1950s, $75.00 pair. *Courtesy Nelda Shelton.*

Political

20" porcelain Danbury Mint First Lady Rosalyn Carter, dark hair, painted eyes, open/closed mouth with teeth, gold earrings, wears pale blue chiffon skirt, gold beaded bodice, sleeveless coat of matching brocade, gold trim, circa 1990s, $225.00. *Courtesy Cornelia Ford*

20" porcelain Danbury Mint First Lady Barbara Bush, painted eyes, closed mouth, in two-tone blue inaugural gown, white wig, pearl earrings, pearl necklace, carries blue evening purse, circa 1990s, $225.00. *Courtesy Cornelia Ford.*

20" porcelain Danbury Mint President First Lady Jacqueline Kennedy, dark wig, brown painted eyes, pearl earrings, wears long white cape over white sheath inaugural gown, carries white purse, circa 1990s $225.00.
Courtesy Cornelia Ford.

12" vinyl Suzanne Gibson First Lady Mamie Eisenhower, dark wig, blue glass eyes, closed mouth, hang tag, in long pink sequined dress, circa 1985, $75.00.
Courtesy Cornelia Ford.

20" porcelain Danbury Mint First Lady Pat Nixon, dark blond wig, painted eyes, open mouth with teeth, earrings, gold sheath dress with gold short beaded jacket top, hands painted to represent gloves, circa 1990s, $225.00.
Courtesy Cornelia Ford.

20" porcelain Danbury Mint First Lady Bird Johnson, dark hair, painted eyes, open/closed mouth with teeth, pearl earrings, pearl necklace, gold fur-trimmed coat over gold inaugural dress, circa 1990s, $225.00.
Courtesy Cornelia Ford.

20" porcelain Danbury Mint First Lady Nancy Reagan, brown wig, painted eyes, eyeshadow, open/closed mouth with teeth, earrings, white coat over beaded one shoulder gown, hands painted white to represent gloves, circa 1990s, $225.00.
Courtesy Cornelia Ford.

18" vinyl Wes Soderstrom Teddy Bear, vinyl face of Teddy Kennedy, painted brown eyes, big smile, painted teeth, plush body, marked "Teddy Bear//Wes Soderstrom Bear//Woodland Hills, CA//P.O. Box 60//91365," plush teddy bear body, circa 1981, $150.00.
Private collection.

16" vinyl Wes Soderstrom President Ronnie Bear, vinyl face of Ronald Reagan, tag reads "President Ronnie Bear//Wes Soderstrom//Woodland Hills, CA//P.O. Box 60//91365," vinyl Ronald Reagan face, painted blue eyes, big smile, painted teeth, plush teddy bear body, circa 1981, $150.00.
Private collection.

Cloth Dolls

Cloth dolls have gained immensely in popularity with collectors recently. Because the doll is made of cloth, children have always favored them for their soft cuddly appearance. This category again presents a wide variety for the collector and while prices have sky-rocketed in the past 10 years, there are still good buys to be found in some of the lesser known dolls that collectors have overlooked in their pursuit of more well-known examples.

What to look for:
Clean dolls with high color on the cheeks, not soiled, ripped, or torn, with original labels, tags, brochures, or boxes. A worn dirty doll will retain little value, so the buyer should consider again that main factor, the condition, before purchasing. Do not pay huge prices for dolls that have rips, soil, fading, or other flaws — even if you do love it.

Alphabetically by Manufacturer

21" Gund Mfg. Co. Nancy Lou, blue painted side-glancing eyes, closed mouth, rosy cheeks, yellow yarn hair, green, red, and navy plaid dress with matching hat, oilcloth feet, circa 1960s, $150.00.
Courtesy Mary Evelyn Graf.

18" Gund Mary Lou with mask face, floating celluloid googly eyes, yarn hair, original bonnet and clothing sewn to make body of doll, wears identifying pinback button with name, $75.00, some wear.
Courtesy Yvonne Burgess.

19" Gund Pollyanna, tagged "Walt Disney's//Pollyanna//Glad Doll//by Gund," mask face, blue side-glancing painted eyes, closed mouth, freckles, yellow yarn hair in braids, cloth body, Gund used the earmarks on tags from WWII until the mid 1960s, circa 1960s, $250.00.
Private collection.

13" Bruckner Topsy-Turvy, marked "Topsy-Turvy//E.I. Horsman," mask face, painted eyes, reversible doll, black doll under one skirt, white doll under the other, all original, made by Horsman for Bruckner, circa 1901–1927, $1,000.00.
Courtesy Nelda Shelton.

32" brown velvet Norah Wellings cloth Islander with label on foot, "Made in England//By//Norah Wellings," black mohair wig, painted eyes, mouth with teeth, bright yellow trousers, yellow plastic necklace and earrings, circa 1950s – 1960s, $850.00.
Courtesy Cornelia Ford.

16" Molly'es girl, painted mask face, blue painted side-glancing eyes, yellow yarn hair, cloth body, original white dress and bonnet with blue flowers and rickrack, no shoes, circa 1950s, $125.00.
Private collection.

13" cloth Molly'es child, mask face, blue painted side-glancing eyes, closed mouth, yellow yarn hair, mitt hands, all-cloth body, red pants and cap with blue trim, white shirt with blue flowers, circa 1930, $35.00.
Courtesy Joanna Smith.

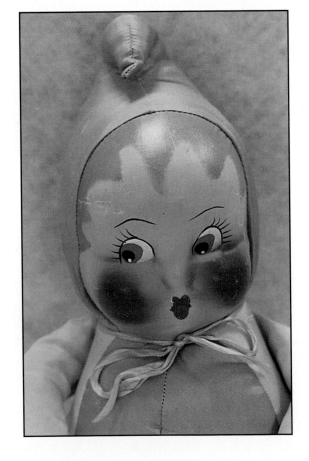

13½" unmarked mask face baby by unknown maker, painted features, side-glancing eyes, painted lashes above, very ruddy cheeks, closed mouth, lavender cap forms head as does sewn-on lavender and yellow clothing, some wear, a charming childhood soft doll of the 1940s, $50.00.
Courtesy Yvonne Burgess.

Comic Dolls

Comic characters are great collectibles and this category presents huge potential for the collector who is looking for something away from the mainstream. Not only characters from the comic pages of the newspapers, but comic books, movies, and television cartoon characters are included. These may come in many different mediums and the collector may wish to include associated paper goods or other accessories with the dolls.

What to look for:

Again condition is king when choosing collectibles. Dolls should be clean, with good color, little crazing if composition and preferably with tags, boxes, labels, original clothing, all intact. Have fun looking for these dolls at garage and estate sales, on eBay, or in thrift shops — comic characters are a great collectible that men seem to like.

13" cloth Georgene Dolls Becassine, stockinette mask face, painted eyes, no mouth indicated, cloth body jointed at shoulders, hips, hang tag, all original, mint in box, circa 1953, $925.00.
Courtesy McMasters Doll Auctions.

14" all-composition Herman Cohen and The House of Puzzy, Inc. comic character Puzzy, unmarked, painted eyes to side, freckles, open/closed mouth, painted teeth, molded/painted red hair, known as the Good Habit kids (images used on soap, toothbrushes, other grooming items) black and white outfit, red ribbon tie, all original, circa 1948, $325.00; left, 9" Steiff Hexie, silver Steiff button, inset eyes, black floss nose, swivel head, circa 1957+, $85.00.
Courtesy McMasters Doll Auctions.

Comic Dolls

Marge comic characters, all cloth, original hang tags, circa 1944 – 1964.

Left: 12" Alvin, cloth mask face, mint in box, $2,000.00.

Center: 14" Little Lulu, cloth mask face, near mint in box, $1,300.00.

Right: 14" Tubby Tom, cloth mask face, mint in box, $2,000.00.
Courtesy McMasters Doll Auctions.

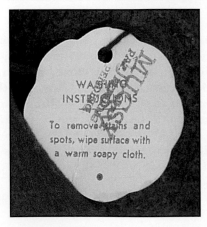

16" cloth Trixy Toy Mugsy with painted cloth face, red patched overalls, blue shirt, original hang tag, no hat, possibly 1950s, $50.00.
Courtesy Debbie Crume.

Composition Dolls

Composition dolls have been made since the 1890s and possibly earlier. Cold press composition describes the method of putting a mixture of ingredients (composition) into molds. The recipe for composition varied with each manufacturer, but at first glue was used to bind together such things as flour, shredded cardboard or paper, and rags. Later recipes used wood pulp as manufacturers learned how to bake the composition in multiple molds in the hot press method. The mixture was more soupy when poured into molds than when pressed and the ingredients differed somewhat.

These doll heads were first described as indestructible as compared to the bisque and china heads that could be easily broken. The dolls were dipped in tinted glue baths to give a flesh tone and then later the features and coloring were air-brushed. Humidity made it difficult for the dolls to dry correctly in early production procedures, but later techniques were refined to reduce this problem. The big problem with composition dolls was their glycerin and glue base — when the surface became saturated with water, it would disintegrate. Extremes in heat and humidity cause bacteria to grow on the surface and destroy the painted finish.

Collectors need to keep composition dolls away from direct sunlight, avoid extremes in temperature, and keep a gauge in their cases to check the relative humidity. When the relative humidity exceeds 85%, bacteria have opportune conditions to grow and destroy the painted surfaces. Composition dolls should not be stored in plastic, but wrapped in cotton fabric that has been washed and well rinsed to remove any soap or conditioner. Collectors who had this type of doll as a plaything in their childhood can, with a little caution, enjoy some of the wide variety of dolls still available. Included in this category are composition dolls by unknown makers or little known companies.

What to look for:

Great composition dolls should have no crazing, cracking, peeling, or lifting of paint. They should also have rosy cheek color and original wig and clothes. They may have blush on knees, hands, and arms. Added incentives would be tags, labels, brochures, or labeled boxes. Consider dolls with major flaws only if they have pluses like tagged original costumes, brochures, hang tags, or boxes, and they should be priced accordingly.

15" Eugenia Doll Co. Inc. girl, tagged dress, blond mohair wig, nylon dress with attached slip and panties, pink center snap shoes, circa 1940s, $250.00.

Courtesy Gay Smedes.

Composition Dolls

17" Eugenia Doll Co. Roberta, mohair wig, original tagged outfit, circa 1940s, excellent condition, $300.00.

Courtesy Betty Jane Fronefield.

28" Halco mama doll, doll is unmarked, box reads "Super Halco Brand//Quality Dolls," shoulder plate, blue sleep eyes, real lashes, feathered brows, painted lower lashes, open mouth, four upper teeth, brown human hair wig, cloth body, crier, composition arms and legs, blue pleated dress, flowered bodice, matching hat, underclothing, socks and shoes, unplayed with condition, original with box, circa 1940, $245.00.

Courtesy McMasters Doll Auctions.

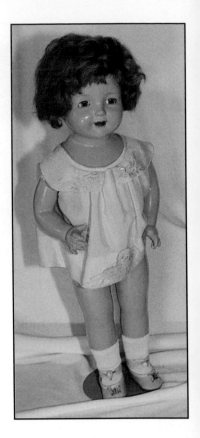

21" K & K marked (K & K Toy Company affiliated with Borgfeldt) shoulder-head, sleep eyes, mohair wig, open mouth with teeth, cloth body, composition limbs, old dress, circa 1930s, $275.00.

Courtesy Oleta Woodside.

14" Reliable Toy Co. Her Highness Coronation, marked "Reliable Doll//Made in Canada" on head, blue sleep eyes, eyeshadow, open smiling mouth, four upper teeth, auburn saran wig, five-piece body, white gown, gold trim, dark red velvet cape lined with white satin, gold paper crown, red sash reads "Her Highness Coronation Doll," unplayed with in original box, circa 1953, $210.00.

Courtesy McMasters Doll Auctions.

15" Reliable celebrity skater, Barbara Ann Scott, marked "Reliable//Made in Canada," blue sleep eyes, real lashes, eyeshadow, unusual eyebrows with short dashes, open mouth with teeth, reddish mohair wig, redressed, circa 1948 – 1953, $300.00.
Courtesy Oleta Woodside.

17" Reliable Royal Canadian Mountie, molded painted hair, painted blue eyes, closed mouth, straw stuffed cloth body and legs, composition arms, marked "Reliable//Made in Canada," original Mountie uniform, replaced hat, circa 1936, $300.00.
Courtesy Oleta Woodside.

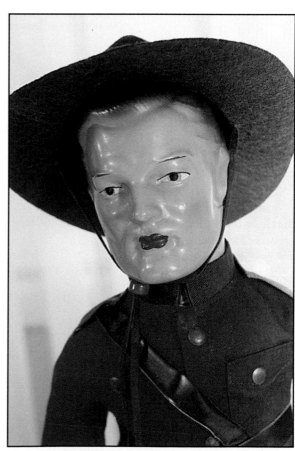

Composition Dolls

16" Roberta Doll Co. girl, marked on torso with an "X," her box is marked "Roberta Doll//Quality Products//of Roberta Doll Co. Inc. New York, U.S.A.," blue glassene sleep eyes, real lashes, eyeshadow above, open mouth with four upper teeth, rosy cheek color, red mohair wig, five-piece jointed composition body, original long pink organdy dress with lace trim, attached slip, underwear, tan oilcloth-type tie shoes, mint in box, circa 1940s, $300.00.
Courtesy Flo Burnside.

18" Sayco Mary Ann, marked "R&B" on back of head, hang tag reads "Dolls of Quality//Mary Ann//A Sayco Doll," sleep eyes, open mouth with two teeth, mohair wig, white baby dress, blue jacket, black hat, late 1930s, $350.00.
Courtesy Sally DeSmet.

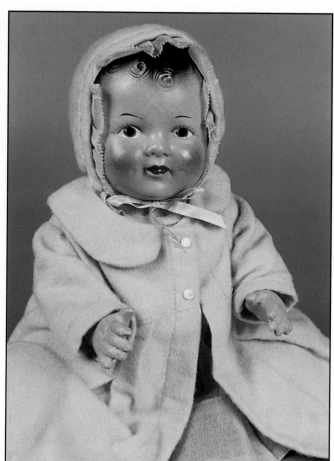

Composition Dolls

12" unmarked baby, painted blue eyes, single stroke brows, painted upper lashes, open/closed smiling mouth, molded dimples, rosy cheeks, molded painted dark hair, composition bent-limb baby body, original pink and white organdy dress, pink organdy slip, flannel diaper, socks, original pink flannel coat and bonnet, near mint, circa 1910+, $155.00.

Courtesy McMasters Doll Auctions.

17" Webber's Doll, marked "Webber's Dolls" in center of back, blue sleep eyes, closed mouth, blond synthetic wig, red plaid skirt and tam, red jacket, red shoes, white knee high socks, circa late 1940s, $225.00.

Courtesy Angie Gonzales.

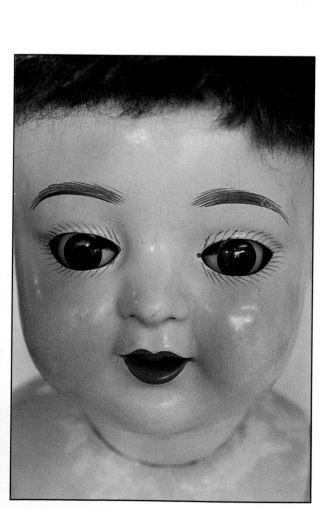

21" Zaiden Baby, marked "H2 mark//Zaiden//American// Superior Doll," glass sleep eyes with lashes, auburn mohair glued on wig, open mouth, tongue, fully jointed composition body, circa 1915, $150.00.

Courtesy Nelda Shelton.

Composition Dolls

18" unmarked Patsy-type, tin eyes, open/closed mouth, molded painted hair, fully jointed composition body, red dress, circa 1928+, $250.00.
Courtesy Lee Ann Beaumont.

25" unmarked mama doll, glassene eyes, shoulder plate, open mouth with two teeth, brown human hair wig, composition arms, cloth body, swing legs, crier, yellow dress, orange/brown trim, hat, all original, circa 1920s, $300.00.
Courtesy Sally DeSmet.

17" unmarked girl, sleep eyes, open mouth with two teeth, felt tongue, red mohair wig, five-piece composition body, circa 1928+, $175.00.
Courtesy Flo Burnside.

17" unmarked child with blond mohair wig in pigtails, brown sleep eyes with eyeshadow over real lashes, painted lashes below, open mouth, original costume, circa 1940s, $175.00.
Courtesy Lynda Towler.

13" McGuffey Ana-type doll from unknown maker, marked only with size number on back, open mouth with four upper teeth, sleep eyes with eyeshadow, mohair wig, original red and white costume, circa 1939 – 1940, $175.00.
Courtesy Yvonne Burgess.

11" unmarked girl, blue sleep eyes, closed mouth, blond mohair wig, original pink dress with lace, white lace petticoat, replaced hat, circa 1940s, $175.00.
Courtesy Sheryl Schmidt.

22" Snow White by unknown maker, brown glass eyes, open mouth with teeth, two dimples, black mohair wig with blue ribbon, all composition, circa 1939, $325.00.
Courtesy Shawna Goodwin.

14" unmarked rabbit doll, socket head, light blue painted eyes, closed mouth, five-piece composition body jointed at shoulders and hips, each piece of the entire doll is covered with rabbit fur so it is well jointed and moves freely, ears are of rabbit skin, hands and feet are composition, circa 1920s, $160.00.
Courtesy McMasters Doll Auctions.

Deluxe Reading

Deluxe Reading manufactured dolls from 1957 to 1965 that were sold at supermarkets as premiums — a reward for purchasing something else or groceries totaling a certain figure. They were marketed with several names: Deluxe Premium Corp., Deluxe Reading, Deluxe Topper, Deluxe Toy Creations, Topper Corp., and Topper Toys. They were of stuffed vinyl, jointed at the neck only, with sleep eyes and rooted hair. The dolls were inexpensively dressed, often as brides, in long formals, or in street dresses which included a hat in the 50s and 60s. They also made 8" vinyl Penny Brite dolls with side-glancing eyes and a vinyl carrying case.

What to look for:

More and more of these dolls are showing up, often still packed in their original box. Unfortunately those that were played with often had problems with the stuffed vinyl rupturing at the neck. The costumes or accessories on some of these dolls make them an interesting and overlooked collectible.

22" vinyl Candy Fashion, box marked "The Dream of Every Girl//Better Toys For Young America," four complete outfits with accessories, dressed in green outfit with matching hat, sunglasses, mint in box, circa 1960s, $150.00.
Courtesy Iva Mae Jones.

8½" vinyl Penny Brite, rooted blond hair, painted eyes, with blue rigid plastic see-through case, missing shoe, original dress, marked "Deluxe Reading Corp, © 1963," circa 1963, $35.00.
Courtesy Michele Lyons.

7" vinyl Suzy Cute, sleep eyes, closed mouth, blond hair, yellow plastic crib with rattle and two booklets, wearing two-piece blue outfit, mint in box, circa 1964, $45.00.
Courtesy Leslie Tannenbaum.

25" vinyl Suzy Smart, sleep eyes, closed mouth, rooted blond ponytail, hard plastic body, red, green, and black checkered skirt, white blouse, black tam and shoes, box reads "My Name Is Suzy Smart, The Talking School Doll," desk, chair, easel, blackboard, and school accessories, mint in box, sold through food markets during the 1962 Christmas season, $300.00.
Courtesy Vanessa Mebel.

Disney

Walter Ellas Disney, was born in 1902 in the Chicago area, but grew up on a Missouri farm, and had his first art lessons at age 13. His family moved back to Chicago in 1917, and he entered the Chicago Academy of Fine Art and studied under cartoonist Leroy Gossitt. During World War I, at age 16, he was an ambulance driver in France. After the war, he worked for an advertising firm doing animation.

With his brother, Roy, Disney came to Hollywood where they set up their own animation studio, and in 1927 his first character, Oswald the Lucky rabbit, appeared in a silent cartoon series. Finding he did not own the rights to his cartoon, they were held by the distributor, Disney determined he would not lose control of his own creations again. He then created a new mouse character, first named Mortimer, but later named Mickey by his wife.

Charlotte Clark designed and made the first Mickey Mouse doll and won Disney's approval for this copyrighted character. The demand soon overcame her production capabilities and the Disney brothers asked a major toy distributor, George Borgfeldt in New York, to mass produce and market the doll. Unfortunately, these dolls proved inferior to Clark's dolls, so the Disneys got the idea to make a pattern and have people make their own dolls. McCalls offered pattern #91 to make a stuffed Mickey Mouse in 1932.

After Mickey and Minnie Mouse came Donald Duck, Pluto, Red Riding Hood, the Wolf and the Three Little Pigs and then, Snow White and the Seven Dwarfs, Cinderella, and Pinnochio. Some of the early firms who produced dolls for Disney include Lenci and Lars of Italy, Steiff, Chad Valley, Dean's Rag, Gund, Crown, Knickerbocker, Ideal, Horsman, Borgfeldt, Krueger, and Alexander. Because Disney retained the copyright for these dolls, he demanded high quality in the production and costuming of the dolls — and defended infringement on the use of his copyrights. Disney dolls are great collectibles and their high quality has been appreciated over the years.

What to look for:

Because of the popularity Disney theme parks and the following explosion of related dolls sold in their gift shops, a collector could just have a collection of just Disney dolls. The early cloth dolls should be clean and bright, and have original clothing. Because early cloth dolls like Mickey Mouse were so loved, they are hard to find in excellent condition but even worn dolls have some value. These dolls still turn up in estate and garage sales — what child did not bring home a memento from their Disneyland visit?

15½" composition Ideal Snow White, painted brown side-glancing eyes, closed mouth, molded blue bow in black molded hair, all-composition body, original yellow taffeta dress, velvet bodice, circa 1938 – 1939, $300.00.
Courtesy Oleta Woodside.

12" cloth R.G. Kruger Doc, tag reads "Authentic Walt Disney character exclusive with R.G. Kruger, New York," dark blue hat, glasses, orange jacket, mint in box, circa 1930s – 1940s, $500.00 each, $3,500.00 set of seven.
Courtesy Sharon Kolibaba.

12" cloth R.G. Kruger Grumpy, tag reads "Authentic Walt Disney character exclusive with R.G. Kruger, New York," orange hat, blue jacket, yellow pants, mint in box, circa 1930s – 1940s, $500.00 each, $3,500.00 set of seven.
Courtesy Sharon Kolibaba.

12" cloth R.G. Kruger Dopey, tag reads "Authentic Walt Disney character exclusive with R.G. Kruger, New York," lavender hat, yellow jacket, mint in box, circa 1930s – 1940s, $500.00 each, $3,500.00 for set of Seven Dwarfs.
Courtesy Sharon Kolibaba.

Effanbee

Bernard Fleishaker and Hugo Baum formed a partnership, Fleishaker and Baum, in 1910 in New York City that would eventually be known as Effanbee. They began making rag and crude composition dolls and even had Lenox make some bisque heads for them. They developed a very high quality composition doll with a high quality finish. This characterizes their dolls of the 1920s and 1930s and until after the World War II, when the company was sold to Noma Electric. The company declined with the death of Hugo Baum in 1940, but had remarkable success with a series of dolls, including Bubbles, Grumpy, Lovums, Patsy, and Dy-Dee. Effanbee was a very entrepreneurial company during its prominent years using the talents of free-lance doll artist, Bernard Lipfert who created Bubbles, Patsy, and Dy-Dee as well as Shirley Temple for Ideal, the Dionne Quintuplets for Alexander, and Ginny for Vogue. Today, Effanbee Doll Company is owned by Stanley and Irene Wahlberg who have re-introduced many of Effanbee's 1930s favorites in vinyl, painted to give a composition look.

What to look for:
Effanbee's early composition dolls are classics and the painted finish was the finest available in its day. Unfortunately, the finish on played-with dolls was prone to scuffs and bumps, not to mention that these playthings have been stored for 70 years or more and subject to varying degrees of heat, cold, and moisture. The biggest threat to composition dolls is changes in relative humidity. When the humidity is over 85 percent, conditions are ripe for the growth of bacteria that cause the paint to decompose, flake, or peel. Also avoid direct sunlight to minimize fading. It is necessary to keep composition dolls clean and in a stable environment avoiding high humidity. Composition dolls should be clean, with rosy cheeks, costumed in original or appropriate costumes. These were some of the greatest dolls of the composition era and a treasure when you find them.

Later hard plastic and vinyl dolls also have problems with cleanliness and high relative humidity that allows the growth of bacteria. You can, however, still find all-original dolls with labeled or tagged costumes and good color and condition.

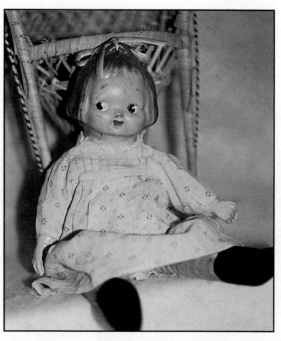

11" early composition child with heavily molded hair and loop for bow, painted side-glancing heart eyes, closed mouth painted eyebrows, wears old, possibly original, dress, marked "F+B" on back of head, cloth body with disk joints, black shoes part of feet, composition hands, circa 1911, $100.00.
Courtesy June Stepanski.

19" composition American Child designed by Dewees Cochran, marked "Effanbee//American Children" on head, "Effanbee//Anne-Shirley" on back, painted brown eyes, closed mouth, human hair wig, five-piece composition child body, blue flowered dress, white collar and bodice, white leather shoes with tassels, all-original, circa 1936 – 1939+, $1,000.00.
Courtesy McMasters Doll Auctions.

21" composition Barbara Lou designed by Dewees Cochran, one of the American Children series, marked "Effanbee//Anne-Shirley" on back, brown sleep eyes, real lashes, multi-stroke brows, painted lower lashes, open mouth, four teeth, auburn human hair wig, five-piece composition body, original blue jumper, white blouse, matching romper, white apron, socks, black leatherette fringe tie shoes, circa 1936 – 1939, $350.00.
Courtesy McMasters Doll Auctions.

21" all-composition American Child Barbara Ann marked "Effanbee//Anne Shirley," sleep eyes, open mouth, human hair wig, five-piece body, old perhaps original dress, light crazing, circa 1936 – 1939+, $450.00.
Courtesy McMasters Doll Auctions.

22" composition Betty Bee, marked "Effanbee//Patsy Lou" on back, sleep eyes, open mouth with teeth, human hair wig, original tagged dress with matching hat, all original with box, circa 1932, $400.00.
Courtesy Carol Elder.

Effanbee

14" composition Baby Grumpy, marked "Effanbee//Mark Deco (in circle)//Grumpy," painted side-glancing intaglio eyes, frowning eyebrows, heavily molded painted hair, composition hands, cloth body, legs, and feet, tagged Effanbee clothes, circa 1915+, $250.00.
Courtesy Nelda Shelton.

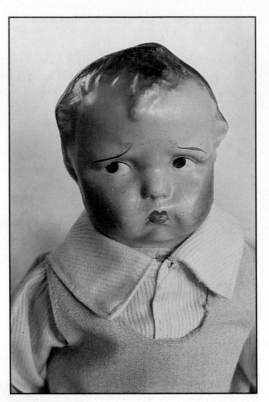

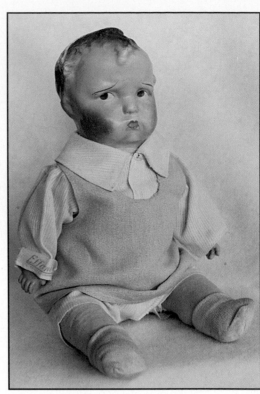

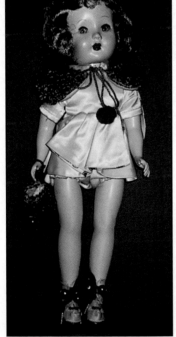

14" hard plastic Honey Walker skater, blue sleep eyes, closed mouth, saran wig, hard plastic body with walking mechanism, all-original white satin skating outfit, missing one pompon, circa 1952+, $300.00.
Courtesy Flo Burnside.

15" composition smiling Grumpy, mold 104, heavily molded hair, intaglio eyes, open/closed mouth with two painted teeth, cloth body, composition lower arms, circa 1915, $425.00.
Courtesy Janet Hill.

21" composition Honey, flirty sleep eyes, closed mouth, rosy cheeks, auburn human hair wig, all-composition jointed body, pink dress with white lace, white shoes and socks, all-original, circa 1947 – 1948, $400.00.
Courtesy Bev Mitchell.

14" composition Suzanne, mohair wig, blue sleep eyes, closed mouth, marked "Suzanne" on head; "Effanbee//Made in USA" on back, dressed in hand knitted cowgirl costume, circa 1940s, $200.00.
Courtesy Elizabeth Surber.

21" composition Effanbee Little Lady, marked "Effanbee//Anne Shirley" on back, blue sleep eyes, original yarn wig, five-piece composition body, original light blue nylon dress, some touch-up, circa 1940s, $200.00.
Courtesy McMasters Doll Auctions.

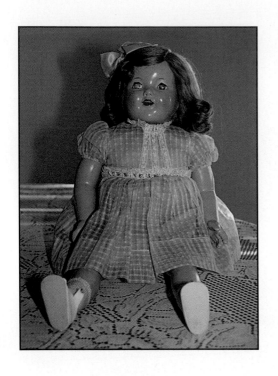

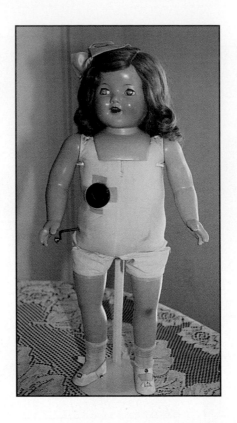

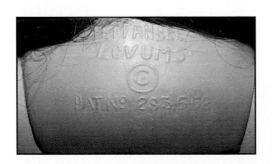

25" composition Lovums Phonograph Doll, marked "Effanbee Lovums//©//Pat. No. 1293558" on shoulder plate, sleep eyes, open mouth with teeth, cloth body with swing legs, composition arms and legs, pink ribbon in hair, original pink dress, with an unusual metal mechanism to place five wax cylinder records – *Easy Mary, Rock-a-bye Baby, London Bridge, Now I Lay Me Down to Sleep,* and *Old Mother Hubbard,* all-original in box, circa 1928, $650.00.

Courtesy Pat Schuda.

The Patsy Family

Another one of Effanbee's great success stories was the Patsy doll designed by Bernard Lipfert and advertised in 1928. She almost was not named Patsy. Identical ads advertised her as Mimi late in 1927 and then as Patsy in 1928 *Playthings* magazines. Patsy was one of the first dolls to have a wardrobe manufactured just for her by Effanbee and other manufacturers. She was made of all-composition and her patent was hotly defended by Effanbee. What was actually patented was a neck joint that allowed the doll to pose and stand alone. She portrayed a three-year-old girl with short bobbed red hair with a molded headband, painted side-glancing eyes, pouty mouth, bent right arm, and she wore simple classic dresses closed with a safety pin. She had a golden heart charm bracelet and/or a gold paper heart tag with her name. Patsy was so popular she soon had several sisters, many variations, and even a boyfriend, Skippy.

Effanbee promoted Patsy sales with a newspaper *The Patsytown News* that went to a reported quarter million children. Effanbee also had an Aunt Patsy who toured the country promoting their dolls. In addition, it formed a Patsy Doll Club and gave free pinback membership buttons to children who wrote in or bought a Patsy doll. Effanbee tied its doll line to popular current events such as producing George and Martha Washington for the bicentennial of George's birth. The company costumed a group of dolls like the *White Horse Inn* operetta that toured the U.S. During the war years, Effanbee fashioned military uniforms for the Skippy dolls and also costumed dolls in ethnic dress (Dutch) or after characters in books like *Alice in Wonderland*.

The death of Hugo Baum in 1940 and the loss of income during the war years threw Effanbee into a decline. In 1946, Effanbee was sold to Noma Electric who reissued a 1946 Patsy and later a new 17" Patsy Joan. Effanbee has changed owners several times. Stanley and Irene Wahlberg reissued vinyl Patsy family dolls during the 1990s. Effanbee again has new management in 1999. Limited editions of Patsy Ann and Skippy dolls were issued during the 1970s, and Patsy reappeared in vinyl in the 1980s. Effanbee reissued Patsy Joan in 1995, and are continuing in 1996, 1997, and 1998 with a new group of Patsy, Skippy, and Wee Patsy dolls in vinyl painted to look like the old composition ones. These are already becoming collectibles for the modern collector.

Patsy Baby

7" composition Tinyette Toddler $450.00, and Baby Tinyette, all-original, circa 1934, $300.00.
Photo by Scott Gladden.
Courtesy Ellen Sturgess.

Effanbee

7" composition Baby Tinyette Twins, painted blue eyes, closed mouths, molded and painted hair, composition bent-limb baby body, original clothes, circa 1934, $275.00. *Courtesy McMasters Doll Auctions.*

11" composition Patsy Baby, set eyes, molded painted hair, "Effanbee//Patsy Baby" on head, magnet hands to hold bottle and ball, original costume, good condition, fine crack below right eye, circa 1931, $275.00. *Courtesy McMasters Doll Auctions.*

Wee Patsy

5½" composition, advertised only as Fairy Princess, original striped beach pajamas with matching hat, doll castle box with peek-through window, circa 1935, $400.00. *Private collection.*

5½" composition, advertised as Fairy Princess, box reads "Fairy Princess//The Colleen Moore//Doll House//Doll," in trousseau box with extra wardrobe, painted features, molded hair, jointed, molded shoes and socks, pin on dress reads "Colleen Moore//Fairy Princess," circa 1935, $425.00. *Private collection.*

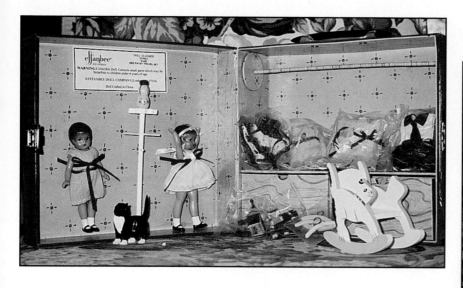

5½" vinyl Wee Patsy Brother and Sister dollhouse trunk set, six outfits, toys, molded hair, painted features, jointed, box says "Effanbee//Doll Classics Series//V528//Wee Patsy Travel Set," circa 1996, $115.00.
Courtesy Lilian Booth.

5½" vinyl Wee Patsy club doll, came with pin, box says "Effanbee Doll Company//Wee Patsy//V571," painted features, pink dress with white pinafore, pink ribbon, matching ribbon in hair, circa 1997, $35.00.
Private collection.

Effanbee

Patsyette

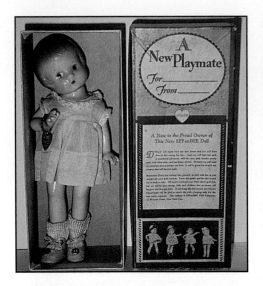

9½" composition Patsyette, marked "Effanbee//Patsyette Doll" on back, painted brown side-glancing eyes, molded painted hair, typical pink dotted Swiss dress, all-original with box, circa 1931+, $350.00.
Courtesy Carol Elder.

9½" composition Patsyette with a suitcase full of clothing consisting of three factory dresses and several homemade outfits, circa 1931, $850.00.
Courtesy McMasters Doll Auctions.

Patsy

14" composition Patsy, marked "Effanbee Patsy" on head, blue glassene sleep eyes, closed mouth, red mohair wig, original blue print dress, tagged "Effanbee Durable Dolls," socks and shoes, circa 1932, $425.00.
Courtesy Janet Hill.

13" new vinyl Patsy Cowgirl, painted side-glancing eyes, molded painted hair, costume re-created from the original 1936 Texas Centennial Costume, hang tag, circa 1997, $60.00.
Courtesy Lilian Booth.

Three 14" composition Patsys, circa 1928+. Left to right: Patsy in tagged dress with roller skates, $500.00; black in snow suit, $700.00; in red silk dress, $500.00.
Photo by Scott Gladden.
Courtesy Ellen Sturgess.

Patsy Joan

Black Patsyette, circa 1930, $450.00; 11" black Patsy Baby, circa 1931, $575.00; 19" Patsy Ann, circa 1929, $750.00; and 14" composition black Patsy, circa 1928, $700.00.
Photo by Scott Gladden.
Courtesy Ellen Sturgess.

16" composition Patsy Joan, sleep eyes, closed rosebud mouth, brown wig, blue dress with pleats and matching bonnet, white side snap shoes, all-original, circa 1931, $550.00.
Courtesy Martha Sweeney.

Effanbee

Patsy Ann

19" composition Patsy Ann marked "Effanbee//"Patsy Ann"//© Pat. #1283558" on back, brown sleep eyes, closed mouth, molded painted hair in bob, five-piece composition child body, green dress with embroidered flowers, matching one-piece under-clothing, old socks, new leather shoes, circa 1929, $300.00.

Courtesy McMasters Doll Auctions.

19" composition Patsy Ann dressed in "Dolly//Tog//Melrose//Mass." tagged Girl Scout uniform, sleep eyes, closed mouth, molded/painted hair, all composition. Patsy Ann, nude would be priced $500.00, the Girl Scout uniform, tagged, complete with hat to fit her, $300.00, circa 1930s.

Courtesy Ann Sutton.

Left: 16" vinyl Patsy Ann, blue sleep eyes, closed mouth, molded painted hair, white dress over pink slip, pink shoes, circa 1976, $300.00.

Right: 19" composition Patsy Ann, molded hair, sleep eyes, metal heart bracelet, circa 1929, with 1935 book *Patsy Ann, Her Happy Times*, by Mona Reed King, Rand McNally & Co., $400.00.

Courtesy Kate Treber.

Patsy Lou

22" composition Patsy Lou, marked "Effanbee//Patsy Lou" on back, brown sleep eyes, closed mouth, light brown mohair wig, re-dressed in handmade clothes, circa 1930, $600.00.

Courtesy Sue Robertson.

Patsy Ruth

26" composition Patsy Ruth, marked "EFFANBEE//PATSY RUTH" on head, "EFFANBEE//LOVUMS//c. PAT. NO. 1283558" on shoulder plate, brown sleep eyes, real and painted lashes, closed pouty mouth, brown human hair wig, cloth body, crier, swing legs, original red flocked white organdy dress, matching combination undergarment, circa 1934, $1,800.00+.
Private collection.

Patsy Mae

30" composition Patsy Mae, marked "Effanbee//Patsy-Mae" on head, "Effanbee//Lovums//©//Pat. No. 1,283,558" on shoulder plate, brown sleep eyes, closed mouth, brown human hair wig, cloth body, composition arms and legs, crier, swing legs, tagged white organdy dress with red trim and print, leather button shoes, metal heart bracelet, all original, circa 1934, $800.00.
Courtesy McMasters Doll Auctions.

Patricia

15" composition Patricia marked "EFFANBEE//PATRICIA," brown sleep eyes, closed mouth, auburn wig, vintage navy blue dress with white polka dots, trimmed with red and white lace, blue hat, circa 1935, $400.00.
Courtesy Lee Ann Beaumont.

Skippy

13½" composition Skippy with painted molded hair, painted side-glancing eyes, cloth torso, composition molded black shoes and socks, marked on head "Effanbee//Skippy//©//P.L. Crosby," original sailor costume, advertised only as Sailor, small paint flake on eye, circa 1940s, $535.00.
Courtesy Debbie Crume.

14" composition Effanbee Skippy Fireman, marked "Effanbee//Skippy//©//P.L. Crosby" on head, painted features, molded painted hair, cloth body, composition hands, arms, and feet, felt hat, no crazing, almost mint condition, circa 1929+, $550.00.
Courtesy Gay Smedes.

14" composition Skippy marked "Effanbee//Skippy//©//P.L. Crosby" on head, "Effanbee//Patsy//Pat.Pend.//Doll" on body, painted blue side-glancing eyes, molded painted blond hair, original Skippy pin, circa 1929, $400.00.
Courtesy Carol Elder.

Ethnic Dolls

Collectors sometimes refer to dolls dressed in regional or national costumes as ethnic or tourist dolls as they were commonly available in shops visited by tourists looking for a souvenir. Dolls dressed in national costume at times were touted as "educational" by showing the costume or dress of that country.

Today some collectors are trying to identify many of these ethnic dolls which are often quite charming and passed over for the better-known collectible dolls. One doll club has taken on the project researching certain groups of dolls. After one year's study, they became so engrossed, they decided to continue for another year. This is an area with little research and is well worth continued interest. Dolls in national costume were made of many mediums, including bisque, cloth, composition, hard plastic, and vinyl. During the 1930s, 1940s, 1950s, and later, many dolls dressed in regional costumes could be purchased cheaply as souvenirs in different areas. A wide variety of these dolls are unmarked or made by little known companies. This category is sometimes a catchall for dolls that have little history and no category. Many were cheaply made and mass produced for the tourist market, but some were extremely well made and are whimsical and charming and make an interesting and eclectic collection.

What to look for:

The workmanship and the costuming make these dolls valuable. Look for clean, all original dolls with boxes, labels, and/or tagged clothing. Try for dolls with very well-made clothing that is clean, has bright colors, no fading or soil. This category has big potential for collectors as it is not as popular with older collectors, who seek more conventional dolls in ethnic costumes. Acquire dolls that are appealing to you, but always look for well-made dolls of good color and original costume.

American Indian

8" brown bisque Ernst Heubach mold 1901 Indian girl, horseshoe mark "1901//15/0," glass eyes, open mouth with teeth, black braided wig, five-piece composition body, painted shoes, original outfit, circa 1901, $300.00.
Courtesy Phyllis Cook.

11½" cloth Eskimo doll, painted features, elk-hide coat and head covering, brown dress with beaded necklace, closed sewn fingers, circa 1930s – 1940s, $200.00+.
Courtesy Stella May Baylis.

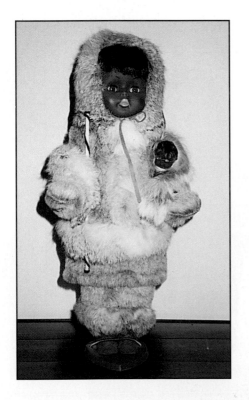

18" vinyl unmarked Eskimo, with baby and stand, brown sleep eyes, closed mouth, black rooted hair, all original, circa 1980s, $75.00.
Courtesy Sue Robertson.

14½" composition Reliable Indian, shoulder head, painted brown eyes, closed mouth, yarn braided wig over molded hair, cloth body and legs, composition arms, felt clothing, circa 1940s, $175.00.
Courtesy Oleta Woodside.

17" cloth Navajo Indian, made on reservation, stitched features, headband, black yarn hair, red shirt, white pants, circa 1950s, $75.00.
Courtesy Diana Jenness.

15" cloth Navajo Indian, made on reservation, stitched features, black yarn hair, green top, green and orange skirt, bead necklace, circa 1950s, $75.00.
Courtesy Diana Jenness.

8" composition Indian Girl, marked "Seaside Oregon" on foot, painted side-glancing eyes, closed mouth, black braided mohair wig, red headband, jointed at shoulders only, molded shoes, brown skirt, circa 1950s, $65.00.
Private collection.

Skookums, 1914 – 1950+

Skookums was designed and patented by Mary McAboy in 1914. The first doll heads were reported to be made of dried apples, then composition and later plastic. They were manufactured first as a cottage industry for the Denver H.H. Tammen Company and then by Arrow Novelty Co. They had side-glancing painted eyes, molded and painted features, horsehair wigs, and padded cloth over stick bodies which was formed by wrapping and folding an Indian blanket to suggest arms. The label on the bottom of the flat wooden feet reads *Trade Mark Registered (Bully Good) Indian//U.S.A.//Patented.* Later dolls had plastic molded feet. Dolls range in size from 6" to 36" store displays. Typical figures represent a chief, squaw with papoose, and child. The dolls were made for the tourist markets and sold through the Tammen Company catalogs and elsewhere. They are a nostalgic piece of Americana.

10" composition Skookums squaw with papoose, painted side-glancing eyes, mohair wig, blanket wrapped padded stick body, wooden feet, circa 1930s – 1940s, $245.00.
Courtesy Tricia Tompkins.

3½" composition Skookum papoose, designed by Mary McAboy, painted features, side-glancing eyes, black mohair wig, head wrapped in blanket, no body, red carry bag, circa 1930s – 1940s, $45.00. *Private collection.*

6" composition Skookums child, painted side-glancing eyes, mohair wig, blanket wrapped padded stick body, wooden feet, circa 1930s – 1940s, $98.00. *Courtesy Tricia Tompkins.*

32" composition Skookum Indian, squaw, and papoose, designed by Mary McAboy, painted features, side-glancing eyes, black mohair wigs, cloth figure wrapped in Indian blanket, with folds representing arms, wooden feet, moccasins, woman has baby on back, circa 1930s, $2,000.00+ for Indian, $1,750.00 for squaw with papoose. *Courtesy Jane Horst.*

Africa

7" black hard plastic doll with inset plastic gold brown eyes, closed mouth, all original with brown vinyl leather costume with beaded decoration, molded hair, with painted red spot on top, purchased in the African Congo circa 1958 – 1961, $45.00.
Courtesy Nancy Ritchey.

10" brown felt cloth, tagged, Republic of South Africa, made to fight TB, felt features, elaborate beaded headdress, skirt, bracelets, applied ears, a mother with a cloth blanket over her bodice carrying baby peeking over shoulder in cloth on back, tagged "Made at Dunstan-Farrell//Santa Centre//Hibberdene//Thank you //You have helped// to combat TB," other side "Republic of South Africa," circa 1958 – 1961, $150.00.
Courtesy Nancy Ritchey.

14½" brown felt with felt features, elaborate beaded native costume with headdress, bracelets, ankle bands, skirt, has molded bosom, applied ears, tagged, "The SA Red Cross Society Durban//This is a product of the Red Cross Rehabilitation Centre. We thank you for purchasing it and hope that you and your friends will continue to support us. H&GF DSN," other side: "Name of Doll//Mfihleni//Hide Her Away," circa 1958 – 1961, $250.00, *Courtesy Nancy Ritchey.*

Austria

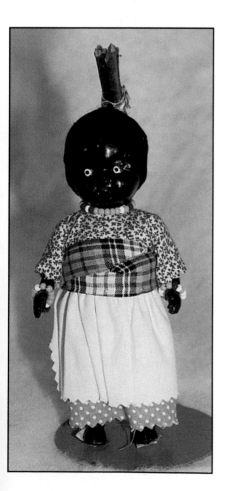

5½" hard plastic black South African child with painted features, mark by eye, all-original costume, circa 1958 – 1961, $25.00. *Courtesy Nancy Ritchey.*

7" vinyl Austrian girl with painted features, synthetic blond braided wig, black hat, blue apron, white blouse, rose skirt, felt covered padded armature body, tagged "Saltzburg, made in Austria," circa 1958 – 1961, $25.00. *Courtesy Nancy Ritchey.*

Baitz

The Baitz firm first started in Germany in 1912. After World War II, the firm moved to Austria where it became Camillo Gardtner and Company in 1963. It is still producing well-made dolls dressed in regional costumes.

Baitz dolls are 9" tall and the head appears to be painted hard plastic or composition. Since Coleman's *Collector's Encyclopedia of Dolls* refers to composition as "made of various ingredients," most collectors equate the term composition with heads made from recipes of wood pulp mixtures.

Baitz dolls are very appealing with their side-glancing painted brown eyes, open round surprise or kissing mouth, and attractive costumes. They have single-line painted eyebrows, and two brown eyelashes painted from the upper corner of the eye. They have glued-on mohair wigs with curls or braids for the girls and short hair for the boys. Their bodies are felt-over-wire armature with simple mitt felt hands. They have a red and black heart-shaped paper hang tag with BAITZ on it. On the back of the hang tag is a gold foil sticker that reads *Made in Austria* and the name of the doll or region it represents. They come in cream floral pattern boxes also with a gold foil sticker. The clothing is cotton with felt used for accent and hats. All dolls have hats or some headdress. The feet have simple black gathered cloth shoes and white cotton knit stockings. The clothing does not have fasteners or openings for removal. They come dressed both as boys and girls.

9" painted hard plastic Baitz Zorich girl, painted features, mohair wig, side-glancing eyes, round open/closed mouth, felt over wire body, original regional outfit, Baitz heart tag, sticker "Made in Austria," circa 1970s, $75.00.
Private collection.

Bermuda

7" brown hard plastic tagged "A Chiquita Doll//from//Bermuda" advertising doll with elaborate fruit headdress, earrings, sleep eyes, straw skirt with trim, shoes molded to feet, circa 1958 – 1961, $45.00.
Courtesy Nancy Ritchey.

China

12" vinyl Chinese child, painted eyes, closed mouth, synthetic rooted hair, marked "Shindana" on head, original outfit, circa 1972, $65.00.
Courtesy Carolyn Hancock.

Czechoslovakia

13" celluloid pair in regional costume, Yugoslavia, circa 1960s, $75.00 pair.
Courtesy Martha L. Metz.

11" composition Dream World doll, box marked "32 Chech," painted blue side-glancing eyes, long painted lashes, closed mouth, blond mohair wig, in Czechoslovakian costume with peach skirt, lace apron, circa 1940s, $75.00.
Courtesy Carolyn Sisson.

Hawaii

8" hard plastic unmarked doll believed to be Pam by Fortune Doll Company, brown sleep eyes, closed mouth, black synthetic wig, box is marked "Mapelas at Waikiki," original crepe paper hula skirt and lei accessories, circa 1950s, competitor to Ginny, $100.00.
Courtesy Peggy Millhouse.

7" brown hard plastic unmarked Hawaiian with sleep eyes, black mohair wig, molded shoes, wears grass skirt, lei, circa 1958 – 1961, $35.00.
Courtesy Nancy Ritchey.

Hungary

13" celluloid girl, marked "18/105/ 32cm//Hungaria//Made in Germany//U.S. Zone," blue sleep eyes, closed mouth, rosy cheeks, dark blond braided wig, in Hungarian dress, red boots, all original in box, circa 1944+, $175.00.
Private collection.

India

8" cloth unmarked Indian woman, very well crafted with individual fingers and toes, red spiritual dot in center forehead, painted toes, applied nose and ears, all original, on black stand, circa 1958, $50.00.
Courtesy Nancy Ritchey.

Israel

9" bisque Bride of Bethlehem marked "Germany 9," black glass eyes, open mouth with four teeth, brown mohair wig, composition body, wears coins on Tarboosh headpiece to show her wealth, all original, circa 1900+, $225.00.
Private collection.

Ethnic Dolls

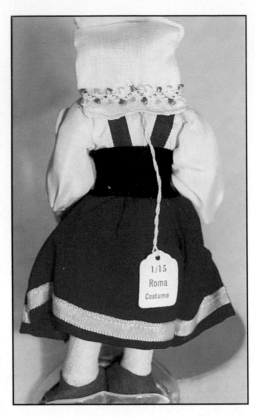

Italy

6" composition Italian girl with original costume, side-glancing painted eyes, black mohair wig, earrings, red skirt, green apron, cloth body, marked paper hand tag reads, "1/15 — Roma Costume" and another tag that reads "Made in Italy," circa 1958 – 1961, $20.00.
Courtesy Nancy Ritchey.

Jamaica

Mexico

14" stockinet cloth unmarked Mexican woman with painted features, yarn hair, bead earrings, cloth body, national dress, sequins on red skirt, circa 1950s, $125.00.
Courtesy Oleta Woodside.

6½" black cloth primitive doll marked "Jamaica" on waist, painted features, straw hat, original costume, cloth body, circa 1958 – 1961, $20.00.
Courtesy Nancy Ritchey.

Morocco

7½" painted hard plastic Moroccan girl, painted features, original costume, passport in English, German, French, Spanish, and other language, circa 1958 – 1961, $25.00.
Courtesy Nancy Ritchey.

Pakistan

8" composition Pakistani doll with cloth body, painted features, earrings, red dot on forehead, jewel on forehead, unmarked, all original, gold braid trim on pink and red costume, circa 1958 – 1961, $25.00.
Courtesy Nancy Ritchey.

Peru

6½" composition unknown woman marked "Made in Peru," painted face, dressed in black, holding black shawl over face, circa 1930s, $65.00.
Courtesy Nelda Shelton.

Poland

7½" hard plastic Virga Ana of Poland, painted blue eyes, closed mouth, rosy cheeks, blond mohair wig, bright color, original costume, marked "487//Ana of Poland" and "Virga" on pink windowpane box, circa 1946 – 1950, $75.00.
Courtesy Cheryl Hoyer.

Portugal

Puerto Rico

6" hard plastic girl with sleep eyes, mohair wig, molded black shoes, blue and floral costume straw hat marked Puerto Rico, circa 1958 – 1961, $25.00.
Courtesy Nancy Ritchey.

6" celluloid unmarked girl from Portugal, painted eyes, molded hair, original costume, has six petticoats, red apron, blue skirt, black hat/cape, gold chain, circa 1958 – 1961, $50.00.
Courtesy Nancy Ritchey.

Russia/ Soviet Union

7" cloth Russian girl of unknown maker, tag reads "Made in Soviet Union," painted blue eyes, painted features, reddish-blond hair, spoon hands, wire in arms, cotton dress, brown shawl, straw shoes, circa 1930s, $175.00.
Courtesy Nelda Shelton.

7" cloth Russian farmer of unknown maker, tag reads "Made in Soviet Union," painted features, spoon hands, wire in arms, cotton clothing, white shirt, blue pants, straw hat, wooden shoes, circa 1930s, $175.00.
Courtesy Nelda Shelton.

6½" cloth Russian girl of unknown maker, tag reads "Made in Soviet Union," painted features, black yarn hair, spoon hands, wire in arms, pink cotton dress, red knitted cap, circa 1930s, $175.00.
Courtesy Nelda Shelton.

161

Ethnic Dolls

Scotland

11" all-composition unmarked Scottish boy, in black jacket, red plaid kilt, black cap, painted eyes, closed mouth, molded hair, circa late 1930s – early 1940s, $75.00.
Courtesy Elizabeth Surber.

6" hard plastic Roddy Scottish boy, marked "Roddy, Made in England" on back, sleep eyes, closed mouth, molded painted hair, movable arms, black felt tam with medal, shoes painted over feet, circa 1950s, $25.00.
Courtesy Rita Mauze.

Spain

12" cloth Molly'es girl, hang tag says "Spain," mask face, brown painted side-glancing eyes, black yarn hair, cloth body, black oil cloth shoes, multicolored skirt and top, red apron, circa 1940s, $100.00.
Private collection.

12" composition unmarked Dream World International doll dressed as Spanish lady with painted side-glancing eyes, circa late 1930s, $100.00.
Courtesy Nancy Ritchey.

6" and 7" clay Marin Company of Spain Spanish Flamenco dancers, painted faces, molded painted hair, wire arms and bodies, designed by Jose Marin Verdugo, circa 1970s, $25.00 each.
Private collection.

24" vinyl Marin Company of Spain Spanish senorita, seated, painted side-glancing eyes, open mouth, painted teeth, black mohair wig, earrings, necklace, aqua dress, many of the faces designed by Jose Marin Verdugo were inspired by Sophia Loren, circa 1970s, $125.00.
Private collection.

Ukraine

18½" composition Jaunin matador, in marked box and hat, sleep eyes, eye shadow above real lashes, painted lashes below, open mouth with two teeth, with elaborate well made matador costume trimmed with sequins, embroidery, and braid, added extra ski outfit with poles and skis, circa 1950s, $400.00.
Courtesy Sue Waldron.

15" cloth lady, original tag reads "Ukrania" on one side and "Sophia" on the other, cloth pressed face, painted features, mohair wig, one-piece cloth body, red cloth boots, circa 1950s, $200.00.
Courtesy Sharon Kolibaba.

World's Fair Tourist Dolls

In Judds' *Compo Dolls, 1928 – 1985,* they report finding a 13" composition doll tagged *A Doll Craft Product.* The Judds' believe the dolls were made in the late 1930s by a factory that sold them to different marketing firms that dressed and sold them to different stores and catalog companies. It has been reported that the dolls were offered for sale at the 1939 New York World's Fair at the different pavilions representing different countries participating in the Fair.

These dolls were 8½" or 13" tall with painted side-glancing eyes, molded hair under mohair wigs, and original costumes with hang tags. The dolls are jointed all-composition with gently curved arms, pouty mouths, one line painted eyebrows, and eyelashes painted above their brown irises. A dot of white accents the right of each black pupil. The fingers are molded together and the composition is well finished, but cruder than Effanbee's Patsy family. Each has a yellow hang tag stating her name and country that her costume represents, such as "I am Katrinka from Holland," "I am Marguerita from Romania," or "I am Maria from Italy."

All-composition 13" dolls such as these with clean bright original costumes, little or no crazing, good color, complete with hang tags, in excellent condition would be priced $250.00, more if costume is elaborate or with accessories, much less if no tag, not original, or faded with heavy crazing. The 8" ones would be priced at $175.00, less for played with or soiled, depending on condition.

What to look for:

These examples of tourist dolls from the late 1939 World's Fair are charming and great collectibles. Revived interest in ethnic and tourist dolls make them a nifty collecting niche. Dolls with fine costuming with intricate details are more in demand. Look for composition dolls with little crazing, all dolls with good facial color, original costumes, hang tags, boxes, or labels. This remains a category that needs more study and research and poses a good avenue for new collectors to pursue and enjoy.

8½" composition Dutch girl, brown painted side-glancing eyes, closed mouth, molded hair under blond wig, molded socks/shoes, blue dress with checked bottom, white apron and hat, 1939 World's Fair tourist doll, $100.00.
Courtesy Dorothy Bohlin.

Gene

Created by magazine illustrator, Mel Odom, a native of North Carolina now living in New York, Gene is marketed by Ashton-Drake Galleries. She is a 15½" vinyl fashion doll and comes complete with her own history. Making her debut in 1995 as Gene Marshall, an actress of the 1940s and 1950s, she reminds you of Betty Grable, Rita Hayworth, or Gene Tierney. Born in the east, Gene comes west to Hollywood and wins starring roles as well as performs on USO tours. Glamour and personality make Gene a favorite among collectors, but the well-made clothing, accessories, and presentation make her one of the hottest competitors for Barbie in the new millennium. The Gene team leader is Joan Greene who says the making of Gene is a labor of love — something few large corporations ever claim. Besides the excellent presentation of the doll, costumes, and accessories, the Gene team in 1996 came up with an inspiring new program, Young Designers of America. This concept challenges young high school students to create a scenario and costume for Gene. Each participant is honored with a special certificate of achievement, a sterling silver pin, and a Gene doll. Winners receive a cash prize, see their design produced, and receive professional royalties. This program alone makes Gene a winner for collectors, young designers, and also for Ashton-Drake.

Eight to ten dolls are introduced annually with about that many or more new costumes. Dolls retail for $79.95 and up, dressed as Simply Gene offered for $49.95. It has been a long time since a doll offered so much excitement to the doll-collecting world.

What to look for:

Check eBay, the Internet, doll shows, and your local doll shop for the latest.

15½" vinyl Gene, marked "Gene™//© 1995 Mel Odom" on head, painted eyes, blond rooted synthetic wig, jointed fashion type body, wearing Premiere, a two-piece evening gown, velvet jacket fully lined with gold lamé, black lace over antique gold taffeta skirt with beads and sequins from the 1941 era designed by Tim Kennedy, issued 1995, retired in 1996, $700.00+.
Photo courtesy Ashton-Drake Galleries.

Gene

IN RED VENUS

15½" vinyl Gene, marked "Gene™//© 1995 Mel Odom" on head, red rooted synthetic wig, wearing Red Venus, a ruby taffeta off-the-shoulder gown, dramatic asymmetrical draping across the hips, a boa of gathered tulle layered in two colors, matching shoes, hose, jewelry from the 1944 era designed by Tim Kennedy, issued 1995, $69.95 for doll and costume.
Photo courtesy Ashton-Drake Galleries.

IN MONACO

15½" vinyl Gene, marked "Gene™//© 1995 Mel Odom" on head, brown rooted synthetic wig, wearing Monaco, a bridal ensemble, bodice of lace over satin with collar, cuffs, and belt of satin, layered tulle skirt with ribbon roses, net slip, pearl-trimmed headpiece and veil, seamed hose, from the 1950 era designed by Tim Alberts, issued 1995, retired 1997, $85.00 – 105.00+.
Photo courtesy Ashton-Drake Galleries.

15½" vinyl Gene, marked "Gene™//© 1995 Mel Odom" on head, blond rooted synthetic wig, wearing Blond Lace, a tuxedo with tailored jacket, slacks, lace-trimmed halter top, lace cuffs, black velvet beret, tiny boutonniere, matching shoes, pearl-topped cane, from the 1941 era designed by Tim Kennedy, issued 1995, doll $69.95, costume $29.95, costume retired in 1998.
Photo courtesy Ashton-Drake Galleries.

15½" vinyl Gene, marked "Gene™//© 1995 Mel Odom" on head, brown rooted synthetic wig, wearing Pink Lightning, a midnight blue taffeta with a portrait neckline, pink organdy draped at the bosom and around the shoulders, matching shoes, clutch handbag, from the 1956 era designed by Tim Kennedy, issued 1995, doll $69.95, costume $29.95, costume retired in 1998.
Photo courtesy Ashton-Drake Galleries.

15½" vinyl Gene, marked "Gene™//© 1995 Mel Odom" on head, dark brown rooted synthetic wig, wearing Love's Ghost, a white blouse with deeply-ruffled neckline, lace edging, hook and eye fastenings on front, matching skirt, net slip, flowered cummerbund, straw hat, from the 1946 era designed by Doug James, issued 1995, doll $69.95, costume $29.95.

Photo courtesy Ashton-Drake Galleries.

15½" vinyl Gene, marked "Gene™//© 1995 Mel Odom" on head, blond rooted synthetic wig, wearing Striking Gold, a golden knit sheath with portrait neckline, rhinestones at bustline, matching golden knit gloves, tasseled beaded stole, golden star jewelry, from the 1943 era designed by Timothy Alberts, issued 1995, doll $69.95, costume $29.95, costume retired in 1998.

Photo courtesy Ashton-Drake Galleries.

15½" vinyl Gene, marked "Gene™//© 1995 Mel Odom" on head, blond rooted synthetic wig, wearing Usherette, a four-piece uniform of velveteen piped with satin, accented with pearls, jacket, tap pants, matching long pants, pillbox hat, shoes, tiny flashlight, from the 1941 era designed by Tim Kennedy, issued 1995, doll $69.95, costume $29.95.

Photo courtesy Ashton-Drake Galleries.

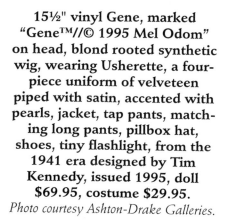

15½" vinyl Gene, marked "Gene™//© 1995 Mel Odom" on head, brown rooted synthetic wig, wearing Blue Evening, twilight-blue satin strapless gown, deep rose accents at draped bosom, pink net slip, rhinestone pin, pearl earrings, pink chiffon stole, beaded choker, hose, matching shoes, from the 1953 era designed by Timothy Alberts, issued 1995, doll $69.95, costume $29.95.

Photo courtesy Ashton-Drake Galleries.

Gene

15½" vinyl Gene, marked "Gene™//© 1995 Mel Odom" on head, blond rooted synthetic wig, wearing The Kiss, marabou-trimmed pink satin peignoir lined in silver lamé, matching gown with diamond pin, earrings, high-heeled mules, from the 1946 era designed by Tim Kennedy, issued 1995, doll $69.95, costume $29.95.
Photo courtesy Ashton-Drake Galleries.

15½" vinyl Gene, marked "Gene™//© 1995 Mel Odom" on head, auburn rooted synthetic wig, wearing Crimson Sun, one-piece halter top knit swimsuit, floral-print sarong, matching hat, beach tote, golden ankle-wrap sandals, matching belt, earrings and matching bracelet, from the 1943 era designed by Doug James, issued 1995, doll $69.95, costume $29.95.
Photo courtesy Ashton-Drake Galleries.

15½" vinyl Gene, marked "Gene™//© 1995 Mel Odom" on head, blond rooted synthetic wig, wearing Good-Bye New York, two-piece suit in crepe and tweed with fur accents, jersey blouse, fur hat and muff, scatter pin with chain, earrings, gloves, seamed hose, hat box, teddy bear, from the 1946 era designed by Doug James, issued 1995, doll $69.95, costume $34.95.
Photo courtesy Ashton-Drake Galleries.

15½" vinyl Gene, marked "Gene™//© 1995 Mel Odom" on head, blond rooted synthetic wig, wearing Blue Goddess, a strapless gown in aqua chiffon, attached stole, accented with hand beading, matching shoes, hose, aqua necklace, drop diamond earrings, rhinestone and aqua bracelet from the 1945 era designed by Tim Kennedy, issued 1996, doll $69.95, retired in 1999.
Photo courtesy Ashton-Drake Galleries.

15½" vinyl Gene, marked "Gene™//© 1995 Mel Odom" on head, blond rooted synthetic wig, wearing Crescendo, emerald taffeta gown, separate fuchsia underskirt, fuchsia crystal buttons, white lace hand-beaded bodice, miniature violin, sheet music, matching hose, shoes, jewelry, hanky, from the 1946 era designed by Doug James, issued 1996, doll $69.95, costume $39.95. *Photo courtesy Ashton-Drake Galleries.*

15½" vinyl Gene, marked "Gene™//© 1995 Mel Odom" on head, brown rooted synthetic wig, wearing El Morocco, a plum taffeta sheath, overskirt of black tulle, jet buttons, black velvet bow, matching hat with veil, clutch handbag, diamond scatter pins, bracelet, hose, shoes, from the 1955 era designed by Timothy Alberts, issued 1996, doll $69.95, costume $29.95. *Photo courtesy Ashton-Drake Galleries.*

15½" vinyl Gene, marked "Gene™//© 1995 Mel Odom" on head, brown rooted synthetic wig, wearing Pin-Up, black laced satin teddy, accented with pink ribbon, ribbon lacing in back, lace trimmed negligee and laced heels, from the 1944 era designed by Tim Kennedy, issued 1996, doll and costume retired in 1999, $75.00 – 95.00+. *Photo courtesy Ashton-Drake Galleries.*

15½" vinyl Gene, marked "Gene™//© 1995 Mel Odom" on head, brown rooted synthetic wig, wearing Afternoon Off, gray twill jacket lined in royal blue, tweed skirt, sweater with beaded trim at neckline, gray shoes, hose, miniature copy of Screen Look — a classic movie fan magazine, from the 1947 era designed by Doug James, issued 1996, doll $69.95, costume retired in 1998, costume $35.00 – 50.00+. *Photo courtesy Ashton-Drake Galleries.*

15½" vinyl Gene, marked "Gene™//© 1995 Mel Odom" on head, brown rooted synthetic wig, wearing Holiday Magic, a limited edition of 2,000 evening gown, satin bodice, snow-white tulle skirt with blue satin bows, white gloves, jewelry, hose, shoes, from the 1956 era designed by Tim Kennedy, issued 1996, doll $69.95, costume retired 1996, costume $300.00 – 350.00+.
Photo courtesy Ashton-Drake Galleries.

15½" vinyl Gene, marked "Gene™//© 1995 Mel Odom" on head, blond rooted synthetic wig, wearing Atlantic City Beauty, the convention exclusive costume, limited edition of 250, lavender/pink floral print two-piece halter swimsuit, matching sunshade hat, clutch purse, beach towel, shoes, pearl earrings, from the 1943 era designed by Doug James, issued at 1996 Convention, $100.00.
Photo courtesy Ashton-Drake Galleries.

15½" vinyl Gene, marked "Gene™//© 1995 Mel Odom" on head, rooted synthetic wig, wearing Sparkling Seduction, a strapless black gown with a furled hemline, glittering with applied pailettes, full-length cape of claret velvet, sleeves of faux fur, amethyst necklace, bracelet, earrings, from the 1948 era designed by Shelley Rinker, issued 1997, doll and costume $79.95.
Photo courtesy Ashton-Drake Galleries.

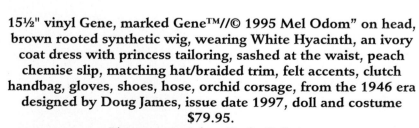

15½" vinyl Gene, marked Gene™//© 1995 Mel Odom" on head, brown rooted synthetic wig, wearing White Hyacinth, an ivory coat dress with princess tailoring, sashed at the waist, peach chemise slip, matching hat/braided trim, felt accents, clutch handbag, gloves, shoes, hose, orchid corsage, from the 1946 era designed by Doug James, issue date 1997, doll and costume $79.95.
Photo courtesy Ashton-Drake Galleries.

15½" vinyl Gene, marked "Gene™//© 1995 Mel Odom" on head, brown rooted synthetic wig, wearing Iced Coffee, gown with shaped gathered café-au-lait chiffon bodice, worn above creamy satin, bodice extends into a swagged sash fastened at the hip with a rhinestone pin, gloves, hose, shoes, from the 1946 era designed by Laura Meisner, issue date 1997, doll and costume $79.95.
Photo courtesy Ashton-Drake Galleries.

15½" vinyl Gene, marked "Gene™//© 1995 Mel Odom" on head, brown rooted synthetic wig, wearing The King's Daughter, limited edition of 5,000, eighteenth century style gown, blue velvet embellished with lace and golden braided trim, patterned lilac underskirt with hand beading, tiara, hose, matching shoes, designed by Michele Gutierrez, issued and retired 1997, $200.00 – $250.00+.
Photo courtesy Ashton-Drake Galleries.

15½" vinyl Gene, marked "Gene™//© 1995 Mel Odom" on head, blond rooted synthetic wig, wearing Bird of Paradise, a showgirl ensemble, crystal beading over net bodysuit, beaded swags from hips with pink tulle, turban of lavender iridescent fabric, crystal drops, spangled hose, shoes, from the 1949 era designed by William Ivey Long, issue date 1997, doll and costume $79.95.
Photo courtesy Ashton-Drake Galleries.

15½" vinyl Gene, marked "Gene™//© 1995 Mel Odom" on head, blond rooted synthetic wig, wearing Promenade, orchid suit accented with navy and white gingham, fully lined jacket, sleeveless blouse, trumpet skirt with flared hemline, matching shoes, veiled hat, gloves, hose, from the 1945 era designed by Tim Kennedy, doll $79.95, costume issued in 1997, retired in 1998, $29.95.
Photo courtesy Ashton-Drake Galleries.

15½" vinyl Gene, marked "Gene™//© 1995 Mel Odom" on head, blond rooted synthetic wig, wearing Personal Secretary, gray taffeta ensemble, wide collar of white organdy, matching cuffs, white buttons on bodice, hat and drawstring handbag in crochet pattern of violets, hose, white shoes, from the 1957 era designed by Tim Kennedy, doll issued 1997, $79.95, costume $34.95.
Photo courtesy Ashton-Drake Galleries.

15½" vinyl Gene, marked "Gene™//© 1995 Mel Odom" on head, brown rooted synthetic wig, wearing Mandarin Mood, Chinese pajamas featuring silk jacket flared beneath waist, wide pants, piped in navy satin, frog closures on jacket, coin earrings, tiny chopsticks in hair, gold sandals, from the 1946 era designed by Tim Kennedy, doll issued 1997, $79.95, costume $34.95.
Photo courtesy Ashton-Drake Galleries.

15½" vinyl Gene, marked "Gene™//© 1995 Mel Odom" on head, blond rooted synthetic wig, wearing Blossoms in the Snow, The Retailers Exclusive Costume, limited edition of 5,000, pink satin gown, white fur accents/rose blossoms, muff, hanky, jewelry, hose, shoes, from the 1953 era designed by Tim Kennedy, doll $79.95, issued and retired 1997, costume $44.95.
Photo courtesy Ashton-Drake Galleries.

15½" vinyl Gene, marked "Gene™//© 1995 Mel Odom" on head, auburn rooted synthetic wig, wearing Tango, multi-layered coral chiffon dancer's dress, exotic beaded accents at the draped bosom, attached stole, matching shoes, hose, golden bracelet, gypsy hoop earrings, from the 1951 era designed by Tim Kennedy, doll $79.95, costume issue date 1997, costume $39.95.
Photo courtesy Ashton-Drake Galleries.

15½" vinyl Gene, marked "Gene™//© 1995 Mel Odom" on head, brown rooted synthetic wig, wearing Sea Spree, nautical outfit with a middy halter top, sailor collar, matching wide-leg pants, nautical button detailing, loose-fitting jacket, matching shoes, jewelry, hair ribbon, from the 1943 era designed by Tim Kennedy, doll $79.95, costume $34.95, issue date 1997.
Photo courtesy Ashton-Drake Galleries.

15½" vinyl Gene, marked "Gene™//© 1995 Mel Odom" on head, brown rooted synthetic wig, wearing My Favorite Witch, Convention Exclusive Doll, limited edition of 350, strapless satin dress slit to knee, black tulle overdress/velvety polka dots, matching witch's hat, broom, mask, necklace, earrings, hose, black shoes, from the 1952 era designed by Tim Kennedy, issue date 1997 Convention Doll, $1,500.00 – 1,700.00.
Photo courtesy Ashton-Drake Galleries.

Gene Hot Day in Hollywood accessory set includes a miniature table fan, phone, two miniature movie scripts, and Gene's own rhinestone-studded black sunglasses, issued 1997, $34.95.
Photo courtesy Ashton-Drake Galleries.

15½" vinyl Gene, marked "Gene™//© 1995 Mel Odom" on head, blond rooted synthetic wig, wearing Midnight Romance, First NALED exclusive, blue gown with rhinestones, bodice of satin and tulle with bows, skirt is layered tulle in two shades of blue, wide satin bow in back, jewelry, hose, shoes, from the 1954 era designed by Timothy Alberts, edition closed 1997, $150.00 – 175.00.
Photo courtesy Ashton-Drake Galleries.

Gene

15½" vinyl Gene, marked "Gene™//© 1995 Mel Odom" on head, brown rooted synthetic wig, wearing A Night at Versailles, FAO Schwarz Exclusive, violet satin gown accented in lavender, inverted pleat tailoring, beaded ribbon roses, gloves, chiffon stole, jewelry, shoes, hose, from the 1952 era designed by Timothy Alberts, edition closed 1997, $175.00 – 250.00+.
Photo courtesy Ashton-Drake Galleries.

Gene White Christmas accessories is a 21" white-flocked Christmas tree with a musical base that plays White Christmas, a gift from the Holiday Magic producer and crew, includes star topper and four dozen hand-blown glass ornaments in a special gift box, from the 1956 era, issue date 1997, $44.95.
Photo courtesy Ashton-Drake Galleries.

15½" vinyl Gene, marked "Gene™//© 1995 Mel Odom" on head, auburn rooted synthetic wig, wearing Creme de Cassis, cocktail ensemble of slim lilac bodice and full skirt is overlaid with black lace, large bow belt, bow at neckline, veiled ribbon hat, jewelry, hose, velvet strap shoes, from the 1953 era designed by Timothy Alberts, 1998 doll and costume $79.95.
Photo courtesy Ashton-Drake Galleries.

15½" vinyl Gene, marked "Gene™//© 1995 Mel Odom" on head, rooted synthetic wig, wearing Gold Sensation, bubble gown ensemble, strapless gold satin, with lined overskirt, circlet rhinestone at waist, bow at knee, shawl, gloves, headpiece, purse, hose, shoes, circlet earrings, from the 1957 era designed by Tim Kennedy, doll $79.95, 1998 costume $39.95.
Photo courtesy Ashton-Drake Galleries.

15½" vinyl Gene, marked "Gene™//© 1995 Mel Odom" on head, blond rooted synthetic wig, wearing Forget-Me-Not, a lingerie ensemble, long-line bra, panties, garter belt, seamed stockings, mules, necklace/earrings, satin slip, crinoline, satin trim, eyelet lace, satin bows, corset hooks, from the 1954 era designed by Timothy Alberts, doll $79.95, 1998 costume $39.95.
Photo courtesy Ashton-Drake Galleries.

15½" vinyl Gene, marked "Gene™//© 1995 Mel Odom" on head, brown rooted synthetic wig, wearing Embassy Luncheon, black lined sheath of wool crepe, high collar with black beads, matching belt, lined fur stole, petal hat/gloves, earrings, nylons, suede heels, beaded purse, from the 1951 era designed by Laura Meisner, doll $79.95, 1998 costume $34.95.
Photo courtesy Ashton-Drake Galleries.

15½" vinyl Gene, marked "Gene™//© 1995 Mel Odom" on head, brown rooted synthetic wig, wearing Cameo, gold and white brocade strapless cocktail dress, sweetheart fitted bodice, short cuffed jacket, fully lined, cameo pin, gold stud earrings, seamed nylons, matching open-toed shoes, from the 1951 era designed by Kate Johnson, doll $79.95, 1998 costume $29.95.
Photo courtesy Ashton-Drake Galleries.

15½" vinyl Gene, "Gene™//© 1995 Mel Odom" on head, created to portray a movie star, blond synthetic wig, with marked Gene stand, wearing Destiny, the Annual Edition Doll, limited edition to 1998, strapless teal green taffeta ballgown, gold lamé lace, attached gold mesh underskirt, gloves, barrette, necklace earrings, shoes, from the 1954 era designed by Mark Esposito, circa 1998, $90.00.
Photo courtesy Ashton-Drake Galleries.

Gene

15½" vinyl Gene, marked "Gene™//© 1995 Mel Odom" on head, blond rooted synthetic wig, wearing Hello Hollywood Hello, blue wool suit, matching fur, sleeveless blouse/lace neckline, silk rose bouquet, heart-shaped hat, muff, jewelry, hose, gloves, shoes, includes a billboard by Mel Odom, from the 1941 era designed by Doug James, 1998 doll and costume $79.95.
Photo courtesy Ashton-Drake Galleries.

15½" vinyl Gene, marked "Gene™//© 1995 Mel Odom" on head, auburn rooted synthetic wig, wearing Love After Hours, black taffeta fitted short-sleeve lined bodice, full skirt, pink organza crinoline, golden-edged fan, silk flowers, necklace, earrings, gloves, hose, matching shoes, from the 1957 era designed by Tim Kennedy, doll $79.95, 1998 costume $34.95.
Photo courtesy Ashton-Drake Galleries.

15½" vinyl Gene, marked "Gene™//© 1995 Mel Odom" on head, blond rooted synthetic wig, wearing Incognito, sleeveless red floral print cotton summer frock, red buttons, organza collar, cotton petticoat, purse/gold chain, red polka-dot chiffon scarf, sunglasses, nylons, earrings, shoes, from the 1955 era designed by Timothy Alberts, 1998 doll and costume $79.95.
Photo courtesy Ashton-Drake Galleries.

15½" vinyl Gene, marked "Gene™//© 1995 Mel Odom" on head, auburn rooted synthetic wig, wearing Champagne Supper, copper evening gown, fox collar and cuffs on jacket, cream rose corsage, gold netting under skirt, jewelry, lined clutch purse/chain strap, gloves, nylons, shoes, from the 1957 era designed by Tim Kennedy, 1998 doll and costume $79.95.
Photo courtesy Ashton-Drake Galleries.

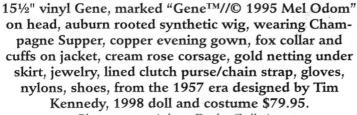

15½" vinyl Gene, marked "Gene™//©
1995 Mel Odom" on head, blond
rooted synthetic wig, wearing Smart
Set, red sleeveless lined sheath dress
of wool crepe, patterned silk bow,
lined bolero jacket, black buttons,
black felt chapeau, white felt feather,
gloves, earrings, hose, shoes, from
the 1948 era designed by Doug
James, doll $79.95, 1998
costume $39.95.
Photo courtesy Ashton-Drake Galleries.

15½" vinyl Gene, marked
"Gene™//© 1995 Mel Odom" on
head, brown rooted synthetic wig,
wearing Covent Garden, NALED
Exclusive, floor-length gown of
white satin and tulle, lace-up black
velvet bodice with bow and sash
train, opera cape, velvet choker
with silk blossoms, from the 1948
era designed by Tim Kennedy,
1998 doll and costume $80.00 –
105.00+.
Photo courtesy Ashton-Drake Galleries.

15½" vinyl Gene, "Gene™//©
1995 Mel Odom" on head,
auburn synthetic wig, with
marked Gene stand, wearing
Warmest Wishes, FAO Schwarz
Fall Exclusive, knit dress with
pocket, lined coat, twist-style
hat, matching muff, closed-toe
shoes, gift box with tiny soldier,
hose, earrings, from the 1948
era designed by Tim Kennedy,
circa 1998, $140.00+.
Courtesy Elizabeth Surber.

15½" vinyl Gene, marked "Gene™//© 1995 Mel
Odom" on head, painted eyes, black rooted synthetic
wig, wearing Midnight Gamble, Retailer's Exclusive,
limited edition of 9,500, navy blue lined sheath, blue
silk pleats on bodice, trapeze-style jacket, sequins,
beads, silver metallic embroidery, gloves, silver shoes,
earrings, from the 1953 era designed by Doug James,
1998, $105.00 – 140.00+.
Photo courtesy Ashton-Drake Galleries.

Gene

15½" vinyl Gene, marked "Gene™//© 1995 Mel Odom" on head, black rooted synthetic wig, wearing Daughter of the Nile, hand-beaded Egyptian gown of white sheath silk crepe, pleated chiffon robe, gold metallic sandals, beaded bracelets, head and arm bands, earrings, from the 1952 historical epic movies era designed by Timothy Alberts, 1998 doll and costume $79.95.
Photo courtesy Ashton-Drake Galleries.

15½" vinyl Gene, marked "Gene™//© 1995 Mel Odom" on head, brown rooted synthetic wig, wearing On the Avenue, FAO Schwarz Spring Exclusive, soft green silk chiffon dress, picture hat with flowers, hatpin, gloves, strap sandals, necklace, bracelet, earrings, from the 1955 era designed by Tim Kennedy, issued and retired 1998, $135.00 – 180.00+.
Photo courtesy Ashton-Drake Galleries.

15½" vinyl Gene, marked "Gene™//© 1995 Mel Odom" on head, auburn rooted synthetic wig, wearing Hi-Fi, green sleeveless lined silk blouse with amber beads, matching sweater, decorative buttons, brown wool worsted gabardine Capri pants, earrings, hair bandeau, bracelet, shoes, from the 1954 era designed by Doug James, doll $79.95, 1998 costume $34.95.
Photo courtesy Ashton-Drake Galleries.

15½" vinyl Gene, marked "Gene™//© 1995 Mel Odom" on head, blond rooted synthetic wig, wearing Safari, khaki bush jacket, leopard pattern lining, sleeveless white cotton blouse, khaki linen slacks, pith helmet, belt, earrings, sunglasses, shoes, leopard pattern chiffon scarf, from the 1951 era designed by Timothy Alberts, doll $79.95, 1998 costume $39.95.
Photo courtesy Ashton-Drake Galleries.

15½" vinyl Gene, marked "Gene™//© 1995 Mel Odom" on head, auburn rooted synthetic wig, wearing Midnight Angel, pale rose dress with leg-o-mutton sleeves, lace collar, cummerbund, looping appliqué, crinoline, blue wool coat/gold piping, tie bonnet, hose, earrings, shoes, rose brooch, from the 1946 era designed by Nicole Burke, doll $79.95, 1998 costume $39.95.
Photo courtesy Ashton-Drake Galleries.

15½" vinyl Gene, marked "Gene™//© 1995 Mel Odom" on head, blond rooted synthetic wig, wearing Ransom in Red, Retailer's Exclusive, limited edition of 7,500, red peplum sheath dress, halter bodice with split train, bracelet, three-tiered earrings, gloves, hose, red ribbon strap shoes, from the 1954 era designed by Tim Kennedy, doll $79.95, costume issued 1998, $50.00 – 75.00+.
Photo courtesy Ashton-Drake Galleries.

15½" vinyl Gene, marked "Gene™//© 1995 Mel Odom" on head, brown rooted synthetic wig, wearing Rain Song, pink hooded silk and linen blend lined raincoat, pink buttons, belt, gloves, gray and white patterned scarf, earrings, miniature newspaper, shoes, gray nylon galoshes, from the 1953 era designed by Doug James, doll $79.95, 1998 costume $29.95.
Photo courtesy Ashton-Drake Galleries.

15½" vinyl Gene, marked "Gene™//© 1995 Mel Odom" on head, chestnut rooted synthetic wig in bouncy flip, wearing USO, dark green woolen dress uniform, khaki shirt, necktie, purse, lace up shoes, garrison cap, hose, earrings, officially licensed by the USO, Inc, from the 1944 era designed by Doug James, 1999 doll and costume $79.95.
Photo courtesy Ashton-Drake Galleries.

Gene

15½" vinyl Gene, marked "Gene™//© 1995 Mel Odom" on head, black rooted synthetic wig, wearing Song of Spain, 1999 Annual Edition Doll, gold satin lined matador costume in black/gold brocade, golden beads accent top, toreador pants, bolero jacket, matching circle cape, hair net, matador's hat, shoes, earrings, from 1943 era designed by Tim Kennedy, 1999, $99.95.
Photo courtesy Ashton-Drake Galleries.

15½" vinyl Gene, marked "Gene™//© 1995 Mel Odom" on head, blond rooted synthetic wig, wearing Tea Time at the Plaza, an FAO Schwarz Exclusive, A-line navy blue dress, white braid accents, headband-style hat with ribbons, pump shoes, clutch purse, hose, earrings, bracelet, from the 1943 era designed by Lynne Day, 1999 doll and costume $99.95.
Photo courtesy Ashton-Drake Galleries.

15½" vinyl Simply Gene, marked "Gene™//© 1995 Mel Odom" on head, long red, blond, and brunette hair suitable for styling, bendable knees, comes with a guide to changing Gene's hairstyles, circa 1999, $49.95.
Photo courtesy Ashton-Drake Galleries.

15½" vinyl Gene, marked "Gene™//© 1995 Mel Odom" on head, auburn rooted synthetic wig, wearing Stand Up and Cheer, a patriotic dance costume, red bodysuit with sequins, blue jacket with long tails, lined with gold satin, matching cuffs, red and blue top hat, red, white, and blue boots, from the 1944 era designed by Dolly Cipolla, doll $79.95, 1999 costume $44.95.
Photo courtesy Ashton-Drake Galleries.

15½" vinyl Gene, marked "Gene™//© 1995 Mel Odom" on head, blond rooted synthetic wig, wearing On the Veranda, tea-length peach dress, scattered flowers on skirt, matching wide brim picture hat, shoes, pearl earrings, from the 1955 era designed by Lynne Day, doll $79.95, 1999 costume $49.95.
Photo courtesy Ashton-Drake Galleries.

15½" vinyl Gene, marked "Gene™//© 1995 Mel Odom" on head, auburn rooted synthetic wig, wearing Press Conference, two-piece fitted day suit of chiffon lined peach pattern top, chiffon lined brown crepe skirt, gloves, corsage, bracelet, earrings, matching headpiece, hose, shoes, purse, from the 1944 era designed by Dolly Cipolla, doll $79.95, 1999 costume $44.95.
Photo courtesy Ashton-Drake Galleries.

15½" vinyl Gene, marked "Gene™//© 1995 Mel Odom" on head, auburn rooted synthetic wig, wearing Farewell Golden Moon, halter-style evening gown of gold lamé, long tulle wrap, gloves, shoes, hose, earrings, brooch, golden laurel wreath headpiece, from the 1944 era designed by Tim Kennedy, doll $79.95, 1999 costume $44.95.
Photo courtesy Ashton-Drake Galleries.

15½" vinyl Gene, marked "Gene™//© 1995 Mel Odom" on head, blond rooted synthetic wig, wearing Love, Paris, gray linen suit, deeply-gored skirt, satin lining, black organza underskirt, rose suede hat, purse, earrings, hose, shoes, custom stand, from the 1947 era designed by Jose Ferrand, 1999 doll and costume $79.95.
Photo courtesy Ashton-Drake Galleries.

15½" vinyl Gene, marked "Gene™//© 1995 Mel Odom" on head, blond rooted synthetic wig, wearing Breathless, a Retailer Exclusive Doll, limited edition of 9,999, strapless celestial blue evening gown, beads, stars, and gold metallic embroidery, beaded shawl, necklace, earrings, hose, crinoline, 1956 era designed by Stephanie Bruner, 1999 doll and costume $99.95.
Photo courtesy Ashton-Drake Galleries.

15½" vinyl Gene, marked "Gene™//© 1995 Mel Odom" on head, platinum rooted synthetic wig, wearing Unforgettable, Ashton-Drake Exclusive Doll, plum evening gown flares in a rounded petal mermaid-style cut, lace scarf, gloves, necklace, bracelet, drop earrings, hose, matching shoes, from the 1957 era designed by Dolly Cipolla, 1999 doll and costume $99.95.
Photo courtesy Ashton-Drake Galleries.

15½" vinyl Gene, marked "Gene™//© 1995 Mel Odom" on head, auburn rooted synthetic wig, wearing Sunset Celebration, orange dupioni silk ensemble flares to a full skirt, diagonal hem length satin sash, jeweled at bodice, matching clutch, earrings, necklace, bracelet, hose, shoes, from the 1955 era designed by Vince Nowell, doll $79.95, 1999 costume $39.95.
Photo courtesy Ashton-Drake Galleries.

15½" vinyl Gene, marked "Gene™//© 1995 Mel Odom" on head, brown rooted synthetic wig, wearing Picnic in the Country, day dress of red and white gingham check, matching bolero jacket, band style hat accented with cherry bead jewelry, shoes, hose, bracelet, pin, earrings, from the 1946 era designed by Lynne Day, doll $79.95, 1999 costume $39.95.
Photo courtesy Ashton-Drake Galleries.

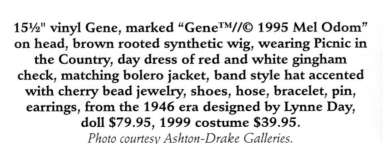

15½" vinyl Gene, marked "Gene™//© 1995 Mel Odom" on head, brown rooted synthetic wig, wearing Pool Side, white cotton sunsuit and matching beach coat with a multicolored confetti-spangled pattern, button accents, shoes, button earrings, sunglasses, button bracelet, from the 1954 era designed by Vince Nowell, doll $79.95, 1999 costume $34.95. *Photo courtesy Ashton-Drake Galleries.*

15½" vinyl Gene, marked "Gene™//© 1995 Mel Odom" on head, red rooted synthetic wig, wearing Priceless, FAO Schwarz Exclusive, strapless black evening gown with button accents, slit in front, long white fur stole, black evening gloves, black shoes, necklace, earrings, hose, designed by Jose Ferrand, 1999, $110.00. *Photo courtesy Ashton-Drake Galleries.*

15½" vinyl Gene, marked "Gene™//© 1995 Mel Odom" on head, brown rooted synthetic wig, wearing Bridge Club, blue checked gingham day dress, boat neckline, low cut back, veiled picture hat adorned with flowers, gloves, belt, shoes, earrings, necklace, bracelet, matching round purse, from the 1954 era designed by Vince Nowell, doll $79.95, 1999 costume $34.95. *Photo courtesy Ashton-Drake Galleries.*

15½" vinyl Gene, marked "Gene™//© 1995 Mel Odom" on head, brown rooted synthetic wig, wearing An American Countess, NALED Exclusive Doll, sequined/embroidered fuchsia taffeta ball gown, off-the-shoulder sequined organza sleeves, full overskirt, petticoat, tiara, purse, earrings, shoes, hose, 1940s era designed by Christine Curtis, 1999 doll and costume $99.95. *Photo courtesy Ashton-Drake Galleries.*

Gene

15½" vinyl Gene, marked "Gene™//© 1995 Mel Odom" on head, brown rooted synthetic wig, wearing At Home for the Holidays, Retailer Exclusive Costume, cocktail pantsuit of iridescent lavender and ruby taffeta, matching shoes, bracelet, necklace, earrings, from the 1957 era designed by Tim Kennedy, doll $79.95, 1999 costume $49.95.
Photo courtesy Ashton-Drake Galleries.

15½" vinyl Gene, marked "Gene™//© 1995 Mel Odom" on head, auburn rooted synthetic wig, wearing Avant Garde, pink cotton cocktail dress with detached floating sleeves, cap style hat with trim, black lace gloves, black bead earrings/necklace, black heels, from the 1956 era designed by Jose Ferrand, doll $79.95, 1999 costume $39.95.
Photo courtesy Ashton-Drake Galleries.

15½" vinyl Gene, marked "Gene™//© 1995 Mel Odom" on head, brown rooted synthetic wig, wearing Cognac Evening, faux two-piece cocktail dress of tobacco iridescent taffeta, beaded side panel cascades from left hip, feathered cap style hat, purse, earrings, necklace, gloves, shoes, 1951 era designed by Jose Ferrand, doll $79.95, 1999 costume $44.95.
Photo courtesy Ashton-Drake Galleries.

15½" vinyl Gene, marked "Gene™//© 1995 Mel Odom" on head, blond rooted synthetic wig, wearing Black Ribbon, two-piece dress, black charmeuse sheath, overdress set off by horizontal black ribbons, rhinestone horseshoe brooch, black feather fan, veiled hat, hatpin, earrings, heels, gloves, hose, 1949 era designed by Tim Kennedy, doll $79.95, 1999 costume $39.95.
Photo courtesy Ashton-Drake Galleries.

Sunday Afternoon

15½" vinyl Gene, marked "Gene™//© 1995 Mel Odom" on head, brown rooted synthetic wig, wearing Sunday Afternoon, navy blue sleeveless rayon sheath with white polka dots, white jacket with blue and white polka dot trim, wide-brimmed hat, hat pin, pearl necklace/earrings, purse, shoes, 1953 era designed by Abigail Haskell, doll $79.95, 1999 costume $39.95.
Photo courtesy Ashton-Drake Galleries.

Savannah

15½" vinyl Gene, marked "Gene™//© 1995 Mel Odom" on head, brown rooted synthetic wig, wearing Savannah, off-the-shoulder gown, pearl earrings, green shoes, cream-colored ribbon rosettes in hair, dressed as a Southern Belle from the 1860 era designed by Katie McHale, 1999 doll and costume $79.95.
Photo courtesy Ashton-Drake Galleries.

Honeymoon

15½" vinyl Gene, marked "Gene™//© 1995 Mel Odom" on head, brown rooted synthetic wig, wearing Honeymoon, sky blue silk charmeuse nightgown, shirred tulle and iridescent beads adorn the matching lace peignoir, aquamarine earrings, fur-trimmed mules, hair ribbon, 1950 era designed by Jose Ferrand, doll $79.95, 1999 costume $44.95.
Photo courtesy Ashton-Drake Galleries.

Gene

15½" vinyl Gene, marked "Gene™//© 1995 Mel Odom" on head, blond rooted synthetic wig, wearing Lucky Stripe, sheath style dress with sweeping hip sash in a horizontal black and white stripe pattern, black satin picture hat, purse, short red gloves, earrings, hose, shoes, from the 1949 era designed by Tim Kennedy, 1999 doll and costume $79.95.
Photo courtesy Ashton-Drake Galleries.

Lucky Stripe

Somewhere Summer

15½" vinyl Gene, marked "Gene™//© 1995 Mel Odom" on head, blond rooted synthetic wig, wearing Somewhere Summer, crisp white dotted organza, layered over white taffeta, dramatic lantern sleeves, white hat trimmed in black ribbon, white pearl earrings, necklace, gloves, shoes, hose, from the 1952 era designed by Tim Kennedy, doll $79.95, costume $44.95.
Photo courtesy Ashton-Drake Galleries.

15½" vinyl Gene, marked "Gene™//© 1995 Mel Odom" on head, auburn rooted synthetic wig, wearing Secret Sleuth, black crepe sheath, fully lined, topped with detachable cape of black and white plaid wood, matching beret, yellow chiffon scarf and gloves, purse, earrings, sling back shoes, hose, 1948 era designed by Tim Kennedy, doll $79.95, 1999 costume $39.95.
Photo courtesy Ashton-Drake Galleries.

Secret Sleuth

Hard Plastic

Plastics came into use during World War II. The war and shortages of some materials caused great upheavals in the toy industry. Some plants were converted to make items for the war effort. After the war, some companies began to use plastic for dolls. Hard plastic seems to have been a good material for doll use. Relatively unbreakable, it does not deteriorate with time, as did the "magic skin" and other materials that were tried and discarded. The prime years of use, roughly a ten year period (late 1940s – 1950s), produced a wide variety of beautiful dolls that Baby Boomers still remember fondly. With the advent of vinyl, in the late 1950s and early 1960s, less hard plastic dolls were made, although occasionally some manufacturer still presents hard plastic dolls today.

What to look for:

Look for clean dolls with rosy cheek color, original clothing, labels, boxes, hang tags, or brochures. Dirt may have caused the plastic to change chemically with the growth of bacteria when the relative humidity is high. Another way for collectors to find inexpensive dolls is to look for those that are unmarked or by little known companies.

24" Advance Winnie the Wonder Doll, sleep eyes, open mouth, teeth, brown synthetic wig, key wind for walking, push button for talking, original box marked "Winnie, the walking and talking doll," circa 1954, $200.00.

Courtesy Arleen Vines.

6" A & H Doll Mfg. Corp. lady, sleep eyes, blue mohair wig, red dress with lavender ribbon, blue felt hat, molded painted shoes, with box, circa 1950s, $15.00.

Courtesy Nora Fronek.

Hard Plastic

7" Almar Salvation Army pair, marked "ALMAR//DOLLS//
MADE//IN//ENGLAND," blue sleep eyes, boy had painted hair,
girl has red mohair wig, jointed at shoulders only, original navy
blue outfits, circa 1960s, $50.00 pair.
Courtesy Lee Ann Beaumont.

6½" Bal walking girl,
marked "Made in
U.S.A.," missing pull
string, flirty blue sleep
eyes, painted molded
hair, closed mouth, red
and white original dress,
molded and painted
shoes and socks, missing
pull string that allows it
to walk when weight is
hung over table, circa
1950s, $25.00.
Courtesy Terri Parker.

15" Belle Doll & Toy
Corp. of Brooklyn, NY,
doll with sleep eyes,
closed mouth, red hair,
blue taffeta dress,
straw hat with flower
trim, circa 1950s,
$125.00.
Courtesy Sally DeSmet.

13½" Crown Imperial Saucy Walker-
type, blue sleep eyes, closed mouth,
molded hair under auburn synthetic
braided wig, turquoise dress, pink ribbon, white shoes and socks, mint with
box, circa 1950s, $60.00.
Courtesy Sally DeSmet.

10" Block Doll Co. The Baby Walker, blue sleep eyes, blond mohair braided wig, closed mouth, box reads "Style 351, I walk, I sleep, I sit, I turn my head," dress with brown print skirt, white top trimmed in red, brown side snap shoes, mint in box, circa 1950s, $125.00.

Courtesy Bev Mitchell.

8" Doll Bodies Mary Lu, blue sleep eyes, auburn wig, marked on doll's back "Product of Doll Bodies, Inc., New York, N.Y.," package reads "Her hair can be washed, combed, brushed, curled and set," circa 1956, $40.00.

Courtesy Peggy Millhouse.

29" Halco doll, marked "Superb Halco Brand//'Beautiful Dolls'//The Seal of Quality" on label of original box, blue flirty sleep eyes, open mouth, four upper teeth, felt tongue, blond mohair wig, cloth body, composition arms and legs, white nylon dress with metallic dots, taffeta slip, underclothing, socks and shoes, all original in box, circa 1950s, $375.00.
Courtesy McMasters Doll Auctions.

17½" Eugenia Doll Co. unmarked girl, sleep eyes with lines painted at side of each eye, closed mouth, brown wig, jointed at neck, shoulders, and hips, red dress with green, yellow, and red rickrack on bodice, circa 1947 – 1949, $125.00.
Courtesy Lee Ann Beaumont.

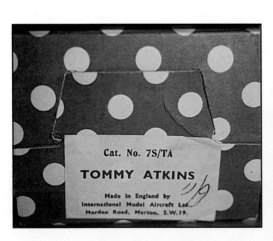

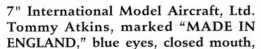

5" Hollywood Dolls Little Girl in white box with blue stars marked "Hollywood Dolls" and labeled "Toy Land Series, Little Girl, Where Have You Been," sleep eyes, closed mouth, red mohair wig, yellow and tan plaid dress, straw hat, circa 1950s, $75.00.
Courtesy Nancy McDonald.

7" International Model Aircraft, Ltd. Tommy Atkins, marked "MADE IN ENGLAND," blue eyes, closed mouth, rosy cheeks, box marked "Cat. No. 7S/TA//TOMMY ATKINS//Made in England by//International Model Aircraft, Ltd.//Morden Road, Merton, S.W.19.," all original with box, circa 1950s, $25.00.

Courtesy Lee Ann Beaumont.

25" Ottolina Italian lady, marked "Ottolina//C&D// Mod-dep//Made in Italy," blue flirty sleep eyes, closed mouth, blond rooted hair, necklace, redressed in 1971 with long black dress, rust colored lace scarf in hair, circa 1948, $150.00.
Courtesy Nelda Shelton.

18" Ratti Alma marked "Ratti Marca Depositat// Made in Italy//Alma 5693/48" on label, synthetic wig, original poodle skirt costume suggests the 1950s, box, $115.00.
Courtesy McMasters Doll Auctions.

24½" Ottolini fashion-type doll made in Italy with pin, Sonia, tagged "Otto Lini//orig. Doll//Made in Italy," blue flirty eyes, molded shoes, blond wig, in original off-white suit, dark brown hat, single strand of pearls around neck, circa 1960, $275.00.
Courtesy Elizabeth Surber.

27" Paris Doll Co. Rita, unmarked walker with open mouth and teeth, sleep eyes with painted lashes below, real lashes above, synthetic wig, original plaid dress with white apron and sleeves, red ribbon trim, circa 1951 – 1954, $225.00. *Courtesy Antoinette Whelan.*

10" Plastic Molded Arts Co. Bride, sleep eyes, closed mouth, blond mohair wig, molded painted shoes, white dress and net veil, with box, circa 1950s, $25.00. *Courtesy Nora Fronek.*

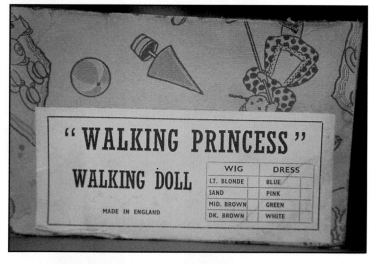

11½" Roddy Walking Princess, marked "RODDY//MADE IN ENGLAND," blue sleep eyes, closed mouth, rosy cheeks, brown mohair braided wig, clenched fists with a separate thumb, original tagged blue dress, all original with box, circa 1950s, $60.00.
Courtesy Lee Ann Beaumont.

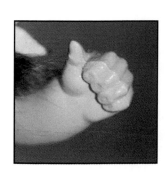

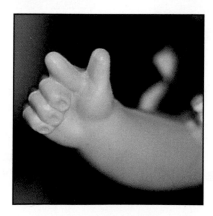

Hard Plastic

6½" Rosebud Company Baby Rosebud, marked "ROSEBUD//MADE//IN// ENGLAND" on back, glassene sleep eyes, molded painted hair, strung, jointed at shoulders and hips only, one-piece body, knitted outfits for Rosebud dolls with full instructions appeared in *Woman's Weekly* magazines, this outfit was knitted by Tricia Smith of England, circa mid 1950s, $55.00.
Courtesy Lee Ann Beaumont.

6½" Rosebud Ltd. Queen, marked "ROSEBUD//MADE IN ENGLAND// PATENTS PENDING" on back, painted sleep eyes, molded hair under auburn mohair wig, head, body, and legs are one piece, jointed arms, dressed as queen in coronation robe and tiara, circa late 1940s to early 1950s, $35.00.
Courtesy Lee Ann Beaumont.

7½" Sarold Co. of England Scottish pair, marked "SAROLD//MADE IN//ENGLAND," blue sleep eyes, closed mouth, blond mohair wig on girl, jointed at neck, shoulders, and hips, dressed in Scottish costumes, molded painted shoes, all original, circa 1950s, $150.00 pair.
Courtesy Lee Ann Beaumont.

7½" Rosebud Ltd. Miss Rosebud, marked "Miss//Rosebud (script) //MADE IN ENGLAND" on back and "Rosebud" in script on head, strung, blue sleep eyes, closed mouth, rosy cheeks, brown mohair wig, dressed in tagged outfit Bride from Amager Denmark, circa mid 1950s, $100.00.
Courtesy Lee Ann Beaumont.

7" Sailor, marked U.S. Navy on cap, molded and painted black shoes, in dark blue Navy uniform, circa 1950s+, $75.00.
Courtesy Kris Panacy.

11" boy (possibly Richwood), blue sleep eyes, molded lashes, black painted hair, jeans, black shoes, plaid shirt with matching cap, all original, circa 1950s, $150.00.
Private collection.

10" Patsy-types made by Australian manufacturer Theo Levy & Co. of Melbourne, Victoria, Baby Patsy on right and Cherub on left, blue eyes, molded painted hair, bent-leg jointed baby body, circa 1950s – 1960s, $50.00 each.
Courtesy Marjory Fainges.

16" Patsy-types made by Australian manufacturer Theo Levy & Co. of Melbourne, Victoria, Cherub on right and Baby Patsy on left, blue eyes, molded painted hair, bent-leg jointed baby body, circa 1950s – 1960s, $100.00 each.
Courtesy Marjory Fainges.

Hard Plastic

16" unmarked girl, blue sleep eyes, eyeshadow, closed mouth, red mohair wig, flat feet, black negligee, bra, and panties, two garters, gold shoes, all original, circa 1950s, $175.00.
Private collection.

14" unmarked Mary Hoyer type doll, red saran hair, blue sleep eyes, eye shadow, closed mouth, lovely color, wears a commercial dress with red with white polka dots, circa 1950s, $200.00.
Courtesy Sheryl Nudelman.

7½" Heart Girl by unknown maker, mint in marked "Heart Girl" box, side-glancing painted eyes, mohair wig, closed mouth, red and white Valentine style dress, white plastic molded shoes, circa 1950s, $75.00.
Courtesy Carolyn Weir.

7" lady, blue sleep eyes, closed mouth, red mohair wig, box reads "A Lovely Miniature Doll//Movable Head//Movable Eyes//Movable Arms//Doll Stand Enclosed," circa 1950s, $10.00.
Courtesy Nora Fronek.

14" Roberta, unmarked, sleep eyes, open mouth with teeth, in original lavender dress with white dots, flowers in hair, circa 1950s, $190.00.
Courtesy Sally DeSmet.

10½" girl, unmarked, sleep eyes with painted lower lashes, closed mouth, blond mohair wig, red and white checked dress with white apron, circa 1950s, $85.00.
Courtesy Nelia Jabara.

19½" Valentine Ballerina, unmarked, blue sleep eyes, closed mouth, rooted red hair, jointed knees, ankles, and waist, blue tutu, rose ballerina shoes, white leotards, circa 1960s, $60.00.
Courtesy Nelda Shelton.

7" Virga Ice Queen, sleep eyes, closed mouth, blond mohair wig, molded/painted socks/shoes, glued on ice skates, box reads "A Virga Doll//Arts Beehler//New York//19//N.Y.//#475//Ice Queen," circa 1950s, $20.00+.
Courtesy Caroline Mohagen.

10" Virga girl, sleep eyes, closed mouth, brunette wig, molded/painted shoes, yellow satin blouse, pleated print skirt, white umbrella, mint-in-box, circa 1950s, $125.00.
Courtesy Peggy Millhouse.

Hasbro

15" vinyl Little Miss No Name, all vinyl, large sad eyes, wears patched burlap dress, bare feet, circa 1965, $65.00. *Courtesy Cathie Clark.*

4½" vinyl Sunday Best with molded blond ponytail with red bow, painted eyes, painted on gloves and molded and painted on socks and shoes, original black and white dress, circa 1965, $25.00. *Courtesy Bertha Melendez.*

G.I. Joe

One of the developments in the doll field has been the action figure, which has produced a whole group of doll collectors who prefer this type of dolls. The most famous of these figures has to be G.I. Joe.

G.I. Joe, 1964 – 1976, 11½" tall
Super Joes, 1976 – 1978, 8½" tall
G.I. Joe, 1982 – on, 3½" tall

11½" vinyl Talking G.I. Joe Adventure Team Commander, blue eyes, brown flocked hair and beard, scar, re-dressed in two-piece outfit, pistol holster with strap, plastic dog tag on metal chain, black boots, worn box, very good condition, circa 1970, $105.00.
Courtesy McMasters Doll Auction.

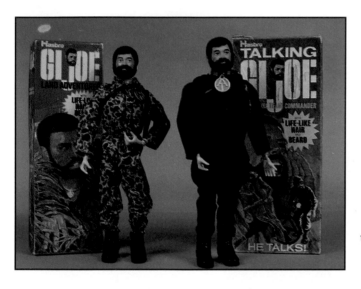

Left: 11½" vinyl G.I. Joe Land Adventurer in box, brown flocked hair and beard, scar, blue eyes, one-piece camouflage suit, extra two-piece camouflage fatigues, black boots, pistol holster with strap, pistol, plastic dog tag on metal chain, very good condition, circa 1970, $115.00.

Right: 11½" vinyl Talking G.I. Joe Adventure Team Commander, blue eyes, brown flocked hair and beard, scar, redressed in two-piece outfit, pistol holster with strap, plastic dog tag on metal chain, black boots, worn box, very good condition, circa 1970, $105.00.
Courtesy McMasters Doll Auction.

Left: 11½" vinyl G.I. Joe Land Adventurer, mint in box, circa 1975, $130.00.

Right: 11½" vinyl Hasbro Talking G.I. Joe Action Soldier, near mint in box, circa 1970, $200.00.
Courtesy McMasters Doll Auctions.

Jem

Jem dolls were produced by Hasbro in 1985 and 1986. They were patterned after characters in the Jem cartoon series which aired from 1985 to 1988, and was later available as reruns. The complete line of Jem dolls consists of only 21 dolls, but there are a lot of variations and rare fashions to keep the collector hunting. All dolls are 12" tall (except Starlight who is 11"), totally posable as the knees and elbows bend, the waist and head turn, and the wrists swivel. They are realistically proportioned like a human figure. They are made of vinyl with rooted hair. They are marked on head *Hasbro, Inc.* Some backs are marked *COPYRIGHT 1985 HASBRO, INC.//CHINA* and some are marked *COPYRIGHT 1987 HASBRO//MADE IN HONG KONG.* Starlight girls are unmarked. The exciting thing about Jem dolls and the appeal to the public may have been the "truly outrageous" flashy mod fashions and startling hair colors that made them so different from other fashion-type dolls of this era.

12" vinyl Jerrica, blond hair, packed with extra costume, flashing star earrings, mint in box, stock #4000, circa 1985, $60.00.
Courtesy Cornelia Ford.

12" vinyl Shana, pink hair, painted features, wears silver coat, pink shorts, pink guitar, music cassette, mint in box, circa 1985, $175.00.
Courtesy Cornelia Ford.

12" vinyl Pizzazz, yellow hair, painted features, black zebra stripe top with chartreuse tie, a Truly Outrageous costume, music cassette and guitar, mint in box, stock #4206, circa 1985, $50.00.
Courtesy Cornelia Ford.

Hitty

Hitty is a character in the book, *Hitty, Her First Hundred Years,* by Rachel Field, published in 1929. It is a story of a 6" doll, Hitty, and her adventures through 100 years. The story remains popular with people who read it as children and give the book to their children and grandchildren. It is charmingly illustrated with pen and ink drawings and early editions also contain some color plates. The original Hitty makes her home in the library in Sturbridge, Massachusetts, while today's artists re-create Hitty for collectors. A Hitty newsletter is published and Hitty get-togethers happen at doll conventions and conferences. See Collectors' Network for information on the Hitty newsletter to keep abreast of latest artist creations.

What to look for:

Re-read the Hitty book to fix in your mind your ideal Hitty and then look for the many artists' interpretations available today. You can find them nude or dressed giving you options on price and the opportunity to make a wardrobe for your own Hitty. You may wish to try carving your own.

6" wood carved Hitty by Judy Brown, painted features, jointed hips and arms, dressed in white lace wedding dress with matching veil, circa 1999, prices range from $310.00 to $425.00 for Hitty and outfit.
Courtesy Judy Brown.

6" wood carved Hitty by Judy Brown, painted features, jointed hips and arms, dressed in blue dress with dark blue coat and matching hat, riding in airplane that says "Spirit of Christmas," circa 1999, prices range from $310.00 – $425.00 for Hitty and outfit.
Courtesy Judy Brown.

Hitty

6" wood carved Hitty by Ruth Brown, light ash-wood, painted features, jointed hips and arms, painted on black boots and white socks, dressed in white flower print dress, circa 1999, $175.00.
Photo courtesy Ruth Brown.

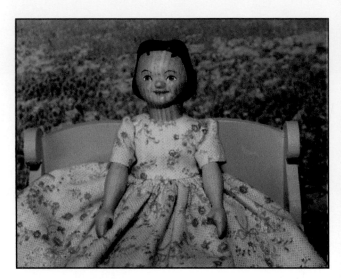

6" wood carved Hitty by Judy Brown, painted features, jointed hips and arms, dressed in blue denim skirt, blue and white checked blouse with white fringe, red cowboy hat, painted on red boots, circa 1999, prices range from $310.00 – $425.00 for Hitty and outfit.
Courtesy Judy Brown.

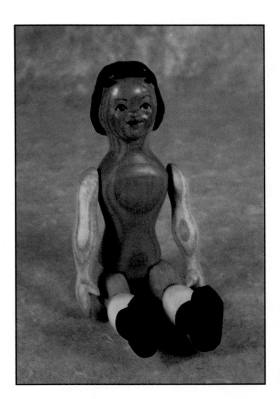

6" wood carved Hitty by Ruth Brown, dark ashwood, painted features, jointed hips and arms, painted on black boots and white socks, circa 1999, undressed Hitty $150.00, dressed $175.00, dresses $15.00 and up.
Photo courtesy Ruth Brown.

6" wood carved Hitty by Ruth Brown, dark ash-wood, painted features, jointed hips and arms, painted on black boots and white socks, dressed in light cotton print dress, bead necklace, circa 1999, $175.00.
Photo courtesy Ruth Brown.

6" wooden jointed Hitty, antiqued to look old, hand carved by Janci doll artists Jill Sanders and Nancy Elliot, painted features, dressed in calico dress of blue and white stripes with flowers, circa 1999, $295.00.
Courtesy Jill Sanders.

6" wooden jointed Hitty, hand carved by Janci doll artists Jill Sanders and Nancy Elliot, painted features, dressed as a bride, circa 1999, $395.00.
Courtesy Jill Sanders.

6" wooden jointed Hitty, hand carved by Janci doll artists Jill Sanders and Nancy Elliot, painted features, calico dress, hang tag reads "Janci Dolls//Hand painted & carved wooden dolls made one at a time with love in Michigan, USA," circa 1999, $295.00.
Courtesy Jill Sanders.

6" wood carved Stockbridge Hitty by Mary Lee Stundstrom, marked on rear "Mary Lee Sundstrom//1-5-98//22/200," limited edition of 200, first 75 were dressed in this outfit from the book, blue dress with blue coat trimmed in lace and flowers with matching hat, body construction is similar to the original Hitty, circa 1998, $595.00.
Courtesy Martha Cramer.

Horsman

Horsman was founded by Edward Imeson Horsman in New York City. It operated from 1865 to 1980+. The E.I. Horsman company distributed, assembled, and made dolls. It merged with Aetna Doll and Toy Co. In 1909 Horsman obtained his first copyright for a complete doll, Billiken. The company later made hard plastic and vinyl dolls many of which are unmarked, some have only a number, and some may be marked *Horsman*. Judds report painted inset pins on the walking mechanism is one means of identification of hard plastic dolls. Some of the hard plastic dolls included Cindy with either a child or fashion-type body.

What to look for:

Composition dolls should have minimal crazing, rosy cheeks, original clothing, labels, or tags when possible. Great characters like the Campbell Kids are always charming. Modern dolls should be perfect and all original. A nifty collecting niche; collectors may find bargains, as later Horsman dolls have not been as popular with collectors.

11½" composition character Billikin with slit eyes, smiling closed mouth, molded painted hair, with original velvet, jointed body tagged "Copyright 1908//The Billikin//Company," circa 1908, $225.00.
Courtesy Connie Lee Martin.

11" composition Campbell Kid Mascot Boy
with tagged gold and black striped shirt
and tan pants, black painted side-glancing
eyes, red accent dots at inner eye and nos-
trils, open/closed mouth, molded painted
light brown hair, disk jointed sawdust
stuffed body, label on sleeve, "The Camp-
bell Kids//Trade Mark//Copyright Camp-
bell Company//Mfg. By E. Horsman Co.,"
paint crack by eye, advertised in 1912,
$250.00.
Private collection.

8½" all-composition
HeeBee-SheBee,
unmarked, two-tone
painted blue eyes, no
brows or lashes,
closed pouty mouth,
large oversize highly
blushed cheeks,
blushed nose and
ears, five-piece body,
molded/painted cloth-
ing on torso, mold-
ed/painted large pink
baby shoes with yarn
ties, paint flaking on
torso and left arm,
circa 1925 – 1927,
$130.00.
Courtesy McMasters Doll
Auctions.

14" composition baby, blue tin sleep eyes,
closed mouth, molded painted hair, cloth
body, composition arms and lower legs,
blue dress and bonnet, knit underclothing,
all original, circa 1930s, $250.00.
Courtesy McMasters Doll Auctions.

Horsman

18" vinyl Pert 'n Pretty, blue sleep eyes, closed mouth, blond hair that grows, comb, pink dress with lace and green ribbon, box says "Most Loved and Played With Dolls Since 1865," mint in box, circa 1988, $35.00. *Courtesy Iva Mae Jones.*

19" composition Betty Ann, blue sleep eyes, open mouth, two teeth, red mohair wig, rubber arms and legs, cloth body, original white baby dress and hat, circa 1930s, $350.00. *Courtesy Kate Treber.*

15" hard plastic Cindy walker, blue sleep eyes, open mouth, four teeth, rewigged in brown human hair wig, re-dressed in black checked dress, white apron with red rickrack, circa 1953, $125.00. *Courtesy Kate Treber.*

15" composition Sweetums, cloth body, drink and wet, with hole in cloth body, mint in box with gown, bonnet, bed jacket, pacifier, and bottle, circa 1930s, $225.00. *Courtesy Sally DeSmet.*

Mary Hoyer

Mary Sensenig Hoyer was born the youngest of 14 children, on October 21, 1901, in Lancaster County, Pennsylvania, to Sallie Whitman and Daniel Sensenig. Her father had a general store and post office in Lancaster, but moved when Mary was six months of age to Mohnton, Pennsylvania, where he again had a store. When she was seven years old the family moved to Reading, Pennsylvania, and she has lived in this area ever since. Her oldest sister, Alice, who did piece work and made cotton sunbonnets with brims of real straw, influenced her.

At age eight, Mary had to be in the hospital with appendicitis, and Alice told her to hurry and get well, because she would buy her a beautiful doll. When she left the hospital, she went home to older sister Alice's house and the doll was waiting for her. Mary remembers the doll being the most beautiful she had ever seen. It had a bisque head with long golden finger curls of human hair, blue eyes, and a smiling mouth with little teeth. The doll was made in Germany and had a jointed body and wore a dress Alice had made for her of blue China silk.

While she was recovering, Alice taught Mary how to knit and crochet and even some simple sewing. Alice eventually opened a store selling yarn, needles, and other related items. Mary, at age 18 attended McCanns Business School, worked for Alice, and began designing and writing knitting instructions.

Mary met William Hoyer in 1923 and they were married in 1926, driving to Canada in a Model T. The honeymooners lived in an apartment until they could build a house nearby in Springmont. Daughter Arlene was born there.

Mary's career began as a designer of knitted and crochetted fashions for children and babies. It seemed a natural outgrowth of that to extend her talents to designing fashions for children's dolls. She first made clothes for her daughter's doll, a 14" heavy composition of unknown maker. Mary soon began dreaming about having an artist make a doll to her own specifications, maybe 14" tall and shaped like a little girl. She first used 13" dolls from Ideal Novelty and Toy Company. Her idea was to sell the nude doll with an accompanying instruction booklet with patterns to knit or crochet outfits for the doll.

About 2,000 of these unmarked Ideal 13" jointed composition dolls were sold before this model was discontinued by Ideal. They had sleep eyes and mohair wigs that came in three different shades; blonde, dark brown, and auburn. The composition bodies had a segmented torso joint just below the arms. The doll sold for $1.50 or you could buy it dressed for $3.00.

In late 1937 Mary met with doll sculptor Bernard Lipfert who had already designed Patsy, Shirley Temple, the Dionne Quintuplets, Ginny, and many other dolls. She told me he did not want to sculpt the doll, but after some conversation and a glass of wine, they came to an agreement. The Fiberoid Doll Company in New York produced the Mary Hoyer doll, but Hoyer retained ownership of the molds. Hoyer estimates approximately 6,500 of the composition dolls were made before the production was discontinued in 1946. Hoyer later discovered that the molds were sold without her knowledge to someone in South America.

Mary Hoyer dolls were unmarked, had painted eyes, and mohair wigs in four shades. The next 5,000 dolls were incised with the mark *THE//MARY HOYER//DOLL.* As soon as

Mary Hoyer

sleep eyes were available for composition dolls, they were used, but at first painted eyes were used.

With World War II hard plastic became a popular material for use in dolls. It was new; it was different; it was *modern!* And it appealed to mothers and children. Hoyer began using this material on the new Mary Hoyer dolls. They were also 14" tall, and first had a walking mechanism. This doll was marked in a circle on the back, *ORIGINAL//MARY HOYER//DOLL.* The walker type of body proved troublesome and was removed leaving those models with two slits in the head.

A variation was introduced in 1950, an 18" Mary Hoyer named Gigi. It has the same hard plastic mark as the 14" dolls. Only about 2,000 of these dolls were made by the Frisch Doll Company and they never gained the popularity of the 14" dolls.

Another variant made in the mid-1950s by Ideal had a vinyl head, rooted hair in a ponytail, and high-heeled feet. This doll was discontinued after only one shipment was made. She originally sold for $6.95.

Mary placed ads in *McCall's Needlework and Crafts* magazine and by 1945, Mr. Hoyer quit his job as purchasing agent for Berkshire Knitting Mills to spend full time managing the mail order business, opening a plant and shipping department. Mary also had a retail shop on Penn Street in Reading and another on the Boardwalk in Ocean City, New Jersey, where granddaughter Mary Lynne Sanders remembers playing under the boardwalk in the summer as a little girl.

Another variation was the all-vinyl Vicky doll made in 1957 for Hoyer by Ideal. She came in three sizes, 10½", 12", and 14". The two larger sizes were discontinued and only the 10½" was continued for any length of time. She was described as having a body that bent at the waist, sleep eyes, rooted saran hair, and high-heeled feet. She came dressed in a bra, panties, high heels, and earrings.

The next year, 1958, the Unique Doll Company made Margie, an all-vinyl 10" toddler with rooted hair and sleep eyes, for Hoyer. In 1961 they added a 10" Cathy, an all-vinyl infant made by the same company. Next came an 8" vinyl baby, Janie. Hoyer continued her main marketing thrust with knitted and crocheted patterns, kits, and dressed dolls as well as her custom-made costumes that were sold mail order and retail. The labels read *Mary Hoyer//Reading//PA.*

In 1960, the Fiberoid Doll Company folded after producing approximately 72,000 of the 14" hard plastic dolls, Mary Hoyer's personal favorite. Hoyers next had the 14" doll copied in vinyl, with rooted hair and some face changes. She was called Becky. Becky had long straight, curly, or upswept hairstyles. The hair could be combed, washed, and set, and came in four shades. The Becky doll was unmarked and was discontinued in 1968.

Granddaughter Mary Lynne Saunders continued the Mary Hoyer Doll Company in the 1980s with a vinyl play doll and characters from *The Doll with the Magic Wand,* a fairy tale written by Mary Hoyer. Her 1990s dolls are now more of a basic play doll with a variety of eye colors, hairstyles, and wardrobe. Some of the more intriguing wardrobe available includes hiking boots, shorts, camping gear, and realistic accessories for the modern girls of today. The dolls, clothing, and accessories are forever popular.

Mary Hoyer was a delightful, talented lady, who turned her designing talents into a wonderful career. Her designs, dolls, and patterns will carry on for generations. The Mary Hoyer Doll Company and mail order business is still thriving: Mary Hoyer Doll Company, PO Box 1608, Lancaster, PA 17603, (717) 393-4121.

What to look for:

One of the hottest collectible dolls this past year has been the 18" hard plastic Gigi with the round Mary Hoyer mark on her back. The prices are high for those with original clothing in excellent condition. Mary Hoyer dolls are a great delight for knitters as they get to use all those patterns that have been reissued and are still on the market. Mary Hoyer dolls are a great collectible to look for in composition and hard plastic, but do not pass up the new ones. Look for rosy cheeks, little crazing if composition, clean hard plastic, and original outfits.

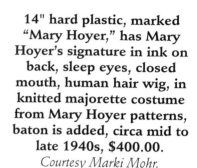

14" hard plastic, marked "Mary Hoyer," has Mary Hoyer's signature in ink on back, sleep eyes, closed mouth, human hair wig, in knitted majorette costume from Mary Hoyer patterns, baton is added, circa mid to late 1940s, $400.00.
Courtesy Marki Mohr.

14" composition, sleep eyes, closed mouth, blond wig, wearing pattern made red skating outfit with ice skates, marked "Mary Hoyer Doll" on back, circa 1940s, $325.00.
Courtesy Elizabeth Surber.

14" composition, marked "The Mary Hoyer Doll" on back, blue sleep eyes, real lashes, painted lower lashes, closed mouth, rosy cheeks, brown mohair wig, five-piece composition body, three-piece navy blue knit outfit, matching panties and hat, socks, black center snap leatherette shoes, outfit made from a pattern made especially for Mary Hoyer dolls, circa 1937+, $325.00.
Courtesy McMasters Doll Auctions.

14" hard plastic Ballerina, marked on back torso, "Original Mary Hoyer Doll," blue sleep eyes, brown wig, closed mouth, mint in box with tagged pink outfit, pamphlet, circa 1953, $750.00.
Courtesy Sally DeSmet.

14" hard plastic girl skater, "Original Mary Hoyer" in circle on back, blue sleep eyes, closed mouth, auburn mohair wig, pink and white crocheted skating outfit, with trunk/more crocheted wardrobe, circa 1947+, $450.00.
Courtesy Sally DeSmet.

14" hard plastic girl, marked "Original Mary Hoyer Doll" inside circle on back, blue sleep eyes, closed mouth, auburn synthetic wig, original tagged dress of pink and white skirt and collar with white bodice, circa 1958, $250.00.
Courtesy Peggy Millhouse.

14" hard plastic, "Original Mary Hoyer" in circle on back, blue sleep eyes, closed mouth, auburn saran wig, pink dress and hat, black cape, circa 1950+, $350.00.
Courtesy Kate Treber.

Ideal

Ideal Novelty and Toy Co. (1906 – 1990+, Brooklyn, NY) produced their own composition dolls in the early years. Morris Michtom started the business making teddy bears in 1906 with his wife, Rose. Michtom also began making composition "unbreakable" dolls about this time. His early comic characters were popular. Ideal also produced licensed dolls for companies to help promote their products such as Uneeda Kid that carried a small box of crackers for the Uneeda Biscuit Company. Some of their big successes were Shirley Temple in composition, Saucy Walker and Toni in hard plastic, and Miss Revlon in vinyl. They also made dolls of cloth and rubber. They used various marks including *IDEAL* (in a diamond) *US of A; IDEAL Novelty and Toy Co., Brooklyn, New York,* and others.

What to look for:

Look for dolls with minimal crazing in composition, good color, original clothing. Hard plastic and vinyl dolls should have very good color, and clean, bright, perhaps tagged original clothing. A wide variety of Ideal dolls are available as they were in business for so many years.

15" composition clapping baby, marked "Ideal (in diamond)//U.S. (around diamond)" on head, blue sleep eyes, painted upper lashes, closed mouth, molded/painted blond hair, cloth body with clapping mechanism in torso, composition hands, white baby dress with lace inserts and trim, lacy bonnet, one-piece underwear, booties, circa 1925+, $115.00.
Courtesy McMasters Doll Auctions.

Ideal

24" composition Plassie, sleep eyes, painted molded hair, re-dressed in white baby gown with blue lace bib, blue ribbon, white lace around hem and sleeves, white lace bonnet, blue and white booties, circa 1942, $150.00.
Private collection.

19" hard plastic pre-Toni girl, blue sleep eyes, closed mouth, brown wig, yellow dress, blue ribbons in hair and around waist, straw hat, all original, marked "P-92" on head, circa 1948, $695.00.
Courtesy Sally DeSmet.

14" hard plastic baby, marked "Ideal Doll Made in U.S.A.," brown sleep eyes, closed mouth, painted hair, blue coat and bonnet, pink dress, purchased from Sears in early 1950s, $85.00.
Courtesy Bev Mitchell.

17" flocked vinyl Baby Dreams, sleep eyes, rooted blond hair, closed mouth, cloth body, vinyl arms and legs, advertised as "The Doll with the Velvet Skin," circa 1975 – 1976, $20.00.
Courtesy Diana McCoy.

12" vinyl Betsy Wetsy, sleep eyes, real lashes, rooted hair, open mouth to accept bottle (a drink & wet type), bent leg body, feet have separate toes, re-dressed, circa 1956, $35.00; sitting in marked cardboard 10" x 16" suitcase $50.00.
Courtesy Eileen Hanrahan.

42" vinyl Daddy's Girl, marked "© Ideal Toy Corp.// G-42-1" on head, "© Ideal Toy Corp. //G-42" on back, blue sleep eyes, lashes, closed smiling mouth, rooted brunette saran hair, swivel waist, jointed ankles, original red plaid dress, large white collar, attached half slip, replaced panties, black one-strap shoes, red straw hat with flower trim, circa 1961, $735.00.
Courtesy McMasters Doll Auctions.

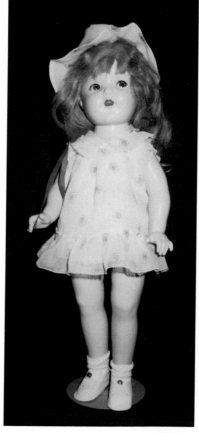

18" composition Ginger, brown flirty sleep eyes, open mouth with teeth, human hair wig, jointed composition body, white print dress with matching hat, all original, circa 1934, $225.00.
Courtesy Martha Sweeney.

17" vinyl Movin' Grovin' Crissy, with swivel waist and growing hair, rooted hair, original orange dress and boots, boxed, circa 1971, $75.00.
Courtesy Michele Lyons.

Ideal

21" vinyl Harmony, marked "H-200 © 1971-Ideal" on head, inset brown eyes, long rooted hair, fingers strum guitar, sound comes from the changeable record in her amplifier, with box, circa 1972, $35.00.
Courtesy Sue Robertson.

25" vinyl Miss Ideal, blue sleep eyes, real lashes, feathered brows, closed smiling mouth, blond rooted nylon wig, rigid vinyl body jointed at shoulders/waist/hips/ankles, marked "© Ideal Toy Corp. SP-25-S" on head, "P-25" on back, original pink dress with black checked top with lace, black shoes, promotional paper *Hair Styling Hints*, wrist booklet, playwave kit, comb, curlers, hair wave lotion, mint with box, circa 1961, $350.00.
Courtesy McMasters Doll Auctions.

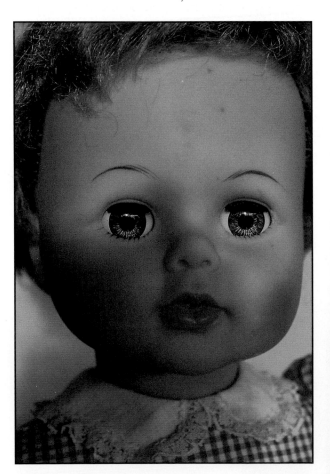

22" vinyl Kissy, marked "©IDEAL CORP.//K-21-L" on head, blue sleep eyes, rooted saran hair, jointed wrists, press hands together and mouth puckers up and makes a kiss with kissing sound, hard vinyl body, tagged red checked dress, red t-strap plastic shoes, all original, circa 1961 – 1964, $135.00.
Courtesy Nelda Shelton.

18" vinyl Miss Revlon, marked "Ideal Doll//IT-18," blue sleep eyes, earrings, closed mouth, rooted saran hair, with hair net, blue taffeta street dress, blue high heels, with sunglasses, hang tag, circa 1956 – 1959, $350.00.
Private collection.

35" vinyl Patti Play Pal, marked "Ideal Doll//G-35" on head, hard to find orange-red rooted saran hair with bangs, walker, wears original orange and green print school dress, circa 1960 – 1961, $500.00.
Courtesy Cornelia Ford.

21" vinyl Miss Revlon, rooted synthetic hair, sleep eyes, original dress with Revlon ribbon tag, marked "Ideal Doll//VT/V-22" on head and body, circa 1956 – 1959, $100.00.
Courtesy Maria Traver.

Ideal

25" vinyl Talkytot, mask face, brown eyes, gold wool hair, dressed in plaid dress and hat, hand crank makes doll say phrases like "Rock-a-bye baby on a tree-top," mint in box, circa 1953, $85.00.
Courtesy Leslie Tannenbaum.

19" vinyl Princess Mary, blue sleep eyes, closed mouth, dark blond wig, red plaid dress, gold and red flowers in hair, hard plastic body, circa 1954, $175.00.
Courtesy Kate Treber.

28" vinyl Saucy Walker rooted blond saran hair, blue sleep eyes, closed smiling mouth, original red dress with marked pinafore, marked, head "Ideal Toy Corp.// T28X-60 © Ideal Toy Crop, 1-28 Pat. Pend." circa 1960 – 1961, $175.00.
Courtesy Cornelia Ford.

9" vinyl Pepper, side-glancing painted eyes, freckles on nose, closed mouth, rooted hair, rigid plastic torso, marked on head "© Ideal Toy Corp," played with condition, circa 1962+, $25.00.
Courtesy Barbara Jones.

14" hard plastic Toni, marked "P-90" on body with original blue velveteen coat, hat, and dress in original box with wave set and curlers, circa 1949 – 1953, $750.00.
Courtesy Ann Sutton.

14" hard plastic Toni, marked "P-90" on body, pale color, blue sleep eyes, closed mouth, blond Dupont glued-on wig, hard plastic jointed body, white pinafore over pink dress, circa 1949 – 1953, $125.00.
Courtesy Beth Edwards.

14" hard plastic Toni with box, wrist tag, play wave set, blue sleep eyes, synthetic wig, beautiful coloring, in original red and green plaid dress, red leatherette center strap shoes, marked "IDEAL DOLL//MADE IN U.S.A." on head, "IDEAL DOLL//P/90" on body, circa 1949+, $575.00.
Courtesy Gloria Sanders.

Ideal

14" hard plastic Toni marked "P-90" on back, sleep eyes, mascara above, painted lashes below, with synthetic wig, in original dress, circa 1949 – 1953, $195.00.
Courtesy Pam Martinec.

14" hard plastic Toni, marked "Ideal Doll//Made in U.S.A.//P-90" on head, blue sleep eyes, rosy cheeks, closed mouth, red Dupont nylon wig, non-walker, white print dress, circa 1949, $300.00.
Courtesy Peggy Millhouse.

Left to right: 14", 16", 14" hard plastic Toni dolls, "Ideal Doll//Made in USA" on head, "P-90" on back of 14", "P-91" on 16", blue sleep eyes, original tagged clothes on blonds, fully jointed, circa 1949, $250.00, $400.00, $135.00.
Courtesy Kate Treber.

16" hard plastic Toni with blue sleep eyes, eyeshadow, real lashes, painted lashes below, closed mouth, strawberry blond wig, in royal blue and cream pique original dress, circa 1949+, $400.00.
Courtesy Maria Traver.

20" hard plastic Bride, marked "Ideal//P92// Ideal Doll//Made in U.S.A.," blue sleep eyes, closed mouth, auburn synthetic wig, all original, circa 1950s, $550.00. *Private collection.*

13" vinyl black Whoopsie with rooted hair, one-piece foam filled body, watermelon mouth, painted eyes, push tummy and braids go up, she makes a whoopsie sound, marked "22/©Ideal Toy Corp.//Hong Kong//1978/H298," $55.00. *Courtesy Antoinette Whelan.*

20" hard plastic Toni with blue sleep eyes, pale blond wig, closed mouth, marked on head "Ideal Doll//Made in USA" and on back, "Ideal Doll//P 92" in original blue dress, lovely coloring, circa 1949+, $575.00. *Courtesy Elizabeth Surber.*

Kenner

The *Star Wars* movie was made in 1977, and the sequel *The Empire Strikes Back* in 1980. Kenner made large Star Wars figures in 1978 in Hong Kong, ranging in heights from 7" to 15". They included Princess Leia Organa, Luke Skywalker, R2-D2, Chewbaca, Darth Vader, and C-3P0. In 1979 Boba Fett, Han Solo, Stormtrooper, Ben (Obi-Wan) Kenobi, Jawa, and IG-88 were added. They also made 3 – 4" small figures starting in 1979.

What to look for:

Kenner has made a variety of modern character dolls such as Bob Scout with Boy Scout uniform and accessories, and sports figures and fashion-type dolls. Look for boxed all-original dolls that are clean with good color. Star War figures are more popular with toy collectors, but are always collectible, as are celebrity dolls such as Six Million Dollar Man figures. Look for them at garage sales, flea markets, and estate sales.

12½" vinyl Darci with red rooted hair, painted blue eyes, with eyeshadow above eyes, open/closed mouth with white teeth, fashion type body, marked "74//Hong Kong//© GMFGI 1978" wears red striped top/ blue cotton skirt, original pack clothes, circa 1978, $35.00.mk,
Courtesy Jaci Jueden.

12½" vinyl Darci with blond rooted hair, painted blue eyes, with eyeshadow above eyes, open/closed mouth with white teeth, fashion type body, marked "74//Hong Kong//© GMFGI 1978," wears yellow jacket marked "Darci," circa 1978, $30.00.
Courtesy Jaci Jueden.

Klumpe

Klumpe made caricature figures of felt over wire armature with painted mask faces in Barcelona, Spain, from 1952 to the mid-1970s. Figures represent professionals, hobbyists, Spanish dancers, historical characters, and contemporary males and females performing a wide variety of tasks. Of the 200 or more different figures, the most common are Spanish dancers, bull fighters, and doctors. Some Klumpes were imported by Effanbee in the early 1950s. Originally the figures had two sewn-on identifying cardboard tags.

What to look for:

These amusing characters may be missing their tags, but are still very collectible. Often passed over by more sophisticated collectors, they can still be found for reasonable prices. Look for those with more accessories, tags, or labels. They should be clean with bright colors. The more intricate the costume and accessories, the more desirable they are to collectors. They must be pristine with all labels to command highest prices. Keep on the lookout at estate sales, antique malls, flea markets, and doll shows for these.

9" mask face Lady Smoker, felt over armature marked "Klumpe," blue painted side-glancing eyes, painted features, mohair wig, black net outfit, black shoes, cigarette in hand, circa 1950s, $125.00.
Private collection.

Klumpe

11" cloth Musician, holds mandolin, foil label, red and green original costume, mint in box, circa 1960, $175.00.
Courtesy Sondra Gast.

11" Going Fishing Girl, hang tag reads "I am a Klumpe Doll hand made in Spain//Distributed by Effanbee," sewn on cardboard tag reads "Klumpe No. 3//Made in Spain," felt over wire armature, painted mask face, red pants, tan shirt and hat, carrying fishing pole, circa 1952+, $125.00.
Courtesy Cherie Gervais.

11" Fish Vendor, made in Spain, felt over wire armature, painted mask face, black pants, white shirt, black hat, carrying fish baskets over his shoulders, circa 1952 to mid 1970s, $95.00.
Courtesy Cherie Gervais.

Lenci

Elena von Konig Scavini was born in Italy in 1886, and after the loss of her firstborn child, she started making cuddly dolls. She called the dolls Lencina or Little Lenci. Her dolls were used as decorative accessories in bedrooms and cars and were carried with designer costumes. Early dolls were characters, tagged with small Lenci button. Many, and some of the most intricate, were made during the 1920s. This era is noted for rooted hair, hand embroidery, and pieced felt costumes with felt flowers. The American stock market crash threw the company into bankruptcy. It was taken over by Pilade Garella who narrowed the product line from clothing, costumes, ceramics, furniture, and handbags to only dolls. The 1930s dolls were simpler and there were fewer styles. Mascottes (7½") and miniature (9") dolls in regional, nursery rhyme, and children's clothing were heavily produced and promoted. Glass flirty eyes were added in 1935. Baby dolls were introduced in the 1930s with two face models, but they were not popular. Boudoir dolls, with elongated arms and legs dressed as celebrities, were very popular and made throughout the company's history. By 1940, Madame Lenci had lost her husband, Enrico, sold her remaining shares in the Lenci Company, and severed all ties to it. In the 1940s, Lenci quality diminished. In 1942, Beppe Garella, Pilade's son came into the business. He became president after his father's death in 1968. In the 1950s, the Lenci dolls' popularity again slowed and the company made dolls of other materials. In 1978, the company again started making felt dolls and this move was profitable. Madame Lenci died in 1974, and in 1993, Beppe Garella died. His daughter Bibija now runs the company.

What to look for:
Lenci dolls are made of felt. With double layer ears and scalloped cotton socks. Early dolls can have rooted mohair wigs, 1930s dolls may have frizzed played with looking wigs, 1940s dolls may have hard cardboard type felt faces. Value depends on condition such as cleanliness, originality, wear, and costumes.

9" flocked hard plastic girl, blue surprise side-glancing eyes, open/closed mouth, dressed in regional felt clothing with nice added details such as embroidery, sandals, circa 1950s, $100.00.
Courtesy Sheryl Nudelman.

Lenci

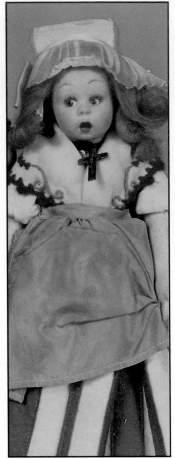

9½" cloth miniature Normandie Mascotte, "Lenci//Torino//Made in Italy// Miniature 110" on round paper tag, "Normandia" on square paper tag stitched on skirt, felt swivel head, circa 1930s, $230.00.
Courtesy McMasters Doll Auctions.

10" cloth Mascotte, pressed felt swivel head, painted side-glancing eyes, felt hair in braids, cloth torso, legs, felt arms, original costume, near mint, circa 1930s, $300.00.
Courtesy McMasters Doll Auctions.

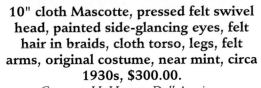

Left: 8" cloth Mascotte, marked "Lenci//Torino//Made in Italy" on tag, pressed felt face, painted brown eyes, original mohair wig, cloth torso and legs, felt arms with stitched fingers, original regional-type costume, circa 1940s, $165.00.

Right: 14" cloth child, pressed felt swivel head, brown eyes painted to side, closed mouth, mohair wig, original turquoise felt dress with white and yellow trim, knit socks, felt shoes, circa 1940s, $225.00.
Courtesy McMasters Doll Auctions.

35" cloth, long-limbed, unmarked, pressed felt swivel head, painted side-glancing eyes, applied ears, mohair wig, felt body, jointed shoulders, hips, knees, original costume, some soil, fading, circa 1930s, $2,500.00+.
Courtesy McMasters Doll Auctions.

16" cloth girl in regional costume, silver label on red skirt, purple stamp on bottom of left foot, some soil on costume, moth holes, circa 1930s, $850.00.
Photo by Scott Gladden.
Courtesy Ellen Sturgess.

14" cloth Tyrolean girl, applied felt ears, blond mohair wig, original outfit, cloth tag reads "Lenci//Made in Italy," "Bambola Italia//Lenci//Torino//Made in Italy" on paper tag, circa 1930s, $250.00.
Courtesy McMasters Doll Auctions.

22" cloth baby, tag on hem of organdy dress, human hair wig, all original, circa 1930s, $3,500.00.
Photo by Scott Gladden.
Courtesy Ellen Sturgess.

18" felt girl, dress tagged "Lenci, Made in Italy," oil painted pressed felt mask face, circa 1940s – 1950s, $300.00.
Courtesy McMasters Doll Auctions.

Lenci

14" cloth child, marked "Bambo-la-Italia//Lenci //Torino//Made in Italy" on paper tag, "Lucia 4" on faded paper tag on coat, "7" on bottom of right foot, pressed felt head, painted brown eyes, closed mouth, applied ears, mohair wig, cloth torso, felt arms and legs, jointed at shoulders and hips, original white felt shirt with gray tie, gray shorts, white cotton socks, rust colored felt shoes, rust colored coat and matching hat, circa 1930s, $525.00. *Courtesy McMasters Doll Auctions.*

21½" cloth girl, painted brown side-glancing eyes, pressed felt face, blond mohair wig, blue coat trimmed in black, black skirt and hat, blue top, moth holes, circa 1930s, $985.00. *Courtesy Suzanne Prince.*

14" pressed felt girl, marked "4" on bottom of right foot, painted brown eyes, painted upper and lower lashes on molded lid, accented nostrils, closed mouth, applied ears, mohair wig, cloth torso with felt arms and legs, ethnic costume, all original, circa 1940s – 1950s, $550.00. *Courtesy McMasters Doll Auctions.*

25" felt Melania with painted blue eyes, two-tone pink lips, synthetic wig, tagged on skirt "Lenci® Made in Italy," wearing pink and mauve-brown wool felt long dress, with pink scalloped hem, matching pink hat, some moth holes, no certificate, reissued circa 1979+, $250.00. *Courtesy Pauletta Patterson.*

25" felt boudoir Smoker, brown painted side-glancing eyes, closed mouth with cigarette, dark blond mohair wig, painted eyebrows, red accent marks at nostrils, holds cigarette in mouth, jointed neck, elongated felt body, blue pantsuit with yellow trim, black stockings, circa 1930s, $1,200.00.
Courtesy Jane Horst.

21" felt Pajama Bag Series 178 Marietta, surprise glass eyes, surprise "O" shaped mouth, molded/pressed face, zipper down back, black hat, clutches a colorful felt rooster, wooden shoes/felt tops, circa 1930s, $2,800.00.
Courtesy Suzanne Prince.

Mattel, Inc.

Mattel was founded in 1945 in Los Angeles, California, and has been a dominant force in the doll industry with their Barbie, Chatty Cathy, and others. The company began when Ruth and Elliott Handler and their friend Harold Mattson founded the Mattel company. The name came from "Matt" for Mattson and "el" for Elliot. They began by first making picture frames, evolving into toy furniture. Mattson left the company because of ill health and Ruth Handler began to handle marketing. She advertised in 1955 on a children's TV show, *The Mickey Mouse Club.* In 1959, they marketed Barbie, named after their daughter, and the company prospered. Barbie (see separate section) has become the number one collectible doll in the world. Mattel also has manufactured quite a list of celebrity dolls as well as characters from TV shows. The Handlers are no longer associated with the company.

What to look for:

These modern vinyl and hard plastic dolls are very collectible because so many kids played with them. Look for those still with boxes and accessories.

10½" vinyl Baby Small Talks Cinderella, blue eyes, auburn hair, open mouth with teeth, hard plastic body, says eight phrases, infant voice, lavender and gold gown, circa 1968 – 1969, $25.00.
Courtesy Bev Mitchell.

7" vinyl Baby Cheerful Tearful, painted blue eyes, blond hair, face changes from smile to frown when arm is raised and lowered, drinks, wets, and cries real tears, never removed from package, circa 1960s, $30.00.
Courtesy Leslie Tannenbaum.

6½" vinyl Buffy & Mrs. Beasley, painted features, rooted blond hair, holds small Mrs. Beasley with vinyl head on cloth body, mint in box, circa 1967 and 1974, $180.00; Buffy Beauty Boutique Case made by Amsco in 1970, $45.00.
Courtesy Leslie Tannenbaum.

10" vinyl Talking Buffy & Mrs. Beasley, painted blue eyes, rooted blond hair, holds 6" Mrs. Beasley, never removed from box, circa 1969 – 1971, $350.00.
Courtesy Leslie Tannenbaum.

Authorized edition of *Family Affair Buffy Finds A Star* by Gladys Baker Bond, illustrated by Michael Lowenbein, published by Whitman Publishing Company, © 1970, $35.00.
Courtesy Jennifer Warren.

22" vinyl Mrs. Beasley talking pull string doll with blue and white dotted print body, rooted blond hair, watermelon mouth, decal type eyes, wears square glasses vinyl hands, in original marked box, near mint, with those hard to find glasses, circa 1967 – 1974, $1,000.00+.
Courtesy Jennifer Warren.

Mattel, Inc.

24" vinyl Charmin' Chatty, closed smiling mouth, hard vinyl body, long rooted hair, five records placed in left side slot play, one-piece navy skirt, white middy blouse with red sailor collar, marked, "Charmin' Chatty//© 1961 Mattel Inc.// Hawthorne, Calif. USA//U.S. Pat.//Pat'd. In Canada// Other U.S. and Foreign//Patents Pending," circa 1963 – 64, $125.00.
Courtesy Connie Lara.

20" vinyl Chatty Cathy, marked "Chatty Cathy T.M.// Patents Pending//© MCMLX//By Mattel, Inc.// Hawthorne, Calif." on back, brown sleep eyes, freckles, open/closed mouth, two upper teeth, rooted brunette hair, five-piece vinyl body, tagged "Nursery School" yellow dress with pink and blue trim, pink velvet shoes, original picture box, booklet, talking mechanism does not work, circa 1960 – 1963, $150.00.
Courtesy McMasters Doll Auctions.

18" vinyl Hot Looks with rooted synthetic hair, decal type eyes, earrings, stockinet body, circa 1986, played with condition $12.00.
Courtesy Marie Rodgers.

23" vinyl Scooba Doo rooted blond hair, heavy eyeshadow, closed mouth, pale lips, cloth body with pull string talker, says 11 phrases, wears striped top, gold necklace, advertised in 1964 Sears catalog, $75.00+.
Courtesy Oleta Woodside.

Monica

Monica was the creation of Mrs. Hansi Share, owner of the Monica Doll Studios of Hollywood, California. Monica dolls were first advertised in 1941. Early dolls were 20" and 24" in size. In 1947, *Toys and Novelties*, a toy trade publication, advertised 15", 17", and 20" sizes. Individual dolls had names like Veronica, Jean, and Rosalind. Hard plastic dolls named Elizabeth, Marion, and Linda were offered by high-end stores such as F.A.O. Schwarz and Neiman Marcus. In October 1949 Monica Doll Studios announced the arrival of an all-plastic Marion doll with rooted hair and sleep eyes. What is remarkable about this doll is the ingenious idea of rooting human hair first in the composition head and then later in the hard plastic one.

Mrs. Share managed to come up with a process to place small portions of fragile human hair in the composition and plastic heads during manufacturing to give the appearance of real rooted hair. Hair rooted into the head became an accepted practice with the use of vinyl for making dolls in the 1960s. The Monica Doll Company made dolls until 1952. The Monica line of dolls is also interesting, as it typifies the reentry of fashion dolls into the world of dolls. Dolls of the 1930s such as Patsy and Shirley Temple had an early child-like all-composition pudgy body. In 1935, Effanbee introduced the Patricia line and advertised them as an older sister of about twelve years of age with just the hint of breasts. In 1940, Effanbee showed Little Lady dolls still with an older child body, but wearing sophisticated negligees over panties and bras. Monica dolls in 1941 had all-composition unmarked bodies with flat feet, and the arms and hands seem somewhat heavy and awkward in contrast to the sophistication of the hair, makeup, and facial features. Monica dolls had painted eyes, eyeshadow, a closed mouth, rosy cheeks, and most important the unique rooted human hair. All of this makes the composition dolls dramatic and appealing. In hard plastic, Monica is not as striking as the features become softened. The dramatic look given by the painted eyes diminishes with sleep eyes. These dolls had sophisticated wardrobes and came dressed in fancy short dresses, suits, long evening dresses, or as brides. Additional costumes were available separately. Neiman Marcus's 1945 Christmas catalog featured Monica with a white peasant blouse, red peasant skirt and bolero, fruit-trimmed hat, and black ballerina slippers. Montgomery Ward's 1947 catalog pictures an all-composition Monica in net dress with ruffles, rayon underskirt, rayon panties, and long stockings with her rooted human hair wig. Monica, appearing first in composition and making the transition to hard plastic is an example of a doll that spans the gap from the 1930 child dolls to the more glamorous dolls of the 1950s. She has the same mystique as today's Gene dolls with her sophisticated Hollywood glamour makeup. Her short life, unique features, and Hollywood presence makes her an interesting and desirable collectible.

What to look for:

Identification tips include rooted hair and painted eyes, although she was later made with sleep eyes. Try to find Monica with great hair and costumes. The small 11" size is hard to find.

Monica

20" all-composition Monica is unmarked and is identified by her unusual rooted human hair wig, widow's peak, and long face, painted blue eyes, dark eyeliner above eyes, light blue eyeshadow, soft rosy cheeks, red accents at inner eye and nose, a profile of her body reveals slightly bent arms, a child-like torso with a slight breast, hands are large and heavy, nicely costumed in a new long red and white dress, circa 1941 – 1947, $500.00.
Courtesy Oleta Woodside.

17" all-composition unmarked Monica doll, painted blue eyes, eyeshadow, rosy cheeks, closed mouth, rooted human hair, original long pink floral dress with gold paper hang tag, replaced flower trim and replaced shoes, circa 1942, $700.00.
Courtesy Myrna McDaniel.

20" all-composition unmarked Monica Bride, painted eyes with eyeliner and mauve eyeshadow above eyes, closed mouth, rooted auburn hair, five-piece composition body, original bride dress, veil and flowers added, circa 1940s, $750.00.
Private collection.

17" all-composition unmarked Monica Bride, painted eyes, eyeshadow, closed mouth, rooted dark blond hair, five-piece composition body, original bride dress, circa 1940s, $550.00.
Private collection.

21" composition Monica, painted eyes, closed mouth, auburn rooted human hair, original costume with white blouse, bolero, and red skirt all trimmed in rick-rack was featured in the 1945 Neiman Marcus catalog, $950.00.
Courtesy Nelda Shelton.

Nancy Ann Storybook

Nancy Ann Storybook Dolls was started in 1936, in San Francisco, California, by Rowena Haskin (Nancy Ann Abbott). The dolls were painted bisque with mohair wigs and painted eyes. Their heads were molded to their torsos, and they had jointed limbs. They either had a sticker on their outfit or a hang tag. They also made a hard plastic 8" Muffie and various sizes of Miss Nancy Ann Style Show, and an 11" Debbie and 7½" Lori Ann with vinyl heads and hard plastic bodies. In the 1950s and 1960s they made 10½" Miss Nancy Ann and Little Miss Nancy Ann, vinyl high-heeled fashion-type dolls.

What to look for:

The newer dolls need to be complete and mint. That is what collectors are looking for. In competition, the older, rare, mint, original, and beautiful doll is the one that catches the judges' eyes. That leaves a lot of played with and soiled dolls with faded clothing or missing accessories that are still collectible, and perhaps you can salvage some great dolls that others have skipped over. You can certainly find enough to collect, but always look for the one with the more intricate costume, prettier coloring, and original clothing, tags, labels, or in boxes.

4½" painted bisque #234 Little Miss Pattycake, baby with star shaped hand, in pink dress-up coat and bonnet, circa 1938, $300.00.

Courtesy Elaine Pardee.

5½" painted bisque Jennie Set the Table on original gold foil bracelet, marked "Story// Book//Doll// USAl," painted features, closed mouth, auburn mohair wig, green checked taffeta dress with eyelet apron/hat, circa 1941 – 1942, $50.00.

Courtesy Diane Graves.

5½" painted bisque Little Joan, marked "Storybook Doll USA," painted eyes, auburn mohair wig, molded painted shoes, pink taffeta dress with plastic blue checked apron, circa 1941 – 1942, $50.00.
Courtesy Diane Graves.

5½" painted bisque Annie at the Garden Gate on original gold foil bracelet, marked "Story//Book//Doll//USA," painted features, cherries/ribbon on auburn mohair wig, white bodice, green taffeta on bottom and across chest, circa 1941 – 1942, $50.00.
Courtesy Diane Graves.

5½" painted bisque Winter on original gold foil bracelet, marked "Storybook Doll USA," painted features, closed mouth, brown mohair wig, white taffeta dress, red felt coat/hat, mint in box, circa 1941 – 1942, $75.00.
Courtesy Diane Graves.

6½" painted bisque Nancy Ann Storybook girl, February, marked "Storybook Doll USA," painted features, blond mohair wig, closed mouth, unusual dress with cheese-cloth like fabric, ruffle, felt hat with feather, circa 1941 – 1942, $65.00.
Courtesy Diane Graves.

5½" painted bisque He Loves Me, He Loves Me Not on original gold bracelet, marked "Storybook Doll USA," painted eyes, blond mohair wig, light pink taffeta dress, magenta felt hat, circa 1941 – 1942, $50.00.
Courtesy Diane Graves.

5½" painted bisque, I'm Going a Milking on original gold bracelet, marked "Storybook Doll USA," painted eyes, blond mohair wig, red taffeta bodice/apron, red/white check skirt, Dutch hat with matching trim, circa 1941 – 1942, $50.00.
Courtesy Diane Graves.

5½" painted bisque Goldilocks, marked "Storybook Doll USA," painted eyes, blond mohair wig, yellow floral skirt trimmed in blue, royal blue taffeta bodice and skirt trimmed in yellow, blue ribbon in hair, circa 1941 – 1947, $50.00.
Courtesy Diane Graves.

5½" painted bisque Polly Put the Kettle On, marked "Storybook Doll USA," painted features, closed mouth, brown mohair wig, red and white taffeta dress, dotted Swiss apron, checked trim to match bodice, headband, circa 1941 – 1947, $35.00.
Courtesy Diane Graves.

5½" painted bisque, Sunday's Child on original gold foil bracelet, marked "Storybook Doll USA," painted features, reddish-blond mohair wig, pink dress, pink hat with brim turned up, mint in box, circa 1941 – 1947, $75.00.
Courtesy Diane Graves.

5½" painted bisque, Thursday's Child on original gold foil bracelet, marked "Storybook Doll USA," painted features, brown mohair wig, closed mouth, red and yellow plaid dress, red felt hat, mint in box, circa 1941 – 1947, $75.00.
Courtesy Diane Graves.

6½" painted bisque, October on original gold foil bracelet, marked "Storybook Doll USA," painted features, brown mohair wig, frozen legs, yellow dress with black lace insert, black felt hat, mint in box, circa 1943 – 1947, $75.00.
Courtesy Diane Graves.

5½" painted bisque A Dillar A Dollar, marked "Story//Book// Doll//USA," painted features, closed mouth, brown mohair wig, unusual light pink taffeta dress, apron with embroidered rickrack, blue felt hat, circa 1941 – 1947, $50.00.
Courtesy Diane Graves.

Nancy Ann Storybook

6½" hard plastic Stardust, marked "Storybook Doll USA//™," painted eyes, auburn mohair wig, magenta dress with silver glitter, matching black lace hat, magenta ribbon, circa 1947 – 1949, $50.00.
Courtesy Diane Graves.

8" hard plastic Muffie, marked "Storybook Dolls//California," blue sleep eyes, auburn wig, painted lashes, strung, straight leg, non-walker, yellow and gray striped dress with white lace trim, circa 1953, $175.00.
Courtesy Peggy Millhouse.

6½" hard plastic, Let Me Call You Sweetheart on original gold bracelet, marked "Storybook Doll USA//™," painted eyes, auburn mohair wig, white lace hat, pink taffeta dress, white net, red felt heart on front, circa 1947 – 1949, $50.00.
Courtesy Diane Graves.

8" hard plastic Muffie, marked "Storybook Dolls//California," rare brown eyes, blond wig, painted lashes, strung, straight leg, non-walker, pink dotted Swiss dress, circa 1953, $200.00.
Courtesy Peggy Millhouse.

18" hard plastic Nancy Ann Style Show non-walker, #2901 Grand Ball, mint in box with tag, white gown with aqua trim, big rose and satin ribbon trim, circa 1950s, $700.00.
Courtesy Elaine Pardee.

8" hard plastic Muffie, #500B, marked "Storybook Dolls// California// MUFFIE," brunette saran wig with ponytails, sleep eyes, painted lashes, closed mouth, walker, hard plastic body, with box, circa 1956, $150.00.
Courtesy Peggy Millhouse.

18" hard plastic Nancy Ann Style Show A Summery Day, unmarked walker, sleep eyes, closed mouth, mohair wig, dress is yellow with pink, black, and red stripes, replaced hat, circa 1950s, $350.00.
Courtesy Diane Graves.

18" hard plastic Nancy Ann Style Show non walker, #2404 Glamorous, pink nylon lace with pink stole, circa 1960s, $600.00.
Courtesy Elaine Pardee.

Nurse Dolls

Some sources believe that as long ago as 4,000 BC temples were used to house the sick and as training schools for doctors. Primarily, the care of the sick fell to religious groups. Usually there was no formal training; apprentices learned from experienced nurses and in turn, passed on the training to others. Nurses provided low-cost service to institutions and then worked in private homes or services.

By 1836, some schools for training nurses were found in Germany. Pastor Fliedner in Kaiserswerth had as one of their pupils, Florence Nightingale. Nightingale was appalled at the lack of sanitation and poorly trained and supervised nurses. When the Crimean War broke out in 1854, she volunteered. She organized nurses and provided some skilled care during this crisis, dropping the mortality rate. At the close of the war in 1860, she founded a nursing school in London, marking the beginning of professional education in nursing.

About this time, a Swiss philanthropist, Jean Henri Dunant, organized world leaders to found societies to care for the wounded in wartime. At a conference in 1864, officials of 12 nations signed the first Geneva Convention specifying rules of treatment for wounded and protection of medical personnel. A symbol of this movement was adopted at this time — a white flag with a red cross. The organization came to be known as the Red Cross, an international humanitarian agency that alleviates suffering from wars and major disasters and performs other public service functions. Clara Barton founded the American Red Cross in 1881. Barton was called the "Angel of the Battle" for setting up a supply service during the Civil War, nursing, and searching for the missing. Congress chartered the Red Cross in 1900.

Little has been documented about nurse dolls as a specific category, but it does rate two pages in *Coleman's Collector's Encyclopedia of Dolls, Vol. II. Coleman's* cites specific nurse dolls from 1885 on. Certainly world events played a role in the popularity of nurse dolls. Before 1900, a nurse was most often portrayed as a nanny who took care of a baby or child. With the advent of World War I, however, dolls with the familiar Red Cross emblem on their costume were seen. In 1934, the birth of the Dionne Quintuplets revived the image of the nurse helping Dr. Dafoe with the quintuplets. Alexander was granted the license to produce the official Dionne Quintuplets. Fruendlich and others jumped on the bandwagon with unlicensed quintuplets and nurse sets. World War II brought again dolls dressed in the image of a nurse in a white uniform, blue cape lined with red, and white cap. They were produced by a variety of manufacturers. Mattel promoted a television character, Julia, as a nurse, circa 1969 – 1971. Still later, Hasbro's military G.I. Joe also had a plastic 10½" GI Action Girl in 1967 authentically outfitted in a white hospital uniform, Red Cross hat, and accessories pack with crutches, bandages, stethoscope, plasma bottle, and more. Nurses as a collectible provide an interesting avenue to pursue and can be a niche category that may be overlooked. The scope and range of this can be as broad or as narrow as you make it

What to look for:

Both antique and modern dolls can be found. An average day on eBay will find over 100 collectibles listed when searching the Nurse category. The more modern the doll, the more complete it has to be — including all accessories. Look for costuming that has added details and for dolls that are clean, bright, tagged, boxed, or labeled.

11" bisque Kestner, mold 154, dolly face, marked "154 DEP," blue sleep eyes, open mouth/two teeth, blond mohair wig, plaster pate, kid body, original costume includes lace trimmed drawers, matching petticoat, pink dress, lace lower sleeves, attached lace apron, white batiste cap, black velvet ribbon on apron and around neck, brown leather shoes, pinned into bodice is gold colored heart shaped medallion with the Lord's Prayer, circa 1897, $400.00. *Courtesy Michele Simpson.*

11" bisque Kimcraft Nurse, possibly Florence Nightingale, painted features, painted gray hair, cloth body, label sewn on black satin undershirt reads "KIMCRAFT//AMERICAN TYPE DOLLS//INDEPENDENCE, MO," painted shoes with plain uppers and black heels, off-white pantaloons trimmed with lace, black taffeta blouse and shirt, lace around head forms bonnet, lace collar, oval black bead, black chiffon shawl, circa 1940s – 1950s, $50.00. *Courtesy Michele Simpson.*

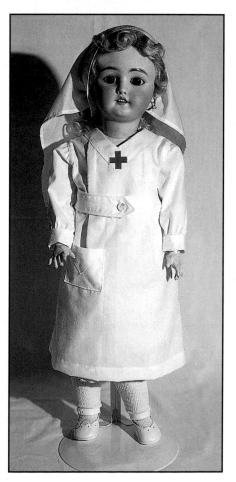

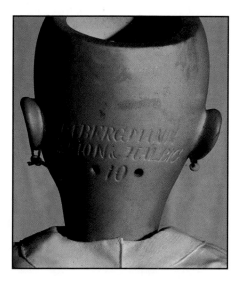

22½" bisque girl, marked "C.M.Bergman//Simon & Halbig//10," brown sleep eyes, painted upper and lower lashes, open mouth with four teeth, dimpled chin, blond mohair wig, pierced ears, ball-jointed composition body, re-dressed by Michele Simpson, circa 1898, $600.00. *Courtesy Michele Simpson.*

Nurse Dolls

22" bisque Armand Marseille mold 370 dolly face, marked "370 DEP," blue sleep eyes, open mouth with four upper teeth, dark blond wig, re-dressed, circa 1900, $475.00.
Courtesy Michele Simpson.

16½" cloth, unmarked, embroidered facial features, base of hair is black stockinet with black wool floss hair, hand-stitched uniform, undershirt is made from old ribbed stocking and edged at top with silk ribbon, dark blue/gray chambray dress, white percale or batiste pinafore with faded red silk cross ribbon stitched on bodice, oilcloth collar, circa 1900+, $750.00.
Courtesy Michele Simpson.

17" bisque Schoenau & Hoffmeister dolly face, marked "S(star)H// 1909//0," blue sleep eyes, open mouth with four teeth, painted upper and lower lashes, high cheek color, dimpled chin, brown human hair wig, composition ball-jointed body, original nurse outfit, lace edged batiste pantaloons and petticoat with lace insertion and lace edging at hem, gauze chemise, blue chambray dress, detachable white cuffs and collar, apron, white cap, circa 1909, $350.00.
Courtesy Michele Simpson.

24" bisque marked "Heinrich Handwerck//Simon & Halbig//Germany" on head, dolly face, brown sleep eyes, painted upper and lower lashes, open mouth with four teeth, tongue, dimple in chin, brown human hair wig, original costume with pin on pocket that reads "GUILD OF ST RADECONDE FOR NURSES 1909," circa 1909, $875.00.
Courtesy Michele Simpson.

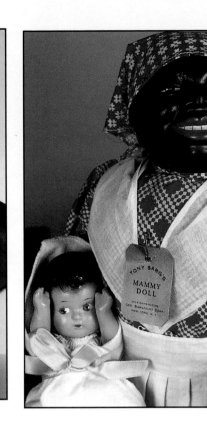

17" composition Tony Sarg's Mammy doll with white compo baby, tag reads "Tony Sarg's// Mammy Doll//Sole Distributors//Geo. Borgfeldt Corp.// New York N.Y," circa 1930s, $1,125.00.
Courtesy McMasters Doll Auctions.

14" cloth Molly'es Jane, an American Nurse, with hang tag marked "Made by Molly'es," painted blue eyes, blond mohair wig, cloth body, all original, circa 1930s, $300.00.
Courtesy Dee Cermak.

8½" composition Patsy-type with hang tag that reads "I am Edith, your Nurse," unmarked, painted features, legs molded to body, similar dolls with hang tags in ethnic costume were sold at the 1939 World's Fair, $90.00.
Courtesy Peggy Millhouse.

10" composition unmarked Patsy-type, painted eyes, wavy molded hair, paper note pinned on uniform says "Student Nurse at LA General Hospital//Presented by Sarah Mowatt," circa 1930s, $175.00.
Courtesy Michele Simpson.

Nurse Dolls

14" composition Madame Alexander Dr. Dafoe, painted eyes, tagged suit, hat, circa 1937 – 1939, $1,400.00; 13" composition Madame Alexander Nurse, tagged dress, cap, circa 1936 – 1937, $875.00. *Courtesy McMasters Doll Auctions.*

9" composition Freundlich nurse and 6½" quintuplets in suitcase box, with extra outfits, advertised Nov. 1935 in *Playthings* magazine with extra dress, socks, bottles, $1,000.00. *Courtesy Donna Hadley.*

16½" wax over porcelain mannequin, unmarked, painted side-glancing eyes, closed mouth, porcelain upper torso and hands, cloth upper arms, lampshade like wire frame covered with black glazed cotton slip from waist down to support skirt, uniform is black silk foulard with white organdy cap, collar and cuffs, straight pin with white glass head to simulate nurse pin, at center of collar there is a serrated edged sequin with a bead in the center, circa 1930s, $175.00. *Courtesy Michele Simpson.*

13" composition Madame Alexander Nurse, blue tin eyes, closed mouth, auburn wig, dress with cloth tag, "Madame /Alexander/NY," all original with original box, circa 1935. *Courtesy Sherryl Shirran.*

244

19" composition Patsy-type, unmarked, brown sleep eyes, open mouth with teeth, dimples, cap with red cross, red and blue cape, red cross hang tag, white socks and shoes, all original, circa 1941 – 1943, $300.00.
Private collection.

10" composition, Arranbee Debu' Teen look-a-like, painted blue eyes, closed mouth, auburn mohair wig, clothes not stapled, original blue nurse uniform with white apron and hat, circa 1941 – 1945, $125.00.
Courtesy Peggy Millhouse.

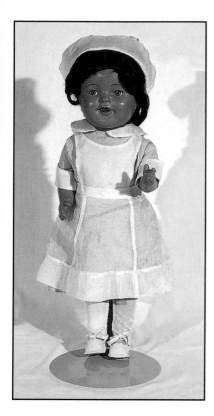

17½" composition unmarked black Shirley Temple-type, sleep eyes, auburn upper lashes, open mouth with four teeth, felt tongue, molded hair with black mohair wig, composition fixed head and shoulder plate, cloth gauze body, original uniform is pale blue-gray silk, cotton cap, collar, cuffs, and pinafore, petticoat, replaced shoes, circa 1940s, $425.00.
Courtesy Michele Simpson.

16" cloth Mollye-type, painted mask face, painted brown side-glancing eyes, closed mouth, rosy cheeks, yellow yarn hair, white dress, apron, and cap, red felt cross on dress and cap, "American" paper label is pinned on sleeve, all original, circa 1940s, $175.00.
Courtesy Michele Simpson.

Nurse Dolls

6½" celluloid unknown French Red Cross nurse with tent and cot, painted blue eyes, blond mohair wig, jointed at shoulders and hips, shoes and socks are painted on, nurse uniform is glued on, red pup tent and cot have vinyl coated wire frame, cot has green cloth with red vinyl blow-up air mattress, green cardboard platform, purchased at Paris flea market in 1994, circa 1940s – 1950s, $65.00.
Courtesy Michele Simpson.

7½" hard plastic, unmarked, pale brown flutter eyes, closed mouth, blond mohair wig, sewn on costume includes eyelet bloomers, removable white plastic shoes, originally had something glued in right hand, circa 1950s, $50.00.
Courtesy Michele Simpson.

19½" hard plastic display doll, bright painted face, molded in one piece with feet that fit onto a wood base, one hand on hip, dressed in white nurse attire — uniform, stockings, shoes and cap, marked "Miss Curity" on hat and dress breast pocket, originally offered to stores selling Curity products, circa 1950s, $75.00.
Courtesy Michele Simpson.

7½" hard plastic Little Nurse Doll Co., mohair wig, sleep eyes, molded painted shoes and socks, original white dress and cap, in box marked, "An Authentic//Little Nurse Doll//Custom Designed and Hand Dressed//For this Hospital//By The//Little Nurse Doll Company//Cedar Rapids, Iowa," circa 1950s+, $75.00.
Courtesy Kris Panacy.

7½" hard plastic Ideal Miss Curity dressed in plastic nurses uniform, with cap reading "Miss Curity" in blue letters, no other marks, sleep eyes, closed mouth, molded painted white shoes and socks, circa 1953, $65.00.
Courtesy Pam Martinec.

14" all hard plastic Ideal Miss Curity, blue sleep eyes, five-piece body, includes play nurse kit, tagged nurse uniform, unplayed with condition in original box, circa 1953, $650.00.
Courtesy McMasters Doll Auctions.

8" hard plastic Vogue Ginny painted lash walker, #31 Nurse, Rain or Shine Series, blue eyes, red hair, nurse's uniform, wrist tag reads "Hi, I'm Ginny," circa 1954, $300.00+.
Courtesy Peggy Millhouse.

7½" hard plastic Ideal Miss Curity dolls, unmarked, blond wigs, sleep eyes (second from left has painted eyes), painted eyelashes, molded and painted shoes/stockings, white nurse's outfits, cap: "Miss Curity," circa 1953, $85.00 ea.
Courtesy Peggy Millhouse.

11½" vinyl Mattel Twist 'n Turn Julia, near mint in box, circa 1969, $165.00.
Courtesy McMasters Doll Auctions.

8" hard plastic Vogue Ginny walker, sleep eyes, closed mouth, long blond braided wig, marked: "Vogue Doll//Inc.// Pat. No. 2687594//Made in USA," circa 1955, $175.00.
Courtesy Lilian Booth.

22" vinyl Deluxe Reading, blue sleep eyes, real lashes above, closed mouth, rosy cheeks, rooted blond hair, stuffed vinyl body, flat feet, in original nurse's outfit with red heart buttons, includes cape and hat, circa 1958, $75.00.
Courtesy Bertha Melendez.

9½" vinyl Reliable Toy Co., Canadian, GK22, blue sleep eyes, closed mouth, rooted dark brown hair, hard plastic body, jointed hips, shoulders, and neck, original Kehagias-Reliable hang tag, circa 1986, $50.00.
Courtesy Peggy Millhouse.

20" cloth, hang tag reads "Lloyderson Dolls: A Joy Forever//Made by Lloyderson Dolls//a division of Lloyderson International LTD," painted mask face with glued on plastic blue eyes, stockinet head and arms, auburn wig, cloth body and legs, felt red cross on blue cape, pinafore and cap, black socks and vinyl shoes, circa 1984, $40.00.
Courtesy Michele Simpson.

8½" porcelain Irish Si-og Doll Florrie Kind Hearted, by Marie Enright, Rathkeale, Co. Limerick, Ireland, marked "N98 F007," the word Si-og means the little Irish people, circa 1998, $60.00.
Courtesy Michele Simpson.

22" cloth Cabbage Patch Kid Nurse Payne, the Professional Camp Nurse, an Edition Within An Edition for Camp Cabbage 1991 Conventioneers, from the Garnet Edition of original Cabbage Patch Kids, born April 24, 1991, with blond kinky yarn hair, blue appliquéd eyes, blue polished cotton uniform, white apron with exclusive peach logo, blue cape, nurse's cap, diaper, tights, shoes with logo on left sole, white plastic Band-Aid box on rope with accessories, circa 1991, $300.00.
Courtesy Michele Simpson.

12½" porcelain Danbury Mint Red Cross Volunteer Nurse with dog by Norman Rockwell from *Life* magazine September 21, 1918, porcelain head, feet, and hands on wire framed cloth body, auburn braided hair, white and orange costume, black dog has matching coat, nurse can hold wooden collection box, circa 1980s, $80.00.
Courtesy Michele Simpson.

Old Cottage Toys

This firm was founded in 1948 by Mrs. Margaret. E. Fleischmann, who fled to England from her native Czechoslovakia during the war years. Mrs. Fleischmann made dolls for her daughter Suzanne and then for sale. The heads are made of a hard composition/hard plastic type material, with bodies of felt over padded wire armature. The features are molded and painted with mohair wigs. Fleischmann registered her trademark in 1948. The dolls have an oval paper hang tag with a cottage picured on one side and marked *Old Cottage Doll Made in England* on the other. They made historical figures, literary figures, and English policemen, guards, and pearly figures. In 1968 she made Tweedledee and Tweedledum for a B.B.C. production of Lewis Carrol's *Through the Looking-Glass*.

What to look for:

This category of dolls is currently sought after, very collectible, and rising in value. Most desired are the literary characters, pearly dolls, and dolls with added detail. Finding Tweedledee or Tweedledum in a box would be very lucky. Dolls should be clean, tagged, and original to command highest prices.

10" composition, painted blue eyes, reddish wig, dressed in elaborate wine court costume with ruffled collar, matching beaded wine hat, circa 1960s, $165.00.

Courtesy Elizabeth Surber.

9" composition, painted eyes, eyeshadow, closed mouth, platinum wig, stuffed felt body, mitt hands, original boy's court costume of white satin, walking stick, has Old Cottage Doll oval tag with house logo, circa 1960s, $175.00.

Courtesy Dorothy Bohlin.

9" composition Pearlie, painted blue eyes, closed mouth, blond mohair wig, felt body, black felt jacket and hat covered with buttons, gray felt pants covered with buttons, circa 1960s, $125.00+.
Courtesy Marilyn Nielsen.

8" composition Elizabethan Lady in black costume with fur trim, gold turban headdress, hang tag reads "Old Cottage Toys/ /Hand Made in Great Britain," circa 1950, $135.00.
Courtesy Sondra Gast.

8"composition Elizabethan Lady in red and white elaborate costume with black trim, hang tag reads "Old Cottage Toys// Made in Great Britain," circa 1950, $135.00.
Courtesy Sondra Gast.

9½" composition, cloth body, hang tag reads
"Old Cottage Doll, made in England,"
tagged "J.B. Altman," circa 1960s, $125.00.
Courtesy Peggy Millhouse.

9" composition, painted eyes, closed
mouth, platinum wig with floral decoration, stuffed felt body, mitt hands,
original costume of blue, pink with
white quilted skirt, has Old Cottage
Doll oval tag with house logo, circa
1960s, $165.00.
Courtesy Dorothy Bohlin.

Quintuplets

Alexander Doll Co. won the license to produce the official Dionne quintuplet dolls after the girls' birth in 1934 to a Canadian farm couple. Designed by Bernard Lipfert, they were all composition with painted eyes, molded hair, and jointed baby bodies. They were also made as toddlers in different sizes. Not to be outdone, other companies came out with their own sets of five babies to try to capitalize on the buying frenzy. Quint collectors have their own newsletter and collect all sorts of related memorabilia as well as the dolls. See Collectors' Network for information on the *Quint News*.

What to look for:

Dolls should be clean, bright, with good color and original clothing. Look for dolls other than Alexanders, as other companies made dolls to compete with the licensee. Other Quints should not be priced as high as Alexanders.

8" composition Madame Alexander Dionne Quintuplets, marked "Alexander" on backs, painted side-glancing eyes, closed mouths, mohair wigs, tagged cotton flowered outfits and hats, circa 1935 – 1939, set of babies, $500.00, set of toddlers, $700.00.
Courtesy Louise Williams.

11" composition Madame Alexander Dionne Quint Marie, brown sleep eyes, closed mouth, brown wig, composition toddler body, dress with matching bonnet, Marie pin, hang tag, all original with box, circa 1937 – 1938, $400.00.
Courtesy Martha Sweeney.

Quintuplets

11" composition Madame Alexander Dionne Quintuplets Emelie, molded painted hair, brown sleep eyes, white baby dress, booties, lavender trim/name embroidered on bib, mint in box, circa 1936, $750.00 each, $4,250.00 for Dionne Quintuplets set with Dr. and Nurse, both re-dressed.
Courtesy Sharon Kolibaba.

11" composition Madame Alexander Dionne Quintuplets Marie, molded painted hair, brown sleep eyes, white baby dress, booties, blue trim/name embroidered on bib, mint in box, circa 1936, $750.00 each, $4,250.00 for Dionne Quintuplets set with Dr. and Nurse, both re-dressed.
Courtesy Sharon Kolibaba.

7" hard plastic Madame Alexander Fischer Quints, used Little Genius doll, blue sleep eyes, molded/painted hair, vinyl body, one boy, four girls, in picture box with pink blanket/bottles, circa 1964, $360.00.
Courtesy McMasters Doll Auctions.

8" composition Madame Alexander Dionne Quintuplet Toddlers, marked "Alexander" on heads, painted brown side-glancing eyes, closed mouths, molded painted hair, five-piece composition toddler bodies, original tagged dresses in five pastel colors, matching bonnets, white leatherette shoes, circa 1935 – 1939, $1,900.00; 14" composition Alexander Dr. Dafoe, painted blue eyes, closed mouth, gray mohair wig, tagged doctor clothing, original box, circa 1937 – 1939, $1,300.00.
Courtesy McMasters Doll Auctions.

Raggedy Ann & Andy

Raggedy Ann and Andy were designed by Johnny Gruelle in 1915, and made by various companies. Ann wears a dress with an apron, Andy a shirt and pants with matching hat.

P.J. Volland, 1920 – 34

Early dolls marked *Patented Sept. 7, 1915.* All-cloth, tin or wooden button eyes, painted features. Some have sewn knee or arm joints, brown or auburn sparse yarn hair, oversize hands, feet turned outward.

Mollye Goldman, 1935 – 38

Marked on chest: *Raggedy Ann and Andy Dolls Manufactured by Mollye's Doll Outfitters.* Nose outlined in black, red heart on chest, reddish orange hair, multicolored legs, blue feet, some have oil cloth faces.

Georgene Novelties, 1938 – 62

Ann has orange hair and a top knot, six different mouth styles, early dolls had tin eyes, later plastic, six different noses, seams in middle of legs and arms to represent knees and elbows, feet turn forward, red and white striped legs. All have hearts that say *I love you* printed on chest. Tag sewn to left side seam, several variations, all say *Georgene Novelties, Inc.*

Knickerbocker, 1962 – 82

Printed features, hair color changes from orange to red; there were five mouth and five eyelash variations, tags were located on clothing back or pant seam.

Applause Toy Company, 1981 – 83

Hasbro (Playskool) 1983+

Raggedy Ann storybooks and dolls remain a favorite with doll collectors. They too, have a newsletter *Rags* devoted to collectors, see Collector's Network for more ins

What to look for:

Dolls that are clean, no rips or tears, original clothing, tags, or labels. Raggedy Ann was so loved that many are too worn to collect, but they are still available and eagerly sought by collectors.

18" cloth P.F. Volland Pirate Chieftain, button eyes, yarn hair and beard, pink felt coat, black belt, purple short pants, striped legs, gold boots, white felt gloves, skull and crossbones on hat, buckle on shoe, tagged: "Made in U.S.A. — The P.F. Volland Company Joliet.// I am a Volland Doll My name is Pirate Chieftain You can read about me in a book called *The Camel with the Wrinkled Knees*," circa 1920 – 1934, $2,500.00.

Courtesy Roberta Hale.

Bernard & Frances Ravca

Bernard Ravca was born in Paris in 1904. He was touring the United States when Germany invaded his country. Ravca, who had already won prizes for his life-size dolls in the 1930s, remained in the U.S. He met and later married Frances Diecks, becoming a citizen of the U.S. Ravca and his wife work primarily in cloth, first making French ethnic type characters and later expanding their lines. They traveled the world lecturing and displaying their dolls and had a museum at one time. They were members of NIADA, and were called sculptors in cotton.

17½" cloth old man with cane, painted features, mohair wig, unjointed body, checked shirt, plaid vest, brown striped trousers, brown hat, wooden shoes, circa late 1930s to 1955, $250.00.
Courtesy Sharon Kolibaba.

17½" cloth old woman with knitting in hands, painted features, mohair wig, unjointed body, green print blouse, plaid skirt/checked apron, red scarf on head, wooden shoes, circa late 1930s to 1955, $250.00.
Courtesy Nelda Shelton.

9" cloth Benjamin Franklin, tagged "Bernard Ravca//Benjamin Franklin," sculptured stockinette face, painted side-glancing eyes, cloth Constitution rolled up under arm, brown felt coat and short pants, red stockings, red vest, pilgrim shoes, glasses, white gloves, circa 1930s, $250.00.
Courtesy Nelda Shelton.

9" cloth Sam Houston, tagged "Sam Houston," sculptured stockinette face, cloth over wire arms, full fingers, blue wool suit, circa 1930s, $250.00.
Courtesy Nelda Shelton.

Bernard & Frances Ravca

9" cloth General Lee, tagged "Bernard Ravca //General Lee," sculptured stockinette face, blue eyes, beard, full fingers, gray felt uniform and hat, circa 1930s, $250.00.
Courtesy Nelda Shelton.

9" composition Mussolini, tagged "Bernard Ravca//Mussolini," molded painted face, full fingers, cloth body, gray wool uniform, black hat, black leather boots, circa 1930s, $1,300.00.
Courtesy Nelda Shelton.

Bernard & Frances Ravca

9" cloth Scarlett, tagged "Bernard Ravca//Scarlett," sculptured stockinette face, side-glancing eyes, smiling mouth, unusual hands and fingers, flowered long dress and straw bonnet, circa 1930s, $225.00.
Courtesy Nelda Shelton.

9" cloth Rhett Butler, tagged "Bernard Ravca//Rhett," sculptured stockinette face, painted eyes, thick eyebrows, black mustache, cloth body, gray felt suit, blue vest, white shirt, polka dot tie, circa 1930s, $225.00.
Courtesy Nelda Shelton.

8" cloth Martha Washington, tagged "Bernard Ravca//Martha Washington," sculptured stockinette face, blond hair, cloth over wire arms, unusual hands, green dress, net shawl, white cap, circa 1930s, $250.00.
Courtesy Nelda Shelton.

Remco

Remco Industries Inc. was founded by Sol Robbins in the 1960s. They made television promotional dolls and advertised heavily on television. The company was later bought by Roth American, but closed in January 1974. The Playcraft Toys Inc. of Canada made some dolls under a license agreement with Remco. Some of their better known dolls include Littlechap Family, Heidi, and the Beatles.

14½" vinyl Remco Littlechap Family, set of four, 14½" Dr. John, 13½" Lisa, 12" Judy, and 10½" Libby, jointed hips, shoulders, and neck, painted eyes, closed mouths, brown wigs on Lisa, Judy, and Libby, molded painted black hair on Dr. John, rare set complete with brochures, mint in box, circa 1963, $325.00.
Courtesy June Allgeier.

4½" vinyl Beatles, Paul McCartney, John Lennon, George Harrison, and Ringo
Starr, synthetic dark wigs, painted molded features, open/closed mouths with
teeth, have oversize heads, rigid vinyl bodies with molded black suits, shoes,
Paul McCartney is larger at 4⅞" tall, plastic guitars have name of individual
members, circa 1964, $105.00 for single figure, $400.00 for set.
Courtesy Sarah Munsey.

5½" vinyl Heidi and friends, left to right: Heidi, Jan Oriental, Heidi, painted side-
glancing eyes, open/closed mouth, rooted hair, all vinyl, press button and dolls
wave, all in original plastic carrying cases, circa 1967, $40.00 each.
Courtesy Leslie Tannenbaum.

Richwood

Richwood Toys, Inc., was located in Annapolis, Maryland. Sandra Sue was produced from the late 1940s through the 1950s. The only marks are numbers under her arm or leg. Sandra Sue was a high quality doll, similar to others produced at this time, but with more attributes than most.

Sandra Sue had sleep eyes with molded lashes, closed mouth, jointed arms and legs. She was made as a walker and non-walker, and had an extensive wardrobe available for her as well as a line of furniture. She had saran wigs and a suggestion of a fashion body with gently molded breasts and a slimmer waist. She was modeled with both flat and high-heel feet. One tip for identification is dark orange painted eyebrows and painted lashes below eyes. The hands are formed with fingers together, separate thumbs, and the palms face in to the body. Her head did not turn when she walked.

Sandra Sue's wardrobe would be the envy of many of the contemporary dolls. It included evening and bridal gowns, sports wear such as ski apparel and skating costumes, skirts and blouses, dresses and hats, coat and dress ensembles with accessories, daytime dresses, and more.

What to look for:

Although she is often dismissed as one of the little hard plastic dolls readily available, you should check your garage sales for Sandra Sue, and her collectible wardrobe. Dolls should be clean, have original clothing, and good facial coloring. Her original box is easily recognizable with a silhouette in an oval and her name marked on top.

8" hard plastic Sandra Sue, sleep eyes, reddish-blond saran wig, flat feet, in red and white striped dress with red rickrack, red hat, red shoes, hang tag and curlers, circa 1952 – 1958, $200.00.
Courtesy Peggy Millhouse.

Five 8" hard plastic Sandra Sue Ballerinas, left two are early Dress Me Dolls dressed by Ida Wood, founder; next two are flat foot, far right is high heeled, circa 1947 – 1958, $125.00 each.
Courtesy Peggy Millhouse.

Five 8" hard plastic Sandra Sue dolls with sleep eyes, saran wigs, all high heel, all dressed in original outfits, circa 1950s, school dress, $175.00; party dress or formal, $200.00.
Courtesy Peggy Millhouse.

Roldan

Roldan Characters are similar to Klumpe figures in many respects. They were made in Barcelona, Spain, from the early 1960s until the mid 1970s. They are made of felt over a wire armature, with painted mask faces. Like Klumpe, Roldan figures represent professionals, hobbyists, dancers, historical characters, and contemporary males and females performing a wide variety of tasks. Some, but not all Roldans, were imported by Rosenfeld Imports and Leora Dolores of Hollywood. Figures originally came with two sewn on, identifying cardboard tags. Roldan characters most commonly found are doctors, Spanish dancers, and bullfighters. Roldan characters tend to have somewhat smaller heads, longer necks, and more defined facial features than Klumpe.

What to look for:

Look for bright and clean doll tags; the more accessories, the more collectible these whimsical characters are.

10½" Caribbean Dancer in white and green trim Carmen Miranda type outfit, with red shoes, holds castanets, paper label "Roldan/ Barcelona — Espana," circa 1960, $100.00.

Courtesy Sondra Gast.

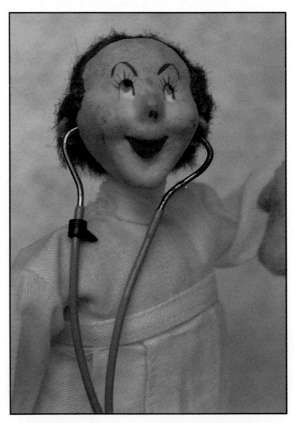

10½" felt over armature mask face Roldan-type doctor, painted blue eyes, painted features, doctors outfit, red plaid pants, stethoscope, black shoes, watch, circa 1960s, $95.00.

Private collection.

Shirley Temple

In 1934, after Shirley Temple stole the show with her performance in *Stand Up and Cheer,* Ideal gained the license to produce Shirley Temple dolls, hired Bernard Lipfert to sculpt a prototype, cast her in composition, and soon had Shirley Temple dolls in red and white polka dotted dresses on the market. The costumes were designed by Mollye Goldman from 1934 to 1936, and show the NRA markings on their labels. The costumes were sold separately as well as with the doll. The composition dolls had sleep eyes, with some flirty eyes, open mouth with six upper teeth, multi-stroke eyebrows, a five-piece jointed body, mohair wig, and soon came in a range of sizes from 11" to 27". The first dolls were packaged with a pinback button and signed photograph. Marked on the head and/or torso, was *SHIRLEY TEMPLE//IDEAL NOV. & TOY CO.* with *SHIRLEY TEMPLE* on the body. In late 1935, a Shirley Temple Baby was introduced followed by baby carriages and accessories. The Shirley Temple dolls were popular through the early 1940s, declining when Shirley reached adolescence.

In 1957, Ideal reissued a vinyl 12" Shirley to coincide with the release of her movies to television audiences and as Temple started her own television series. They have plastic script pins and paper hang tags. In the 1960s, 15", 17", and 19" vinyl dolls were issued. In 1972, Montgomery Wards, to celebrate its 100th anniversary, issued a 15" vinyl Shirley Temple. In 1982, Ideal made 8" and 12" Shirley Temple dolls costumed as *Heidi, Stowaway, Stand Up and Cheer, The Little Colonel, Captain January,* and *The Littlest Rebel.* Danbury Mint has made more recent Shirley Temple dolls, including porcelain 20" dolls designed by Elke Hutchens and costumed from movies. See Collectors' Network for information on several Shirley Temple publications and groups.

What to look for:

Composition Shirley Temples are difficult to find in excellent condition because the painted finish crazes, and so those in very good condition have risen drastically in price. Collectors may wish to search for the vinyl and newer dolls as they, too, will eventually become collectible. Check composition dolls for crazing, vinyls should have good color, and clothing should be clean and bright. Shirley collectors like all Shirley Temple related items such as marked products, paper, and advertising.

Composition

27" Ideal Shirley Temple Baby, flirty green eyes, painted hair, open mouth with two upper and three lower teeth, cloth body with crier, baby dress and matching bonnet, circa 1935, $2,500.00.
Courtesy Martha Sweeney.

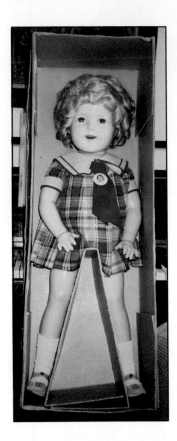

27" Ideal Shirley Temple, mint in box with plaid Bright Eyes dress, pin, flirty eyes, mohair wig, marked "Shirley Temple" on head and torso, dress tagged "Shirley Temple," circa 1934, $2,000.00.
Courtesy Sally DeSmet.

18" Ideal Shirley Temple, marked "18//Shirley Temple// COP//Ideal N.& T. Co." on head, green sleep eyes, open mouth with teeth, dimples, mohair wig, red print dress with white collar similar to style worn in *Captain January*, circa 1936+, $850.00.
Courtesy Iva Mae Jones.

11" Ideal Shirley Temple, in blue dot Curly Top costume, sleep eyes, dimples in cheeks, open mouth with teeth, composition jointed body, center snap shoes, mint in box, circa 1935, $1,950.00.
Courtesy Sally DeSmet.

13" Ideal Shirley Temple, sleep eyes, open mouth with teeth, dimples, curly mohair wig, composition jointed body, in tagged Curly Top pink knife-pleated organdy dress with blue ribbon trim, Shirley Temple pin, white center snap shoes, all original, circa 1935, $1,200.00.
Courtesy Leslie Tannenbaum.

13" Reliable Toy Co. Shirley Temple from Littlest Rebel, marked "SHIRLEY TEMPLE//Cop. Ideal N & T Co." on head, flirty sleep eyes, open mouth with teeth, curly mohair wig, original dress tag reads "A GENUINE//SHIRLEY TEMPLE//DOLL DRESS//RELIABLE TOY CO. LTD//MADE IN CANADA," pin reads "The World's Darling//Genuine Shirley Temple//A Reliable Doll," original cardboard store tag, mint in box, circa 1934+, $3,000.00+.
Courtesy Rachel Quigley.

13" Ideal Shirley Temple in Little Colonel outfit, green sleep eyes, open mouth, teeth, dimples in cheeks, mohair wig, jointed composition body, all original outfit with Shirley Temple pin, circa 1934+, $700.00.
Courtesy Martha Sweeney.

18" Ideal Shirley Temple in rare tagged military style yellow and brown dress from 1935 20th Century Fox film *Little Colonel* complete with matching brown and yellow hat, and pinback button, center snap shoes, $2,500.00+.
Courtesy Rosemary Dent.

16" Ideal Shirley Temple in tagged original pink organdy Little Colonel dress from the 20th Century Fox film of the same name, complete with matching hat and pinback button, circa 1935, $1,600.00.
Courtesy Rosemary Dent.

13" Ideal Shirley Temple, sleep eyes, open mouth with teeth, dimples, curly mohair wig, composition jointed body, in tagged Our Little Girl royal blue music note dress all original, circa 1935, $500.00.
Courtesy Leslie Tannenbaum.

16" Ideal Shirley Temple in tagged Littlest Rebel red print all original costume from the 1935 20th Century Fox film of the same name, complete with cap, and long pantaloon, center snap leatherette shoes, and pinback button, $1,500.00.
Courtesy Rosemary Dent.

22" Ideal Shirley Temple, marked on back and on head, green sleep eyes, open mouth with teeth, dimples in cheeks, curly mohair wig, jointed body, Poor Little Rich Girl blue dress with white collar and cuffs, center snap shoes, circa 1936+, $950.00.
Courtesy Martha Sweeney.

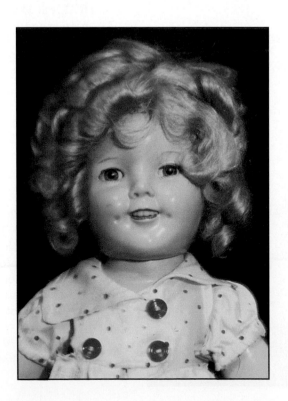

18" composition Ideal Shirley Temple, hazel sleep eyes, open mouth with teeth, gold mohair wig, dressed in silk pajamas from *Poor Little Rich Girl*, pajamas have tiny flocked red polka dots and red plastic buttons, red ribbon in hair, all original, circa 1936, $850.00.
Courtesy Martha Sweeney.

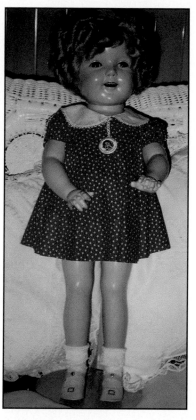

Left, 27" and right, 25" Ideal Shirley Temple dolls, marked "SHIRLEY TEMPLE//COP. IDEAL N & T CO." on head and "SHIRLEY TEMPLE" on body, flirty sleep eyes, open mouth with teeth, curly mohair wig, tagged blue floral print dresses similar to styles from *Poor Little Rich Girl*, circa 1936+, left – $2,200.00, right – $1,300.00.
Courtesy Rachel Quigley.

27" Ideal Shirley Temple marked "Shirley Temple//COP// Ideal N.&T. Co.," green sleep eyes, open mouth with teeth, mohair wig, red dress with white collar and white stars similar to styles worn in *Poor Little Rich Girl*, Shirley Temple pin, circa 1936+, $1,800.00.
Courtesy Iva Mae Jones.

11" Ideal Shirley Temple Texas Rangerette, designed for the 1936 Texas Centennial Celebration, tin eyes, open mouth with teeth, mohair wig, all original, circa 1936, $900.00.
Courtesy Myrna McDaniel.

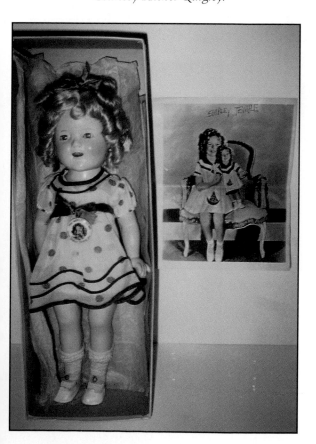

17" Ideal Shirley Temple in Stand Up and Cheer outfit, marked "Cop. Ideal N&T Co." on head, sleep eyes, open mouth with teeth, dimples, curly mohair wig, all original blue-and-white dot costume with box, circa 1934, $1,500.00.
Courtesy Rachel Quigley.

Shirley Temple

25" Ideal Shirley Temple marked "SHIRLEY TEMPLE//COP IDEAL N&T CO." on head and "SHIRLEY TEMPLE" on body, flirty eyes, dressed in rare blue outfit from *Wee Willie Winkie*, circa 1937, $3,500.00.
Courtesy Rachel Quigley.

27" Ideal Shirley Temple Texas Rangerette, green sleep eyes, open mouth with teeth, dimples in cheeks, curly mohair wig, jointed body, all original in mint condition, circa 1936, $1,600.00.
Courtesy Martha Sweeney.

18" Ideal Shirley Temple, green sleep eyes, dimples in cheeks, open mouth with teeth, mohair wig, jointed body, in original Molly'es plaid rain cape with umbrella and original pin, replaced socks and shoes, circa 1934, $750.00.
Courtesy Marki Mohr.

20" Ideal Shirley Temple prototype doll, unmarked except for paper sticker in head, green sleep eyes, open mouth, teeth, dimples in cheeks, mohair wig, jointed composition body, center snap shoes, original dress tagged "Macy's" and matching hat, circa 1934, $900.00.
Courtesy Martha Sweeney.

13" unknown German Shirley Temple marked "S.T.//Germany," sleep eyes, open mouth with teeth, curly wig, wearing red tagged pajamas, mint, circa 1930s, $700.00.
Courtesy Martha Sweeney.

18" Ideal Shirley Temple marked "SHIRLEY TEMPLE// COP. IDEAL N & T CO." on head and "SHIRLEY TEMPLE" on body, sleep eyes, open mouth with teeth, curly mohair wig, wearing tagged riding outfit designed by Mollye, black jacket and pants, yellow shirt and hat, circa 1934+, $950.00.
Courtesy Rachel Quigley.

13" Ideal Shirley Temple marked "13//SHIRLEY TEMPLE" on head, sleep eyes, open mouth with teeth, dimples in cheeks, mohair wig, rare peach floral dress with pale blue ribbon, white center snap shoes, original box, circa 1934+, $825.00.
Courtesy Iva Mae Jones.

Left, 7" celluloid and right, 10" celluloid Shirley Temple types by unknown maker given at carnivals during the 1930s and early 1940s, painted features, molded painted hair, 7" – $200.00, 10" – $275.00.
Courtesy Martha Sweeney.

Shirley Temple

18" Ideal Marama, Ideal used the Shirley Temple mold for this doll representing a character from the movie *Hurricane*, painted side-glancing eyes, painted teeth, brown complexion, black yarn wig, wears grass skirt, Hawaiian costume, all original, circa 1940, $925.00.
Courtesy Martha Sweeney.

Vinyl

Two 12" Ideal Shirley Temple dolls, sleep eyes, open/closed mouth with painted teeth, dimples, rooted hair, both all original with name pin, doll on left is wearing Movie Classics Outfit #9560 Wee Willie Winkie, all original, circa 1960, $225.00; doll on right is wearing Movie Classics Outfit #9564 Captain January, all original in box, circa 1960, $300.00.
Courtesy Leslie Tannenbaum.

12" Ideal Shirley Temple marked "Ideal Doll//ST//12" on head, sleep eyes, synthetic rooted wig, open/closed mouth, teeth, original tagged dress is yellow trimmed with blue lace and ribbons, circa 1957, $225.00.
Courtesy Iva Mae Jones.

15" Ideal Shirley Temple in Heidi costume, with red skirt, marked on neck "ST 15 W" marked on back "Ideal Doll//ST 15" advertised as a "Storybook," circa 1961, with name purse and script pin, $325.00.
Courtesy Maria Traver.

272

15" Ideal Shirley Temple, sleep eyes, open/closed mouth with painted teeth, dimples, rooted hair, in blue print nylon dress with lace trim, black purse and name pin, mint in box, circa 1959 – 1963, $495.00.
Courtesy Leslie Tannenbaum.

17" Ideal Shirley Temple, sleep eyes, open/closed mouth with painted teeth, dimples, rooted hair, in nylon dress with ribbon and lace trim, purse and name pin, mint in box, circa 1959 – 1963, $475.00.
Courtesy Leslie Tannenbaum.

19" Ideal Shirley Temple Walker, sleep eyes, open/closed mouth with teeth, rooted hair, all original in white dress with red polka dots, white socks and shoes, circa 1959 – 1963, $450.00.
Courtesy Martha Sweeney.

Left, 19" Ideal Shirley Temple marked "IDEAL DOLLS//ST-19," flirty (twinkle) eyes, open/closed mouth, teeth, rooted hair, blue nylon lace trimmed dress, white nylon gloves, white socks and shoes, circa 1958 – 1961, $425.00; right, 17" vinyl Ideal Shirley Temple, marked "ST-17-1," sleep eyes, open mouth with teeth, rooted hair, pink lace trimmed nylon dress with blue puff sleeves and collar, hang tag, mint in box, circa 1958 – 1961, $450.00.
Courtesy Martha Sweeney.

Shirley Temple

Three 16" Danbury Mint Shirley Temple dolls, Heidi, Little Colonel, and Rebecca of Sunnybrook Farm, The Shirley Temple Collection sold exclusively at Target stores, all mint in box, circa 1996, $25.00 each.
Courtesy Leslie Tannenbaum.

36" Ideal Shirley Temple, Playpal body with jointed wrists, sleep eyes, open/closed mouth with painted teeth, rosy cheeks, dimples, yellow and white dress, black shoes, all original, circa 1960 – 1961, $2,000.00.
Courtesy Iva Mae Jones.

Porcelain

18" Danbury Mint Shirley Temple sculpted by doll artist Elke Hutchens, Salvation Army motif doll with kettle from a Christmas series, porcelain head, arms and legs, cloth body, circa 1996, $155.00.
Courtesy Marki Mohr.

Shirley Temple Accessories

1930s original doll hanger and tagged pink dress, circa 1930s, $85.00.
Courtesy Marki Mohr.

1930s Playhouse with standing Shirley Paper Doll and accessories. In the drawer are cut and uncut clothes and accessories along with the original box, circa 1935, $125.00.
Courtesy Marki Mohr.

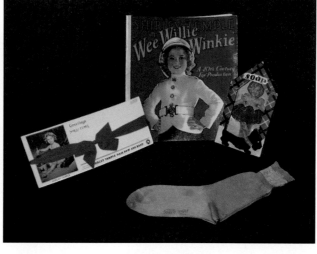

1930s original hair ribbon card with photo, Wee Willie Winkie Book, soap that had Wee Willie on the box (on dog collar), and a pair of socks with Authentic Shirley Temple Style printed on them and a price tag attached reading "Hoffmeyer's Newark, New York, 35¢, size 8," circa 1930s, $100.00.
Courtesy Marki Mohr.

Pink Plastic Ideal Tea Set, unusual because plates and saucers have flower design instead of usual Shirley Temple monogram, mint in box, circa 1959, $525.00.
*Courtesy
Leslie Tannenbaum.*

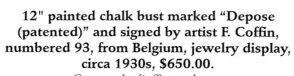

12" painted chalk bust marked "Depose (patented)" and signed by artist F. Coffin, numbered 93, from Belgium, jewelry display, circa 1930s, $650.00.
Courtesy Leslie Tannenbaum.

Terri Lee

Terri Lee was made from 1946 to 1962, in Lincoln, Nebraska, and Apple Valley, California. Dolls were first made of composition, then hard plastic and vinyl. They had closed pouty mouths, painted eyes, wigs, and jointed bodies. They were marked on torso, *TERRI LEE* and the early dolls were marked *PAT. PENDING*.

Recently the molds were acquired to remake Terri Lee dolls, but the company was barred from doing so by legal action from heirs of the founder. See Collectors' Network for more information on collector groups and the bibliography for additional resource material.

What to look for:

Composition dolls are hard to find in good condition as most have crazing in moderate to severe stages. Hard plastic dolls should be clean with rosy face color and original clothing when possible. Hair can be restyled and clothes made for nude dolls. Again a stable environment and cleanliness is needed to avoid deterioration of the plastic materials.

16" soft vinyl Terri Lee, painted brown eyes, closed mouth, auburn saran wig, stuffed vinyl body, original pink dress, circa 1950s, $200.00.
Private collection.

15½" hard plastic Terri Lee, marked "Terri Lee," brown painted eyes, closed pouty mouth, brown braided synthetic wig, jointed hard plastic body, tagged pink Terri Lee dress, pink plastic shoes, circa 1950s, $265.00. *Courtesy Nelda Shelton.*

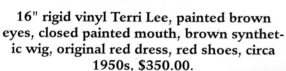

16" rigid vinyl Terri Lee, painted brown eyes, closed painted mouth, brown synthetic wig, original red dress, red shoes, circa 1950s, $350.00.
Private collection.

18" hard plastic Terri Lee Girl Scout, marked "Terri Lee" on back, painted brown eyes, closed mouth, dark brown synthetic wig in unusual style, with hair dress kit and booklet, official Girl Scout uniform, mint in box, circa 1950s, $600.00.
Courtesy Iva Mae Jones.

16" hard plastic Terri Lee, marked "Terri Lee," brown painted eyes, closed mouth, white wig, blue dress with blue checked pinafore, circa 1951+, $300.00.
Courtesy Nickie Maxwell.

10" all hard plastic Tiny Terri Lee, © on head and back, brown inset eyes, real lashes, closed mouth, five-piece body with walking mechanism, tagged long blue taffeta dress, net overlay, panties, white vinyl Cinderella shoes, original with red box marked "Tiny Terri Lee//Manufactured by Terri Lee//(R in circle)//Apple Valley, Calif.," circa 1955+, $255.00.
Courtesy McMasters Doll Auctions.

16" hard plastic Mary Jane, a Terri Lee look-alike, sleep eyes, molded eyelashes, closed mouth, dark brown wig, hard plastic walker, circa 1950s, $225.00.
Private collection.

Robert Tonner Doll Co.

The Robert Tonner Doll Company began in the early 1990s with multi-jointed porcelain fashions dolls, but hit the jackpot when he first licensed Betsy McCall and reproduced her in 14" vinyl. Betsy is reminiscent of the McCall paper doll from the 1950s and is available dressed or with additional outfits.

In 1999 he also produced a vinyl 10" Ann Estelle from the charming character created by Mary Englebreit. Ann Estelle has a blond Dutch bob, blue eyes, and comes dressed in her undies or a special costume. Additional wardrobe is available separately.

Tonner also introduced an 8" vinyl Kripplebush Kid with rooted hair and jointed arms and legs that makes a great travel doll.

Eagerly anticipated before its late 1999 introduction was Tonner's new 16" vinyl fashion doll, Tyler Wentworth. Tonner created a history for Tyler stating that from an early age she was destined to be a high flyer in the world of fashion. During the 1950s, Tyler's great-aunt, Regina Wentworth established the House of Wentworth in New York City and created innovative collections that set the standard for the 7th Avenue fashion design. Years later, Tyler, who had always loved the glamour and excitement of her great-aunt's business, joined the prestigious house's design staff. She proved to be exceptionally talented and it was not long until she was promoted to Regina's first assistant. With the House of Wentworth's reputation firmly established, Regina began to consider passing the reins to a new talent. Spurring her on was her relationship with Carlos, a young artist who had instantly fallen in love with the chic, elegant, older designer. Soon Regina made her decision to move with Carlos to the south of France and she turned the company over to

Tyler. Although young for the job, Tyler quickly showed that she was equal to her new responsibilities. With only a few short seasons of fashion experience, she confidently assumed leadership of the House of Wentworth and received rave reviews over her first collection.

What to look for:

Check eBay, Internet doll shops, doll magazines, and your local doll or gift shop for the latest releases. Limited edition special costumed dolls such as the Roy Rogers Betsy McCall produced for the first Betsy McCall convention or Ann Estelle produced for the UFDC luncheon are available on the secondary market and are increasing in price. Tonner dolls are fun to dress and play with — fun to collect.

10" vinyl Ann Estelle, style No. 99600, blue eyes, closed mouth, blond wig, gold rimmed eyeglasses, rigid vinyl body, basic doll comes in a blue dotted onesie trimmed in white lace, pink rosettes accent the neck and waistline, black shoes, white socks, 1999, $70.00.

Photo courtesy Robert Tonner Doll Company.

Robert Tonner Doll Co.

10" vinyl Ann Estelle style No. 99600, dressed in style No. 99069 May Flowers, blue cherry print overalls, piped in red and white stripes, cotton blouse with zigzag embroidery at the collar and cuffs, bead cherries at the neck, wide brimmed straw hat, hand-painted watering can, 1999, basic doll $70.00, costume $35.00.

Photo courtesy Robert Tonner Doll Company.

10" vinyl Robert Tonner Ann Estelle in Classic Sailor, style No. 99601, white cotton midi top with wide blue collar, red striped inset, red knotted scarf, plaid box pleat skirt, carries a bouquet of flowers matching flowers on hat, straw hat with blue and white polka dot ribbon and flowers, doll and costume, 1999, $70.00.

Photo courtesy Robert Tonner Doll Company.

10" vinyl Ann Estelle, style No. 99600, dressed in style No. 99608 Flower Girl Duty, blush pink seersucker dress, white eyelet overskirt, cuffs and neckline are trimmed with dainty silk flowers, shiny pink satin sash, carries flowers caught up with yellow polka dot ribbon, 1999, basic doll $69.00, costume $35.00.

Photo courtesy Robert Tonner Doll Company.

10" vinyl Ann Estelle in May Day Suit, style No. 99604, butter-colored felt hat and jacket, shiny pearl buttons, sage green scalloped embroidery, underneath is a sleeveless cream shell, dainty pleated skirt, gloves, shoes, pansy corsage, basket of pansies, doll and costume, 1999, $70.00.

Photo courtesy Robert Tonner Doll Company.

10" vinyl Ann Estelle, style No. 99600, dressed in style No. 99606 Thanksgiving Frock, wheat printed dress, trimmed in green rickrack, hemmed with embroidery under a green plaid jumper, jumper is trimmed in green rickrack also, green plaid hairbow, black Mary Janes, 1999, basic doll $70.00, costume $35.00.

Photo courtesy Robert Tonner Doll Company.

8" vinyl Kripplebush Kid Eliza, glass eyes, closed mouth, red wig, marked "Tonner" on back, in denim jumper with striped shirt and leotards, 1998, $55.00 retail.

Courtesy Bev Mitchell.

10" vinyl Ann Estelle in Fairy Costume, style No. 99603, pink satin petal dress with white scalloped satin butterfly sleeves, pink flowers at neckline, fuchsia sash makes a big bow in back, crown of pink flowers and gold glitter rings her hair, starry fairy wand with pink ribbon and flowers, doll and costume, 1999, $70.00.

Photo courtesy Robert Tonner Doll Company.

10" vinyl Ann Estelle, style No. 99600, dressed in style No. 99607 He Sees You When You're Sleeping, flannel print nightgown trimmed with white lace and satin ribbons, crocheted bunny slippers, her favorite teddy bear Melvin wearing his starry nightcap and green striped ribbon, 1999, basic doll $70.00, costume $35.00.

Photo courtesy Robert Tonner Doll Company.

8" vinyl Kripplebush Kid Marni, glass eyes, closed mouth, brunette wig, marked "Tonner" on back, in yellow rain gear, over black check pants, circa 1998, $55.00 retail.
Courtesy Bev Mitchell.

8" vinyl Kripplebush Kid Hanna, glass eyes, closed mouth, blond wig, marked "Tonner" on back, in lime green and blue pant set, circa 1998, $55.00 retail.
Courtesy Bev Mitchell.

16" vinyl Tyler Wentworth, long brown rooted hair in a high pony-tail, glass eyes, closed mouth, hard plastic body, dressed in a white tailored cotton shirt, slim black skirt, black belt with gold buckle, earrings, black fish-net stockings, black shoes, 1999, $80.00.
Photo courtesy Robert Tonner Doll Company.

14" hard vinyl Camellia Girl souvenir doll of the 1998 2 North UFDC Regional A Secret Garden in the Camellia city of Sacramento, CA, marked "© 1998//Robert Tonner," blond curls, pink floral print dress, white apron, basket of flowers, limited edition of 425, $200.00.
Private collection.

16" vinyl Tyler Wentworth, long blond rooted hair, glass eyes, closed mouth, hard plastic body, dressed in a black and white checked suit, jacket is trimmed with black cuffs, collar, and buttons, fitted skirt, gold brooch, bracelet, and earrings, black hat, black fish-net stockings, black high heels, 1999, costume $70.00.
Photo courtesy Robert Tonner Doll Company.

16" vinyl Tyler Wentworth, long rooted hair, glass eyes, closed mouth, hard plastic body, dressed in Wake Up Call, pink satin pajamas, matching housecoat with velour cuffs and collar, matching slippers, 1999, costume $50.00.
Photo courtesy Robert Tonner Doll Company.

16" vinyl Tyler Wentworth dressed in Party of the Season, limited edition of 2,500, long rooted hair, glass eyes, closed mouth, hard plastic body, green gown with gold lace overlay, brooch, necklace, earrings, gold shoes, 1999, $160.00.
Photo courtesy Robert Tonner Doll Company.

Vinyl Dolls

By the mid-fifties, vinyl (polyvinylchloride) was being used for dolls. Material that is soft to the touch and processing that allowed hair to be rooted are positive attractions. Vinyl has become a desirable material and the market has been deluged with dolls manufactured from this product. Many dolls of this period are of little known manufacturer, unmarked, or marked only with a number. With little history behind them, these dolls need to be mint in box and totally complete to warrant top prices. An important factor to remember when purchasing vinyl dolls: all aspects of originality, labeled costume, hang tag, and box are more critical when these dolls are entered into competition.

What to look for:

Clean dolls, all original with good color, vinyl that is not sticky. There can be some real bargains in this area for the collector with limited budget. Often overlooked character and celebrity dolls in vinyl can still be found at garage sales, flea markets, discount outlets and antique malls.

18" Brookglad Co. Goldilocks, marked "BROOKGLAD CO.," blue sleep eyes, dimpled smiling closed mouth, blond synthetic wig, five-piece jointed body, blue flower print dress, white apron with "Goldilocks" embroidered in blue, matching bonnet, all original, circa 1950s, $40.00.
Courtesy Sheryl Schmidt.

16" Dee and Cee Toy Co. Ltd. of Canada high heel doll, marked "D&C" on head, "Dee and Cee" on back, blue sleep eyes, blond rooted synthetic hair, original dress with white top and black checkered skirt with lace, circa early 1960s, $175.00.
Courtesy Carolyn Hancock.

18" Daisy Kingdom Dolls black Pansy Doll, brown painted eyes, closed mouth, molded painted brown hair, white sunsuit trimmed with pink ribbon, white socks and shoes, in package marked "PANSY DOLL//18" Doll//Look for Daisy Kingdom Doll Dress Panels and Patterns by Simplicity®," circa 1999, $12.95 at JoAnne's Fabrics or Wal Mart.
Courtesy Ruby Ward.

17" Furga doll, with wrist tag, still in box, sleep eyes, synthetic hair, closed mouth, wears bright fuchsia velveteen dress and marabou trim, circa 1960s, $50.00.
Courtesy Bella Mohr.

16" Furga doll, with wrist tag, blue sleep eyes, synthetic brunette hair, closed mouth, eyelashes above, painted lashes below, wears red dress, white embroidery trim, daisy at neck, on dress, cream straw hat, tagged "Furga//#1030," circa 1960s, $35.00.
Courtesy Bella Mohr.

Vinyl Dolls

14" Galoob, Inc. Baby Talk, bib marked "Baby Talk," back marked "1985// Galoob, Inc.," blue sleep eyes, open mouth with teeth, blond rooted hair, cloth body with talking mechanism, original pink pajamas with brown bears, pink bib, circa 1985, $75.00. *Courtesy Kathleen Kelly.*

18" Ganz Canadian Royal Mountie, marked "GANZ BROS." on the front of the flange neck, blue painted eyes, closed mouth, molded painted black hair, mohair plush body, molded vinyl hat, leather strap and vinyl boots are part of the body, circa 1960s+, $85.00. *Courtesy Sheryl Schmidt.*

24" Kaysam-Jolly Toy Corporation glamour doll, marked "4373//K// 19©61// KAYSAM," blue sleep eyes, eye-shadow, rosy cheeks, closed mouth, blond root-ed hair, pierced ears, five-piece rigid vinyl high heeled body, wearing dress with full pleated skirt, dark jacket with red lining, red belt, red rayon bow in hair, nylons and high heels, circa 1961, $85.00. *Courtesy Sheryl Schmidt.*

8" Happi-Time girl, unmarked, sold by Sears, blue sleep eyes, closed mouth, rosy cheeks, blond wig, hard plastic body, rigid vinyl arms, socks/panties, pink shoes, mint in box, circa 1950s, $50.00. *Courtesy Bev Mitchell.*

8" Peggy Nisbet Princess Charlotte, blue painted eyes, closed mouth, auburn mohair wig, wearing white lace dress with pink flowers around the skirt and in her hair, with hang tag, all original, $35.00.
Courtesy Sue Robertson.

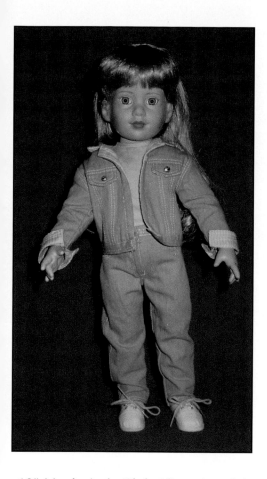

19" Magic Attic Club Alison in original outfit with paperback book, 1997, $100.00.
Courtesy Millie Carol.

8" Suzanne Gibson 1846 American Boy & Girl, #5104, marked "Suzanne Gibson" on heads, blue sleep eyes, rooted brown hair on boy, rooted blond hair on girl, mint in box, circa 1988, $75.00.
Courtesy Sue Robertson.

23" Saikai child with oversize dark blue eyes with no pupil or eyeball, dark blue eyeshadow, closed pale pink mouth, long straight synthetic hair with bangs, original velveteen clothes, marked "Japan" with a symbol and tagged "Sakai & Co.//Japan//#1331," circa 1984, $150.00.
Courtesy Dolores Ortega.

Vinyl Dolls

16" Royal Bride by Miss Elsa of Royal House of Dolls, a limited edition bride, luncheon souvenir, Modern Doll Convention, blue sleep eyes, closed mouth, rooted brown hair, white bride dress, veil and bouquet of flowers, mint in box, circa 1996, $55.00.
Private collection.

17½" Tiger Toys Modilyn, decal eyes, closed mouth, black hair, twist and style outfits, fashion book, styling stand, and comb, mint in box, circa 1990, $25.00.
Courtesy Kathleen Kelly.

15½" Rushton Zippy with black hair and Girlfriend with blond hair, cloth stuffed plush bodies, red corduroy pants, red felt hat, girlfriend in turquoise dress, circa 1955, $65.00 pair with book *Zippy's Birthday Party*.
Courtesy Janet Hill.

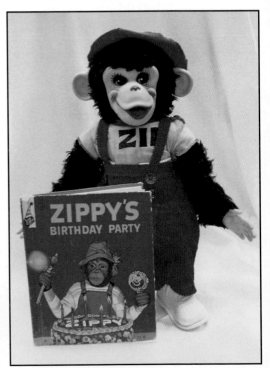

17" Tomy Kimberly, painted blue eyes, closed
mouth, long blond rooted hair, jointed vinyl
body, in original cheerleader outfit, carrying red
and white pompons, red and white plastic
shoes, circa 1984, $65.00.
Courtesy Nelda Shelton.

17" Tyco Thumbelina with hard-to-find
rattle, original tagged outfit, circa 1991,
$45.00.
Courtesy Marie Rodgers.

19" fashion-type doll by unknown maker, marked
"14R" on head (this mark was used on many, usually less expensive dolls made for companies such
as Belle, Deluxe Reading, Eegee, Natural, Rite Lee,
Royal, and Sayco), blue sleep eyes, eyeshadow,
closed mouth, rosy cheeks, pierced ears, blond
rooted Dynel hair, five-piece jointed rigid vinyl
high-heeled body, re-dressed in pink gown with
feather trim, circa 1957 – 1965, $45.00.
Courtesy Sheryl Schmidt.

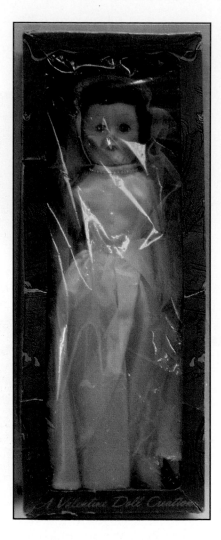

18" Valentine Dolls, Inc. Bride, blue sleep eyes, closed mouth, brown synthetic wig, bride dress and veil, pearl necklace, box reads "A Valentine Doll Creation//I'll Love you (inside heart)// Style #2066," circa 1960s, $95.00.
Courtesy Rita Mauze.

20" Zanini Zambelli child, marked "ZZ//Italy" on head, brown sleep eyes, closed mouth, rooted brunette hair, vinyl arms, legs, cloth body, all original, circa 1980s, $65.00.
Courtesy Sue Robertson.

Vogue

In 1922, Jennie Graves started her Vogue Doll Shop business in Somerville, Massachusetts, by dressing German dolls for department stores. She used cottage industry home sewers as her business expanded. Just before the war, she established a storefront, but depended on home sewers again during the war years, as all able-bodied workers were needed in the defense plants. In 1945, she incorporated Vogue Dolls, Inc., and opened a factory in Medford, Massachusetts. By 1949, she contracted to have an 8" hard plastic doll made with Commonwealth Plastics Company. At no time did she manufacture dolls, but she did open a 15,000 square foot factory where the dolls were dressed and readied for shipment.

Graves designed the costumes for over 20 years. She dressed German Armand Marseille bisque Just Me dolls in early years, and these are highly prized for the costumes today. She also used imported German Kammer & Reinhardt (K*R) dolls to costume and sell as well as composition dolls made by Arranbee and Ideal. In 1937, Graves had doll designer Bernard Lipfert design an 8" composition doll Toddles which she produced until 1948 when she had the doll made in hard plastic named Ginny. In the 1950s, Graves promoted a doll with wardrobe to increase year round sales. Vogue advertising promoted Ginny as a leader in the doll fashion society and noted she had 50 outfits available. This brought such a growth spurt, Graves had to borrow to open another factory in 1953. Her success gave rise to competition such as Ginger by the Cosmopolitan Doll Company. In 1957, Vogue became the largest doll manufacturer in the U.S. In 1958, Vogue purchased Arranbee Doll Company and reported gross sales of over $6 million. Graves retired in 1960 and turned the control of the company over to her daughter Virginia Graves Carlson and son-in-law, Ted Carlson, until 1966 when Virginia retired. In 1972, Vogue was sold to Tonka Corp., who began manufacturing the dolls in Asia. In 1977, the company was purchased by Lesney Products. During the Lesney era the doll was redesigned with a much slimmer body. After several changes of ownership, Meritus (1984) and then R. Dakin in 1986, the rights to Vogue dolls and molds, including Ginny were purchased by Vogue Doll Company, Inc., founded in 1995, by Linda and Jim Smith and Wendy and Keith Lawton (of the Lawton Company) and others. Today President Linda Smith handles marketing while Wendy Lawton oversees designs, making Ginny again a great collectible doll.

What to look for:

Early composition dolls should have minimal crazing and good color. Hard plastic dolls should have good color and original clothing. Hair can be restyled with patience, but clean dolls that have no mold or odor are important considerations. Vogue's Ginny dolls were a big favorite of the baby boomers during the 1950s and remain an appealing collectible with new dolls attracting new as well as older collectors.

Composition

11" all-composition Dora Lee, blue sleep eyes, closed mouth with rather sad wistful expression, blond mohair wig, bathing beauty in red polka dot original outfit, circa 1939, $400.00.
Courtesy Peggy Millhouse.

19½" Jennie, unmarked, sleep eyes, dark eyeshadow above eyes, open mouth with four teeth, composition jointed body, original tagged clothing, white fake lamb coat and muff with red felt trim, blue dress with red felt panel in front, trimmed with pale blue rick-rack, white ankle socks, red and white tie shoes, circa 1943 – 1944, $300.00.
Courtesy Flo Burnside.

Left: 8" Toddles Julie, #8-10B-Play-mate Series, marked "Vogue" on back, blue eyes painted to side, closed mouth, blond mohair wig, tagged green jersey overalls/red felt squirrel, stocking cap, wooden hoe, all original, circa 1948, $155.00.

Right: Toddles Bride, marked "Vogue" on head, "Doll Co." on back, blue eyes painted to side, closed mouth, blond mohair wig, organdy bride dress, net slip, veil, all original, circa 1937 – 1948, $185.00.
Courtesy McMasters Doll Auctions

8" Toddles Bride, painted side-glancing eyes, blond mohair wig, jointed body, in white bridal dress and veil, circa 1937 – 1948, $250.00.
Photo Peggy Millhouse.
Courtesy Lee Beaumont Collection.

8" Toddles, gold foil label, blue painted side-glancing eyes, closed mouth, red mohair wig, jointed body, dressed in gray multicolored striped outfit and cap, mint in box, circa 1940 – 1948, $425.00.
Courtesy Faye Gallagher.

Hard Plastic

8" Ginny walker Dutch pair, all original, marked "Ginny/Vogue Dolls//Inc.//Pat. Pend.//Made in U.S.A.," circa 1950 – 1953, $800.00 for pair.
Courtesy Debbie Crume.

8" Linda, #21 Kindergarten Series, sleep eyes, closed mouth, strung, printed organdy pinafore, trimmed with black ribbon, replaced shoes, missing flowers in hair, circa 1952, $300.00.
Courtesy Peggy Millhouse.

8" Little Red Riding Hood from the fable series, blue sleep eyes, painted lashes, red Dynel wig, strung, floral on white print dress, red cape, carrying basket, circa 1952, $450.00.
Courtesy Peggy Millhouse.

293

8" black Ginny, painted lash straight leg walker, marked "GINNY// VOGUE DOLLS// INC //PAT.PEND// MADE IN USA," brown sleep eyes, black Dynel wig, turning head mechanism, dressed in all-original outfit from My First Corsage series #63, gold velveteen, square neck party dress with dark gray iridescent silk taffeta skirt, net slip with yellow/gold ribbon trim, black straw hat with flower trim, yellow socks, black shoes, circa 1954, $1,000.00.
Courtesy Lee Ann Beaumont.

8" Ginny Ribbon Ballerina, Gadabout Series #45, sleep eyes, red Dynel wig, walker, multicolored ribbon/net tutu trimmed with silver braid, hard to find, circa 1953, $375.00.
Photo Peggy Millhouse.
Courtesy Karen Puck Collection.

8" undressed Ginny Boy, box reads "Vogue Dolls, Inc.// Medford, Mass.//No. 10 Undressed Doll Boy," blue sleep eyes, closed mouth, rosy cheeks, blond Dynel wig, striped under-wear, original with box, circa 1953, $250.00.
Courtesy Lee Ann Beaumont.

8" Ginny Ice Skater painted lash straight leg walker, marked "GINNY//VOGUE DOLLS// INC//PAT.PEND//MADE IN USA," blue sleep eyes, blond Dynel wig, rosy cheeks, turning head mechanism, #50 "For Fun Time" series, green velveteen backed fabric with silver rickrack edg-ing and silver braid and fur trim on skirt hem, fur headband with elastic, circa 1954, $260.00.
Courtesy Lee Ann Beaumont.

10½" Jill, all hard plastic, bend knee walker, all jointed wearing a blue nylon strapless dress, missing is her lined jacket of silver lamé, circa 1958, $125.00.
Courtesy Cathie Clark.

10½" hard plastic Jill in blue denim jeans white shirt, belt and wearing glasses, circa 1958, $175.00. 11" vinyl Jeff in dungarees and a yellow jersey shirt, circa 1959, $75.00.
Courtesy Cathie Clark.

Vinyl

16" Ginny Baby, dry drink and wet nursing doll, unusual because has a closed bottom without tube through body to drain water, rooted hair, blond bob, sleep eyes, open mouth, round belly button on tummy, bent vinyl legs, missing eyelashes, played with condition, circa 1961 – 1963, $7.50.
Private collection.

Ginny, Jeff, and Jill having some winter fun. The two Ginnys are wearing Funtime series outfits.
Courtesy Cathie Clark.

16½" Brikette with rooted orange hair with bangs, green sleep eyes, freckles on face, sharp pointed eyebrows, closed smiling mouth, rigid vinyl, jointed waist body, original green floral dress with white lace trim, marked on head, "Vogue Inc://19©60," circa 1961, $100.00.
Courtesy Cornelia Ford.

10½" Jill, marked "Vogue" on the back of her neck, #603, sleep eyes, blond rooted hair, closed mouth, high heels, wears pink strapless teddy with extra original dress, circa 1962, $150.00.
Courtesy Lee Ann Beaumont.

16" Brikette with very curly blond wig, one-piece torso, no freckles, blue sleep eyes, painted eyelashes below, and real lashes, mint in box with original blue polka dot dress and straw hat, marked "Lesney Prod. Corp.//1978/71679" on back of head, circa 1979 – 1980, $95.00.
Courtesy Antoinette Whelan.

16½" Brikette with rooted platinum hair with bangs, green sleep eyes, freckles on face, sharp pointed eyebrows, closed smiling mouth, rigid vinyl, jointed waist body, original turquoise dress with black stripes, marked on head, "Vogue Inc://19©60," circa 1961, $75.00.
Courtesy Cornelia Ford.

References

No one person can know it all. It is necessary to input data from many sources to bring you this book because of the tremendous scope of this collecting field. With an amazing number of new dolls coming on the market each year and the entire mass of dolls that already exists, more and more collectors are grouping together to share their knowledge and interests. There are clubs, organizations, collectors, Internet chat groups, and others who specializes in one category or type of doll who are willing to talk with others. If you specialize in one of the categories listed in this book and want to share your knowledge with other collectors, please send us your specialty and references or let us know the dolls you would like to see featured.

Collectors' Network

It is strongly recommended when contacting the references below and requesting information that you enclose a SASE (self-addressed stamped envelope) if you wish to receive a reply. Do not ask those who have volunteered to spend money on postage. These collectors may already have many obligations on their time, work schedules, and finances that do not allow them to spend their time and effort to do your research. They might answer if they had an envelope already stamped and addressed.

ACCESSORIES
Best Dressed Doll
P.O. Box 12689
Salem, OR 97309
800-255-2313
Catalog $3.00
Tonilady@aol.com

AMERICAN CHARACTER — TRESSY
Debby Davis, Collector/Dealer
3905 N. 15th St.
Milwaukee, WI, 53206

ANTIQUE DOLLS
Matrix
PO Box 1410
New York, NY 10023
Can research your wants

AUCTION HOUSES
Call or write for a list of upcoming auctions or if you need information about selling a collection.

McMasters Doll Auctions
James and Shari McMasters
PO Box 1755
Cambridge, OH 43725
800-842-35226
614-432-4419
Fax: 614-432-3191

BARBIE
Miller's Fashion Doll
PO Box 8488
Spokane, WA 99203-0488
509 747-0139
Fax: 509 455-6115
Credit Card Subscription
800-874-5201
Six issues $29.95

Dream Dolls Gallery & More
5700 Okeechobee Blvd. #20
West Palm Beach, FL 33417
888-839-3655
dollnmore@aol.com
Jaci Jueden, Collector/Dealer
575 Galice Rd.
Merlin, OR, 97532
fudd@cdsnet.net

Steven Pim, Collector/Dealer
3535 17th St.
San Francisco, CA 94110

BETSY MCCALL
Betsy's Fan Club
Marci Van Ausdall, Editor
PO Box 946
Quincy, CA 95971
Quarterly $15.50 per year

CELEBRITY
Celebrity Doll Journal
Loraine Burdick, Editor
413 10th Ave. Ct. NE
Puyallup, WA 98372
Quarterly, $10.00 per year

CHATTY CATHY, MATTEL
Chatty Cathy Collector's Club
Lisa Eisenstein, Editor
PO Box 140
Readington, NJ 08870-0140
Chatty@eclipse.net
Quarterly Newsletter, $28.00

COMPOSITION
Effanbee's Patsy Family
Patsy & Friends Newsletter
PO Box 311

Deming, NM 88031
patsyandfriends@zianet.com
Bi-monthly, $20.00 per year
Send address for sample copy

COSTUMING
Doll Costumer's Guild of America, Inc.
341 S. McCadden Pl.
Los Angeles, CA 90020
$18.00 per year, bimonthly

French Fashion Gazette
Adele Leurquin, Editor
1862 Sequoia SE
Port Orchard, WA 98366

DELUXE READING — Penny Brite
Carole Fisher, Dealer/Collector
RD 2, Box 301
Palmyra, PA 17078-9738
Rcfisher@voicenet.com

DIONNE QUINTUPLETS
Quint News
Jimmy and Fay Rodolfos, Editors
PO Box 2527
Woburn, MA 01888
Connie Lee Martin, Collector/Dealer
4018 East 17th St.
Tucson, AZ 85711

DOLL ARTISTS
Jamie G. Anderson, Doll Artist
10990 Greenlefe, P.O. Box 806
Rolla, MO 65402
573-364-7347
Jastudio@rollanet.org

Collector's Network

Martha Armstrong-Hand, Doll Artist
575 Worcester Drive
Cambria, CA 93428
805-927-3997

Betsy Baker, Doll Artist
81 Hy-Vue Terrace
Cold Spring, NY 10516

Cynthia Barron, Doll Artist
7796 W. Port Madison
Bainbridge Is., WA 98110
206-780-9003

Charles Batte, Doll Artist
272 Divisadero St. #4
San Francisco, CA 94117
415-252-7440

Atelier Bets van Boxel, Doll Artist
De Poppenstee
ët Vaartje 14
5165 NB Waspik, Holland
www.poppenstee.nl
bets@poppenstee.nl

Cheryl Bollenbach, Doll Artist
P.O. Box 740922
Arvada, CO 80006-0922
303-424-8578
cdboll@aol.com

Laura Clark
PO Box 596
Mesilla, NM 88046

Ankie Daanen Doll-Art
Anton Mauvestraat 1
2102 BA HEEMSTEDE NL
023-5477980
Fax: 023-5477981

Jane Darin, Doll Artist
5648 Camber Drive
San Diego, CA 92117
619-514-8145
Jdarin@san.rr.com
www.janedarin.com

Marleen Engeler, Doll Artist
mílaine dolls
Noordeinde 67 1141 AH Monnickendam
The Netherlands
31-299656814
Mlwent4.2@globalxs.nl

Judith & Lucia Friedericy, Doll Artists
Friedericy Dolls
1260 Wesley Avenue
Pasadena, CA 91104
626-296-0065
Friedericy@aol.com

Originals by Goldie, Doll Artist
8517 Edgeworth Drive
Capitol Heights, MD 20743
301-350-4119

Lillian Hopkins, Doll Artist
2315 29th Street
Santa Monica, CA 90405
310-396-3266
LilyArt@Compuserve.com

Marylynn Huston, Doll Artist
101 Mountain View Drive
Pflugerville, TX 78660
512-252-1192

Kathryn Williams Klushman, Doll Artist
Nellie Lamers, Doll Artist
The Enchantment Peddlers
HC 6 Box 0
Reeds Spring, MO 65737
417-272-3768
Theenchantmentpeddlers@yahoo.com
www.inter-linc.net/TheEnchantmentPeddlers/

Joyce Patterson, Doll Artist
FabricImages
P.O. Box 1599
Brazoria, TX 77422
409-798-9890
Clothdol@tgn.net

W. Harry Perzyk, Doll Artist
2860 Chiplay St.
Sacramento, CA 95826

Daryl Poole, Doll Artist
450 Pioneer Trail
Dripping Springs, TX 78620
512-858-7181
Eltummo@aol.com

Peggy Ann Ridley, Doll Artist
17 Ridlon Road
Lisbon, ME 04250
207-353-8827

Anne Sanregret, Doll Artist
22910 Estorial Drive, #6
Diamond Bar, CA 91765
909-860-8007

Sandy Simonds, Doll Artist
334 Woodhurst Dr.
Coppell, TX 75019

Linda Lee Sutton, Doll Artist
P.O. Box 3725
Central Point, OR 97502

DOLL REPAIRS
Doc. Doc. Assoc.
1406 Sycamore Rd.
Montoursville, PA 17754
717-323-9604

Fresno Doll Hospital
1512 N. College
Fresno, CA 93728
209-266-1108

Kandyland Dolls
PO Box 146
Grande Ronde, OR 97347
503-879-5153

Life's Little Treasures
PO Box 585
Winston, OR 97496
541-679-3472

Oleta's Doll Hospital
1413 Seville Way
Modesto, CA, 95355
209-523-6669

GIRL SCOUTS
Girl Scout Doll Collectors Patch
Pidd Miller
PO Box 631092
Houston, TX 77263

Diane Miller, Collector
13151 Roberta Place
Garden Grove, CA 92643

Ann Sutton, Collector/Dealer
2555 Prine Rd.
Lakeland, FL 33810-5703
Sydneys@aol.com

HASBRO — JEM
Linda E. Holton, Collector/Dealer
P.O. Box 6753
San Rafael, CA 94903

HITTY — ARTISTS
Judy Brown
506 N. Brighton Ct.
Sterling,   VA 20164

Ruth Brown
1606 SW Heather Dr.
Grants Pass, OR 97526

Janci
Jill Sanders/ Nancy Elliot
2442 Hathaway Court
Muskegon, MI 49441-4435

Lotz Studio
Jean Lotz
PO Box 1308
Lacombe, LA 70445-1308
504-882-3482

Friends of Hitty Newsletter
Virginia Ann Heyerdahl, Editor
2704 Bellview Ave
Cheverly, MD 20785
Quarterly, $12.00 per year

IDEAL
Ideal Collectors Newsletter
Judith Izen, Editor
PO Box 623
Lexington, MA 02173
Quarterly, $20.00 per year
Jizen@aol.com

INTERNET
Ebay Auction site
www.ebay.com

About.com Doll Collecting
Denise Van Patten
http://collectdolls.about.com
denise@dollymaker.com

AG Collector List
For American Girl, Heidi Ott, and other 18" dolls,
no selling, just talk
ag_collector_request@lists.best.com

Barbie chat
Fashion-l@ga.unc.edu

Dolls n' Stuff
Dollsnstuff@home.ease.lsoft.com

Doll Chat List
Friendly collectors talk dolls, no flaming permitted, a great group.
E-mail is forwarded to your e-mail address from host, no fees. To subscribe, e-mail: DollChat-Request@nbi.com, type subscribe in body of message.

Not Just Dollmakers
www.notjustdollmakers.com
Information: carls@isrv.com

Sasha
sasha-1-subscribe@makelist.com

Shirley Temple
shirleycollect-subscribe@makelist.com

KLUMPE
Sondra Gast, Collector/Dealer
PO Box 252
Spring Valley, CA 91976
Fax: 619-444-4215

LAWTON, WENDY
Lawton Collectors Guild
PO Box 969
Turlock, CA 95381

Toni Winder, Collector/Dealer
1484 N. Vagedes
Fresno CA 93728
TTUK77B@prodigy.com

LIDDLE KIDDLES
For a signed copy of her book, *Liddle Kiddles*, $22.95 post paid write:
Paris Langford
415 Dodge Ave
Jefferson, LA 70127
504-733-0676

MANUFACTURERS
Alexander Doll Company, Inc.
Herbert Brown, Chairman & CEO
615 West 131st Street
New York, NY 10027
212-283-5900
Fax: 212-283-6042

American Girl
8400 Fairway Place
PO Box 620190
Middleton, WI 53562-0190

Collectible Concepts
Ivonne Heather, President
945 Hickory Run Lane
Great Falls, VA 22066
703 821-0607
Fax: 703-759-0408
ivonnehccc@aol.com

Effanbee Doll Company
19 Lexington Ave.
East Brunswick, NJ 08816
732-613-3852
Fax: 732-613 8366

Gene — Ashton Drake Galleries
9200 N. Maryland Ave.
Niles, IL 60714-9853
1-888-For Gene

Susan Wakeen Doll Company, Inc.
PO Box 1321
Litchfield, CT 06759
860-567-0007
Fax: 908-788-1955
Pkaverud@blast.net

Robert Tonner Doll Company
Robert Tonner Doll Club
PO Box 1187
Kingston, NY 12402
Fax: 914-339-1259
Dues: $19.95
Credit Card: 914 339-9537

Vogue Doll Company
PO Box 756
Oakdale, CA 95361-0756
209-848-0300
Fax: 209-848-4423
www.voguedolls.com

MODERN DOLL COLLECTORS, INC.
Patsy Moyer, Registrar
PO Box 11405
Prescott, AZ 86301
moddol@yahoo.com

MUSEUMS
Arizona Doll & Toy Museum
602 E. Adams St.
Phoenix, AZ 85004
(Stevens House in Heritage Square)
602-253-9337, Tues – Sun, adm. $2.50, closed Aug.

Enchanted World Doll Museum
"The castle across from the Corn Palace"
615 North Main
Mitchell, SD, 57301
605-996-9896
Fax: 605-996-0210

Land of Enchantment Doll Museum
5201 Constitution Ave.
Albuquerque, NM 87110-5813
505-255-8555
Fax: 505-255-1259

Margaret Woodbury Strong Museum
1 Manhattan Square
Rochester, NY 14607
716-263-2700

Rosalie Whyel Museum of Doll Art
1116 108th Avenue N.E.
Bellevue, WA 98004
206-455-1116
Fax: 206-455-4793
www.dollart.com

NANCY ANN STORYBOOK
Elaine Pardee, Collector/Dealer
PO Box 6108
Santa Rosa, CA 95406
707-585-3655

PRESERVATION
Twin Pines
www.twinpines.com

PUBLICATIONS — MAGAZINES
Contemporary Doll Collector
Scott Publications
30595 Eight Mile
Livonia, MI 48152-1798
Subscription: 800 458-8237

Doll Reader
Cumberland Publishing, Inc.
6405 Flank Dr.
Harrisburg, PA 17112
Subcriptions: 800-829-3340
dollreader@palmcoastd.com

Dolls
170 Fifth Ave, 12th Fl.
New York, NY 10010
212-989-8700
Fax: 212-645-8976
snowyw@lsol.net

Miller's Fashion Doll
PO Box 8488
Spokane, WA 99203-0488
509-747-0139
Fax: 509-455-6115
Credit card subscription
800-874-5201
Six issues $29.95

PUBLICATIONS — NEWSLETTERS
Alexander Doll Company
The Review
Official publication of the Madame Alexander Doll Club
Quarterly, plus 2 Shoppers
$20.00 per year
PO Box 330
Mundelein, IL 60060-0330
847-949-9200
Fax: 847-949-9201
www.madc.org

Collectors United
711 S. 3rd Ave.
Chatsworth, GA 30705
706-695-8242
Fax: 706-895-0770
Collun@Alltel.net

Ninsyo Journal — JADE
Japanese American Dolls Enthusiasts
406 Koser Ave
Iowa City, Iowa 52246
vickyd@jadejapandolls.com

Patsy & Friends Newsletter
PO Box 311
Deming, NM 88031
sctrading@zianet.com
$20.00 per year (6 issues), 36 pages

RAGGEDY ANN
Rags newsletter
Barbara Barth, Editor
PO Box 823
Atlanta, GA 30301
Quarterly $16.00

ROLDAN
Sondra Gast, Collector/Dealer
PO Box 252
Spring Valley, CA 91976
Fax: 619-444-4215

SANDRA SUE
Peggy Millhouse, Collector/Dealer
510 Green Hill Road
Conestoga, PA 17516
peggyin717@aol.com

Collector's Network

SASHA
Friends of Sasha
Dorisanne Osborn, Editor
Box 187
Keuka Park, NY 14478
Quarterly Newsletter

SHIRLEY TEMPLE
Australian Shirley Temple Collectors News
Victoria Horne, Editor
39 How Ave.
North Dandenong
Victoria 3175, Australia
Quarterly Newsletter
$25.00 U.S.

Lollipop News
Shirley Temple Collectors by the Sea
P.O. Box 6203
Oxnard, CA 93031
Membership dues: $14.00 year

Shirley Temple Collectors News
Rita Dubas, Editor
881 Colonial Rd
Brooklyn NY 11209
Quarterly, $20.00 year
www.ritadubasdesign.com/shirley/

TERRI LEE
Daisy Chain Newsletter
Terry Bukowski, Editor
3010 Sundland Dr
Alamogordo, NM 88310
bukowski@wazoo.com
$20.00 per year

Ann Sutton, Collector/Dealer
2555 Prine Rd.
Lakeland, FL 33810-5703
Sydneys@aol.com

Betty J. Woten, Collector/Dealer
12 Big Bend Cut Off
Cloudcroft, NM 88317-9411

VOGUE
Ginny Doll Club
PO Box 338
Oakdale, CA 95361-0338
800-554-1447

UNITED FEDERATION OF DOLL CLUBS
10920 N. Ambassador Dr., Suite 130
Kansas City, MO, 64153
816-891-7040
Fax: 816-891-8360
www.ufdc.org/

WOODS, ROBIN
Toni Winder, Collector/Dealer
1484 N. Vagedes
Fresno, CA 93728

Bibliography

Anderson, Johana Gast. *Twentieth Century Dolls*. Wallace Homestead, 1971.

———. *More Twentieth Century Dolls*. Wallace Homestead, 1974.

———. *Cloth Dolls*. Wallace Homestead, 1984.

Axe, John. *Effanbee, A Collector's Encyclopedia 1949 through 1983*. Hobby House Press, 1983.

———. *The Encyclopedia of Celebrity Dolls*. Hobby House Press, 1983.

———. *Tammy and Her Family of Dolls*. Hobby House Press, 1995.

Blitman, Joe. *Francie & her Mod, Mod, Mod, Mod World of Fashion*. Hobby House Press, 1996.

Casper, Peggy Wiedman. *Fashionable Terri Lee Dolls*. Hobby House Press, 1988.

Crowsey, Linda. *Madame Alexander Collector's Dolls Price Guide #23*. Collector Books, 1998.

Clark, Debra. *Troll Identification & Price Guide*. Collector Books, 1993.

Coleman, Dorthy S., Elizabeth Ann and Evelyn Jane. *The Collector's Book of Dolls Clothes*. Crown Publishers, 1975.

———. *The Collector's Encyclopedia of Dolls, Vol. I & II*. Crown Publishers, 1968, 1986.

Cook, Carolyn. *Gene*. Hobby House Press, 1998.

DeWein, Sibyl and Ashabraner, Joan. *The Collector's Encyclopedia of Barbie Dolls and Collectibles*. Collector Books, 1977.

Garrison, Susan Ann. *The Raggedy Ann & Andy Family Album*. Schiffer Publishing, 1989.

Hedrick, Susan & Matchette, Vilma. *World Colors, Dolls & Dress*. Hobby House Press, 1997.

Hoyer, Mary. *Mary Hoyer and Her Dolls*. Hobby House Press, 1982.

Izen, Judith. *A Collector's Guide to Ideal Dolls*. Collector Books, 1994.

Izen, Judith and Stover, Carol. *Collector's Encyclopedia of Vogue Dolls*. Collector Books, 1998.

Judd, Polly and Pam. *African and Asian Costumed Dolls*. Hobby House Press, 1995.

———. *Cloth Dolls*. Hobby House Press, 1990.

———. *Composition Dolls, Vol I & II*. Hobby House Press, 1991, 1994.

———. *European Costumed Dolls*. Hobby House Press, 1994.

———. *Hard Plastic Dolls, I & II*. Hobby House Press, 1987, 1989.

———. *Glamour Dolls of the 1950s & 1960s*. Hobby House Press, 1988.

———. *Santa Dolls & Figurines*. Hobby House Press, 1992.

Langford, Paris. *Liddle Kiddles*. Collector Books, 1996.

Bibliography

Lewis, Kathy and Don. *Chatty Cathy Dolls*. Collector Books, 1994.

Mandeville, A. Glen. *Ginny, An American Toddler Doll*. Hobby House Press, 1994.

Mansell, Colette. *The Collector's Guide to British Dolls Since 1920*. Robert Hale, 1983.

Mertz, Ursula. *Collector's Encyclopedia of American Composition Dolls, 1900 – 1950*. Collector Books, 1999.

Morris, Thomas G. *The Carnival Chalk Prize, I & II*. Prize Publishers, 1985, 1994.

Moyer, Patsy. *Doll Values*. Collector Books, 1997, 1998, 1999.

——. *Modern Collectible Dolls, Vols. I, II & III*. Collector Books, 1997, 1998, 1999.

Niswonger, Jeanne D. *That Doll Ginny*. Cody Publishing, 1978.

——. *The Ginny Doll Family*®, 1996.

Olds, Patrick C. *The Barbie Years*. Collector Books, 1996.

Outwater, Myra Yellin. *Advertising Dolls*. Schiffer, 1998.

Pardella, Edward R. *Shirley Temple Dolls and Fashions*. Schiffer Publishing, 1992.

Perkins, Myla. *Black Dolls*. Collector Books, 1993.

——. *Black Dolls Book I*. Collector Books, 1995.

Robison, Joleen Ashman and Sellers, Kay. *Advertising Dolls*. Collector Books, 1992.

Schoonmaker, Patricia N. *Effanbee Dolls: The Formative Years, 1910 – 1929*. Hobby House Press, 1984.

——. *Patsy Doll Family Encyclopedia, Vol.1*. Hobby House Press, 1992.

——. *Patsy Doll Family Encyclopedia, Vol. II*. Hobby House Press, 1998.

Smith, Patricia R. *Madame Alexander Collector Dolls*. Collector Books, 1978.

——. *Modern Collector's Dolls, Series 1 – 8*. Collector Books.

Tabbat, Andrew. *Raggedy Ann and Andy*. Gold Horse Publishing, 1998.

——. *The Collector's World of Raggedy Ann and Andy*, Gold Horse Publishing, Vol I, 1996; Vol. II, 1997.

Index

Index

Index